Legal Violence and the Limits of the Law

What is the meaning of punishment today? Where is the limit that separates it from the cruel and unusual? In legal discourse, the distinction between punishment and vengeance—punishment being the measured use of legally sanctioned violence and vengeance being a use of violence that has no measure—is expressed by the idea of "cruel and unusual punishment." This phrase was originally contained in the *English Bill of Rights* (1689). But it (and versions of it) has since found its way into numerous constitutions and declarations, including Article 5 of the *Universal Declaration of Human Rights*, as well as the Amendment to the US Constitution. Clearly, in order for the use of violence to be legitimate, it must be subject to limitation. The difficulty is that the determination of this limit should be objective, but it is not, and its application in punitive practice is constituted by a host of extra-legal factors and social and political structures. It is this essential contestability of the limit which distinguishes punishment from violence that this book addresses. And, including contributions from a range of internationally renowned scholars, it offers a plurality of original and important responses to the contemporary question of the relationship between punishment and the limits of law.

Joshua Nichols is an Assistant Professor in the Department of Public Administration at Dalhousie University, Halifax, Canada and a Fellow at the Center for International Governance Innovation.

Amy Swiffen is Associate Professor in the Department of Sociology and Anthropology, Concordia University, Montreal, Canada.

Legal Violence and the Limits of the Law

Edited by
Joshua Nichols and Amy Swiffen

Routledge
Taylor & Francis Group
LONDON AND NEW YORK

First published 2018 by Routledge

2 Park Square, Milton Park, Abingdon, Oxfordshire OX14 4RN
711 Third Avenue, New York, NY 10017

Routledge is an imprint of the Taylor & Francis Group, an informa business

First issued in paperback 2018

British Library Cataloguing-in-Publication Data
A catalogue record for this book is available from the British Library

Library of Congress Cataloging-in-Publication Data
Names: Nichols, Joshua, author. | Swiffen, Amy, author.
Title: Legal violence and the limits of the law / Joshua Nichols, Amy Swiffen.
Description: Abingdon, Oxon [UK] ; New York : Routledge, 2017. |
Includes bibliographical references and index.
Identifiers: LCCN 2017010410 | ISBN 9781138814141 (hardback) |
ISBN 9781317602118 (adobe reader) | ISBN 9781317602101 (epub) |
ISBN 9781317602095 (mobipocket)
Subjects: LCSH: Punishment–Philosophy. | Violence (Law)–Philosophy. |
Punishment–History. | Imprisonment–History. | United Nations. General
Assembly. Universal Declaration of Human Rights. | Capital
punishment–United States. | United States. Constitution. 8th Amendment.
Classification: LCC K5103.N53 2017 | DDC 345/.077301–dc23
LC record available at https://lccn.loc.gov/2017010410

ISBN: 978-1-138-81414-1 (hbk)
ISBN: 978-1-138-34798-4 (pbk)

Typeset in Galliard
by Out of House Publishing

Contents

Figures

Contributors

Adelyn Curran will graduate from Amherst College in 2017.

Kelly Hannah-Moffat is a professor in the Departments of Sociology and Criminology & Sociolegal Studies and is Vice President of Human Resources & Equity at the University of Toronto. She is the co-editor of the international journal *Punishment and Society* and has published several articles and books on risk, punishment, human rights, and detention, parole, gender and diversity, specialized courts, and criminal justice decision making.

Alexandra Hunter is a PhD candidate at the Department of Sociology, University of Toronto, and a Junior Fellow at the Center for Criminology & Sociolegal Studies. Her research focuses on prisons, punishment, gender, and correctional policy. Her dissertation examines the barriers to mental healthcare in Ontario corrections.

Robert Kermes graduated from Amherst College in 2016.

Margaret Kiley graduated from Amherst College in 2016.

Mark Kingwell is Professor of Philosophy at the University of Toronto and is the author of many works on political, cultural, and aesthetic theory. His most recent books are the essay collections *Unruly Voices* (Biblioasis, 2012) and *Measure Yourself against the Earth* (Biblioasis, 2015). He is currently at work on a book about the politics of boredom.

Michael Naas is Professor of Philosophy at DePaul University in Chicago. He works in the areas of ancient Greek philosophy and contemporary French philosophy. His most recent books include *The End of the World and Other Teachable Moments: Jacques Derrida's Final Seminar* (Fordham University Press, 2014) and *Miracle and Machine: Jacques Derrida and the Two Sources of Religion, Science, and the Media* (Fordham University Press, 2012). He is also the co-translator of several works by Jacques Derrida, including *Rogues* (Stanford University Press, 2005) and *Learning to Live Finally* (Melville House, 2007). He is also co-editor of the *Oxford Literary Review*.

Charmaine A. Nelson is Professor of Art History at McGill University. Her research and teaching interests include postcolonial and black feminist scholarship, transatlantic slavery studies and Black diaspora studies. She has made groundbreaking contributions to the fields of the visual culture of slavery, race, and representation, and Black Canadian studies. She has authored six books, including *The Color of Stone: Sculpting the Black Female Subject in Nineteenth-Century America* (University of Minnesota Press, 2007) and *Slavery, Geography, and Empire in Nineteenth-Century Marine Landscapes of Montreal and Jamaica* (Routledge, 2016). She has held several prestigious fellowships and appointments, including a Caird Senior Research Fellowship, National Maritime Museum, UK (2007) and a Fulbright Visiting Research Chair (2010), University of California—Santa Barbara. In 2016, she was named as a Fellow of the Royal Society of Canada, College of New Scholars, Artists, and Scientists.

Robert Nichols is Assistant Professor of Political Theory at the University of Minnesota.

Pablo Ouziel is Assistant Professor of Political Science at the COMSATS Institute of Information Technology in Islamabad, Pakistan. By standing within the tradition of public philosophy, the core of his work is centered on excavating networks of individuals governing themselves in numerous ways that supersede our current structures of representative government.

Keshav Pant will graduate from Amherst College in 2017.

George Pavlich holds a Canada Research Chair in Social Theory, Culture, and Law, and is Professor of Law and Sociology at the University of Alberta. His books include *Justice Fragmented: Mediating Community Disputes under Postmodern Conditions* (Routledge, 1996), *Critique and Radical Discourses on Crime* (Ashgate, 2000), *Governing Paradoxes of Restorative Justice* (Routledge-Cavendish, 2005), and *Law and Society Redefined* (Oxford University Press, 2010). He is a co-editor of *Sociology for the Asking* (Oxford University Press Canada, 2006); *Questioning Sociology* (Oxford University Press Canada, three editions); *After Sovereignty* (Routledge, 2009); *Governance and Regulation in Social Life* (Routledge-Cavendish, 2007); *Rethinking Law, Society, and Governance: Foucault's Bequest* (Bloomsbury, 2001); and most recently *Accusation: Creating Criminals* (UBC Press, 2017). He is currently exploring his social theories of criminal accusation in the context of late nineteenth-century entryways to criminal justice in western Canada.

Austin Sarat is William Nelson Cromwell Professor of Jurisprudence & Political Science and Associate Dean of the Faculty at Amherst College.

Kelly Struthers Montford is a doctoral candidate and Izaak Walton Killam Memorial Scholar in the Department of Sociology at the University of

Alberta, as well as a pre-postdoctoral fellow in punishment, law, and social theory at the Center for Criminology & Sociolegal Studies at the University of Toronto. She has previously been a Social Sciences and Humanities Research Council of Canada Graduate Scholar and 2013–2014 Institute for Critical Animal Studies Hilda Scholar of the year. Her research interests include critical animal studies, philosophy, critical criminology, and social theory. Her work has been published in *philoSOPHIA: A Journal of Continental Feminism*, the *Canadian Journal of Women and the Law*, *Societies*, and *PhaenEx: Journal of Existential and Phenomenological Theory and Culture*.

Christopher Tomlins is Elizabeth Josselyn Boalt Professor of Law at the University of California, Berkeley, where he has taught since July 2014. His most recent book is *Freedom Bound: Law, Labor, and Civic Identity in Colonizing English America, 1580–1865* (Cambridge University Press, 2010), winner of the Bancroft Prize for American History. He is currently at work on a history of the Turner Rebellion and slavery in antebellum Virginia.

Irene Watson is Professor of Law at the University of South Australia and belongs to the Tanganekald, Meintangk/Boandik First Nations Peoples, of what is now known as the Coorong and the south-east of South Australia.

Preface

> [I]f violence, violence crowned by fate, is the origin of law, then it may be readily supposed that where the highest violence, that over life and death, occurs in the legal system, the origins of law jut manifestly and fearsomely into existence.
>
> Walter Benjamin, "Critique of Violence" 286

What is the meaning of punishment today? To begin, we could note the traditional conceptual distinction between punishment and vengeance: punishment being the measured use of legally sanctioned violence and vengeance being a use of violence that has no measure. In legal discourse, this division is expressed by the phrase "cruel and unusual punishment." The origin of the phrase is the *English Bill of Rights* (1689), but it (and versions stemming from it) has since found its way into a wide number of constitutions and declarations, including the 8th Amendment to the US Constitution, section 12 of the *Canadian Charter of Rights and Freedoms*, and Article 5 of the *Universal Declaration of Human Rights*. What is at stake in the phrase is clear: in order for the use of violence to be legitimate, it must be subject to limitation. The difficulty is that the determination of the limit should be objective, but it is not. A number of terms and phrases have developed that attempt to add some degree of precision. It is said, for example, that punishment must respect "human dignity," it must not "shock the conscience of society," and it must respect what is "reasonable in a free and democratic society," but these remain subjective guidelines. Their application in punitive practice is historically located and constituted by a host of extra-legal factors and social and political structures. These factors make punishment—to borrow H.L.A. Hart's phrase—an open textured concept. Given the essential contestability of limit that separates punishment and violence, it is by no means strange that punishment as a concept is difficult to apprehend—it is after all continually redefined.

However, adding to the complexity is the idea that the division between legal violence and non-legal violence is a condition of possibility for law itself. From this perspective, punishment is not just a phenomenon to be analyzed in particular cases; it has a constitutive function in setting the limit that establishes the force of law in the first place. For instance, the limits of legal violence mark a citizen's individual rights and bodily autonomy, while at the same time they mark the difference between a state of war and the rule of law. From this perspective, the significance of the changing nature of the law's use of violence assumes urgency. Recent developments, such as the new distinction between torture and enhanced interrogation, the use of extraordinary rendition, the appearance of "black sites," the use of mass incarceration to control marginalized communities, and the use of humanitarian interventions to justify breaching the sovereign territory of a state, give a sense of the scope and the stakes of the changing face of legal violence. These changes demand that a distinction between punishment and unsanctioned violence be made, yet they also make it difficult to say where that separation lies. An analysis of punishment reveals that we are faced with a crisis in the law's relationship to violence that challenges both the meaning of democratic citizenship and the legitimacy of the state. This being the case, analyzing the meaning of punishment today presents a particular challenge. This book sets out to address this challenge by opening up the question of punishment to scholars who are working in a wide variety of contexts, including the social sciences, law, and the humanities. By engaging a plurality of perspectives and contexts, our aim is to facilitate encounters and develop new approaches to the question of punishment.

The book itself has been organized in such a way that the chapters roughly break down into three approaches. First, Mark Kingwell, Michael Naas, and George Pavlich all take a broader, more philosophical tack to our guiding theme. Second, Robert Nichols, Charmaine Nelson, Christopher Tomlins, and Irene Watson focus on the relationship between the practices of punishment and the processes of colonization. Third, and finally, Austin Sarat, Kelly Hanna-Moffat, and Pablo Ouziel focus their attention on specific debates in the policy and practices of punishment. Overall, the aim of this text is not to offer the reader an exhaustive survey of the current discourse of punishment; rather, it is to provide a series of related, but distinct surveys. Each author approaches the subject matter as an open territory and makes their way through it. By collecting them together, we hope to be able to open up new ways to approach this problem so that we can see it again, from a new series of angles, under different lights, so that we can see the possibilities for it being otherwise than what it currently is.

Acknowledgments

We would like to thank all of the authors, participants, and students who joined us in this project; Concordia University and the Social Science and Humanities Research Council of Canada for providing the funding that made this project possible; and, finally, Eleonora Joensuu for her effective, efficient, and ever-tireless editorial contributions to the book.

Chapter 1

"It's not just a good idea, it's the law"

Rationality, force, and changing minds

Mark Kingwell

Breakin' rocks in the hot sun. I fought the law, and the law won.
(Sonny Curtis)

Changing minds

Can you change someone's mind? Can you change your own?

Philosophers have long thought so. Socrates is the traditional hero of mind-change in the Western tradition. The celebrated *elenchus*, or Socratic Method, involves probing questions that generate counter-examples, expose special pleading, and force self-contradictions out into the open. Particulars are not universals! Exceptions destroy rules! Rational standards are everywhere hidden in plain sight!

But everyone knows that the Socratic interlocutors, in Plato's dialogues anyway, are no better than yes men. They put a feeble show of resistance, then fall into line. The really stubborn opponents—Thrasymachus on justice, Euthyphro on piety—either storm off or slip away. They are not convinced to change; their minds are made up. The cases are instructive. Thrasymachus is a political realist who believes that might makes right. Rational challenge is of no account to him. Euthyphro is a fideist, a man who believes because he has faith in the gods—and yes, since you ask, he *does* have a privileged channel of communication with them.

Consider, then, a combination of these two meta-rational figures: a politician with no regard for truth or argument, who passionately believes in greatness and power (especially his own), and holds himself to no standard except the ones generated by his own megalomania. You do not change the mind of a man like that. He has already done all the changing, and it is, ironically, along the lines attributed to Mohamed Atta: "The world changes first in the mind of the man who decides to change the world."

That is an extreme example—though not so extreme that it defies the possibilities of real-world democratic politics. Meanwhile, confirmation bias, recency bias, cognitive dissonance, post facto rationalization, and layer upon layer of ideological distortion allow all of us to believe we are engaged in rational debate when, in fact, we are simply piling sandbags against the base of our long-held positions. We pursue self-defeating desires; we vote against our interest; we dig in and die. The real drivers are even more primitive: fear, anger, anxiety, and associated pheromonal networks. Otherness of all kinds generates a hackle-raising primate response. Exposed inner contradiction, once thought to spawn change, instead prompts frenzied efforts to scaffold the problem—the mental equivalent of insane astronomical elaborations meant to preserve the geocentric model of the universe.

Moral panic sets in, and the response is feral retrenchment. The gates of our fortress of belief are drawn up, even as heralds on the battlements keep bellowing their slogans of reasoned discourse. We make ourselves easy prey for hucksters and ideologues, the siren call of authority. Yes, we honor epistemic consistency, but how much of *that* is driven by how we want to see ourselves: sensitive soul; staunch protector of the realm; social justice warrior; piratical outsider? Good luck changing anyone else's mind once these various kinds of battlements are manned. Meanwhile, the tenets of *emotional conjugation* show that we always (irrationally) grant more moral flexibility to ourselves than to others. Examples: (1) "I'm firm, you're obstinate, he's a pig-headed fool." (2) "I'm righteously indignant, you're annoyed, he's making a fuss over nothing." (3) "I've reconsidered the matter, you've changed your mind, he's gone back on his word." And of course: (4) "I have an independent mind, you're eccentric, he's round the twist."

When it comes to other people, the best we can hope for is a degree of understanding and, maybe, sympathy for why others believe the things they do. Can one perform the mind-change operation internally, then, cleansing one's mental mechanism of prejudicial sludge and pseudo-rational evasion? Maybe. But recall another part of Plato's Socratic message: the mind is not one coherent thing, nor is it obviously ruled by reason. Imagine instead a sort of lame-duck executive, charged with carrying out directives emanating from a mysterious shadow bureaucracy, spinning them as coherent and responsive to norms of reason.

Or, even better, picture the mind as lacking a central executive altogether, instead being a sort of squabbling, fractious, borderline-insane committee of voices as depicted in the film *Inside Out*, with routine power struggles and multiple internal coups. It is hard enough to resist the siren call of ice cream; how in the world is change in basic belief possible? Results of a now-canonical psychological study: When people are confronted by things they want to believe, the question is "Can I?" When they are confronted by things they don't want to believe, the question is "Must I?"

We can see why *dramatic revelation* is, historically, the preferred method of mind-change. I was struck from my horse and arose a Christian! The word was spoken to me and I turned my back on Babylon! For the rest of us—well, we go on, twiddling our internal dials, trying to find stable platforms in the shifting sands of mental life, and working out our beliefs as best we can. And while it is true that emotion often drives reason, Plato knew that the mind is ever a complex matter of feedback loops, desires for stability, and a powerful (if fragile) alliance between reason, appetite, and will.

Every now and then, with hard work, we can even manage to be rational. And for the rest ... well, what about the application of force? The dark side of Platonic political wisdom—rationality is only rarely the driver of human action—might be echoed in a notorious sentiment that dates, rather obscurely, from Vietnam-era American foreign policy: "When you have them by the balls, their hearts and minds will follow."

The phrase "hearts and minds" may be reliably traced to Theodore Roosevelt. Asked by aide Lt. Douglas MacArthur in 1906 "to what he attributed his popularity," Roosevelt said: "To put into words what is in their hearts and minds but not in their mouths." This makes Roosevelt the poet laureate of politics, at least in his own mind, offering what oft was thought but n'er so well expressed. "Hearts and minds" thus enters the political vernacular, prompting some unknown Green Beret to make up a plaque with the realist update for Charles "Chuck" Colson, general counsel for the Nixon Administration. Or so one story goes. (A reference to this detail appears in the dialogue of *All The President's Men*, citing it as a cartoon rather than a plaque.)

In what follows, I will address the question of force and its relation to changing minds. Can a mind forcibly changed be considered validly changed? What role does the law, both as reality and as figure, play in this everyday psychodrama? If I obey a directive under threat of force but nevertheless convince myself that this is rational, is it rational? We shall find, perhaps sadly but not surprisingly, that "rational," so far from being a strong (if rare) curb on desire and its attendants, is instead an essentially contested concept. In this respect, it resembles such notions as "art" and "democracy" more than it does "circle," "neutron," or even "person."

However, we shall further find that this does not rule out the possibility of changing one's mind for good (i.e., rational) reasons. I mean reasons that are not the results of (a) post-facto rationalization, (b) the distillation or directive of upstream emotions, (c) force *simpliciter*, or (d) the "force of reason" itself, understood as the power of progress toward universal agreement implied in (some) uses of "rational." In other words, the rationality of "rational" can be maintained, but *only when* we acknowledge as fully as possible the essentially contested nature of our use of it. To put it another way, minds can be (justifiably) changed without squeezing anyone's vulnerable parts, as long as we appreciate the vulnerability of the reasons that prompt such change.

As for hearts—well, sometimes they are involved, sometimes not. As Pascal reminds us, "Le coeur a ses raisons que la raison ne connaît point" (no. 423).

Force of law

"It's not just a good idea, it's the law"—that claim, which forms my main title, is made of *gravity* in a rather tired joke. The joke is tired but not bad: you cannot flout the law of gravity because, like other scientific laws of a suitably general extension, it does not brook exceptions. Breaking the law of gravity is impossible; attempts to do so will always be punished, sometimes with grisly results. You can cheat the law, or so it seems when flying in an aircraft or creating a temporary reduction of its value to zero, but these are just fleeting bargains with authority.

The force of human law is not so absolute, much as some would like to have it so, but it is sometimes equally mysterious. Derrida suggests in "Force of Law" that the relations between justice and law, and between obedience and authority, are endlessly unstable. We obey laws, he argues, "not because they are just but because they have authority" (27). And yet, their perceived status as being in the service of justice is an apparently necessary condition of the authority being legitimate. This tangle cannot be resolved—hence the idea, derived in part from Pascal and Montaigne, via Walter Benjamin, that the authority of law is "mystical," the result of a violent intervention executed by a sovereign authority to establish its associated legal order.

This poses an obvious problem. "How are we to distinguish between the force of law of a legitimate power," Derrida wonders, "and the supposedly originary violence that must have established this authority and could not itself have been authorized by any anterior legitimacy so that, in this initial moment, it is neither legal nor illegal—or, others would quickly say, neither just nor unjust?" ("Force of Law"). His answer—which I will not attempt to pursue in detail here—entails a return to paradoxicality and confrontation with aporias which marks deconstruction as itself a form (and perhaps the best form) of justice. This also relates to slightly later forays into the self-contradictory relationship between justice and democracy. The sovereign state, founded on violence and ever capable of its own suspension in the name of the law, opens up the space of "democracy to come."

For the present purposes, it is enough to isolate two core claims: (1) that sovereign authority is violent and "mystical"; and (2) that self-suspension of this authority is always a prerogative of the law. Law is not just a good idea; it is the exercise of implicit force in the name of itself. We may construct various scaffolding narratives to prop up a more palatable version of the situation, but the basic situation remains much the same as when it was first analyzed by Hobbes, Freud, Marx, and other critics of sovereign authority. The state exercises its authority through the law, maintaining monopolies on allowed lethal force and legitimate punishment, even as we recognize that the basis of that authority is not divine right or rational agreement, but fear, desire, and delusion.

I do not wish to quarrel with this basic hermeneutics of suspicion regarding the law and its relation to sovereignty. What I wish to do, instead, is ask whether it is possible even while recognizing the validity of these subtle critiques to have one's mind changed by the law. My answer will be yes; indeed, I will argue that the capacity to change minds is in fact a better account of the law's everyday force than any account, whether rehabilitative or deconstructive, of the law's origins. As a shared interpersonal practice, the law does not need an origin story to justify its force; not needing one, it likewise does not suffer from lacking one.

To illustrate this claim, consider a mundane distinction that is nevertheless essential to the idea of law's force (this example was first devised by Mark Migotti). Imagine two adjacent towns, Priceville and Fineburg. In Priceville, parking is a matter of market negotiation. One parks a car in a certain place and, depending on which group controls the space, pays a certain amount in exchange for the time parked. The price will vary according to the context, including external factors such as popular attractions nearby, special events, and staying in the space past the initially agreed-upon time. For the latter condition, there might be quite high surcharges added to the price, sometimes extracted by withholding the vehicle's release from the space. In Fineburg, by contrast, the parking situation is regulated by law. Tariffs for parking are fixed in advance and do not vary with external factors. Moreover, violations of the tariff—parking without a previously agreed sanction or exceeding the allotted time—result in monetary fines. Sometimes these fines are evaded, but the status of the fine is always maintained as a theoretical curb on ignoring the legal agreements and tariffs.

It should be obvious, first, that the distinction between Priceville and Fineburg is not the cost of parking. The actual amounts surrendered in exchange for parking privileges might be identical from day to day. Nor is this case primarily one concerning the difference between public pricing and private side markets. Private parking deals can stand alongside Fineburg's municipal lots, as when people who live close to a baseball stadium offer their driveways or yards for an often escalated price. Likewise, a private service such as Uber can stand alongside a municipally regulated taxi service—whose fixed "prices" are actually tariffs—and charge amounts that the market will bear.

Such conjunctions may not prove stable, as cities across North America are discovering. Taxi drivers cry foul at the challenge posed to their hard-won monopoly on pay-for-drive services. Customers of such services, meanwhile, elated at the lower costs during off-hours, cannot legitimately complain about drastically higher costs on, say, New Year's Eve. The whole point of taximeter-cabriolet practices was to offer a non-negotiable—that is, non-market—tariff for transportation. A market-based solution to the problem of transportation will, like all markets, generate price fluctuations according to demand.

No, the essential difference between Priceville and Fineburg lies in how "violations" are costed out and understood. In Priceville, staying past the allotted time or not securing an agreement for parking generates, in effect, a further negotiation. In order to secure the release of my car, I will pay what is necessary. In Fineburg, by contrast, I have violated not an implicit contract (fee-for-service), but a law. The cost of the fine necessary to release my car from the pound or wheel-lock may be identical to the negotiated price across the town-line in Priceville, but the existential costs are never the same. The difference that makes a difference is conceptual, not material. A fine is not a price in disguise; it is an indication that you have violated (asymmetrical) authority, not (symmetrical) contract.

Many people may still fail to appreciate the difference. In other words, I might pay my parking fines as more or less the marginal costs of doing business with the world. But the importance remains in that there is a *conceptual* as well as a *material* limit to what you can "pay off" when it comes to the force of law. Beyond a certain limit even of parking violations, one's state-sanctioned privilege of driving itself might be suspended—a reminder that the experience of movement within the state is thoroughly regulated. More seriously, attempts to "price out" law on graver matters might themselves constitute offenses under the law. Nobody sane would try to bribe a police officer to tear up a parking ticket: the price difference is negligible as against simply paying the fine (I might of course attempt persuasion, distress real or feigned, perhaps charm—but not money). At higher reaches of the law's authority, though, a certain kind of character might still believe that offering a subtle incentive to officers of the law might allow him to beat an unacceptable fine with a bearable price. At best, this entails a conceptual confusion; at worst, an actionable crime all on its own.

The root of any confusion about the price/fine distinction is money, since it fosters a dangerous illusion that the law and its sanctions are subject to price. While the law sometimes trades in money for practical reasons, it is decisively not a market. Functionaries of the law may be susceptible to the temptations of pricing, but the law itself is immune from reduction to capital.

Or is it? Surely this view is altogether too optimistic, even naïve, given that the law is administered *by* human agents *over* human agents, using mechanisms and working institutions that are themselves highly imperfect. In formally analogous complex systems—one might think of the game of baseball, a frequent example in legal scholarship—there may be relevantly similar features of rule-governance and enforcement, plus a relevant suspension of market-based norms. Even here, these mechanisms and suspensions are always demonstrating their limits. You cannot "pay off" the umpire to get an on-field call reversed, but of course you can theoretically cut a side-deal, either as a player or as a spectator, to alter actions and outcomes. Thus, the haunting specter of the "thrown game," as in the 1919 World Series "Black Sox" scandal.

The relevant difference is that baseball, while sometimes a matter of livelihood, is never a matter of life and death. For we must never forget that, as Robert Cover puts it, "Legal interpretation takes place in a field of pain and death" (1601). This fact—"blithely ignored," Cover notes, by most scholars of law—puts such interpretation into a special "bonded" relationship. "Legal interpretation must be capable of transforming itself into action," Cover argues, "it must be capable of overcoming inhibitions against violence in order to generate its requisite deeds; it must be capable of massing a sufficient degree of violence to deter reprisal and revenge" (1617). This status of legal interpretation naturally derives from the status of law itself.

There thus exists a shadow, the shadow of law as an idea, between the perpetrator of organized violence, who presumptively acts in the name of rationality and coherence, and the victim of that violence, who experiences the fear, pain, or death that are not byproducts of the law, but its essence. Could we ever expect that the reasons considered by the former person should, via the necessarily distributed mechanisms that execute organized violence, communicate themselves to the latter person?

This should strike us as the essential problem of law's force. From this vantage point, worries about corruption bribery, abuse of power, institutional failure, regulatory capture, and so on are viewed as marginal costs on a system we might otherwise defend as at least minimally rational. The best legal system money can buy might still be, minimally, a functioning legal system. But the violence of actual legal force is a function of the system even (especially) when operating flawlessly. Given this, it is important that the victim of organized violence accept the normative frame of the violence, not merely suffer it. She or he will almost certainly lack the reason-giving style of a legal opinion, but without normative acceptance, the execution of the law's force is no better than torture.

And yet, as Cover insists, it may only be somewhat better even in an ideal case. There is an eerie and unsettling affinity between legal punishment and torture. "Just as the torturer and victim achieve a 'shared' world only by virtue of their diametrically opposed experiences, so the judge and prisoner understand 'punishment' through their diametrically opposed experiences of the punishing act," he writes. "[W]hether or not the judge and prisoner share the same philosophy of punishment, they arrive at the particular act of punishment having dominated and having been dominated with violence, respectively" (1609).

We all know that this violence is more often used to protect the comfortable than to punish the guilty. To use Slavoj Žižek's formulation, our current "legal system and police authority are heavily twisted and not only protect the rich, but are even ready to systematically bend the rule of law to accommodate them." And so "[t]he global capitalist system itself is, in its most fundamental dimension, corruption legalized. The question of where crime begins (which financial dealings are illegal) is not a legal question but an eminently political question, one of power struggle." To ask why a wealthy person takes advantage of this system is to invoke the vulgar inquiry about why a dog licks himself: because he can. These, then, are no longer marginal costs, but the essence of the legal-financial system.

The point forces itself upon us: the very idea of the rule of law is acceptable if and only if we are worse off without than we are with it. Just as the mind of the prisoner must be, in some sense, *of the same mind* as the judge, citizens must acknowledge the authority of the law, not merely suffer before it. This entails a certain kind of narrative – the narrative of mind-change. To see what this might mean, let us consider again the possibility of "rational" conversion.

Minds

There are surely easy cases in the conceptual field before us. I mean ones where the prisoner immediately surrenders, or never had, any extra-legal subject position. "It's a fair cop," the career criminal might allow when caught, ruefully giving this point to the (legitimate) opposition: he was not smart enough, or fast enough, or ruthless enough and so was rightly caught out. There are likewise cases where the prisoner, though bent on a different path, comes to see the error of his ways through the confrontation with the law itself, whether via the process of trial and sentencing or as a result of rehabilitation. We could even count as easy, though tragic, those cases where the charge is false, the victim innocent, and the sentence mistaken. These last are errors of process, not challenges to authority—though, to be sure, such errors may have the effect of undermining authority when perceived as being too frequent.

The really hard case is one where the victim of the law's authority does not want to surrender his resistance to the authority of the law. He may suffer it, even unto death, but does not recognize it as legitimate. Some may dismiss such cases as instances of egomania or arrogance; others will profess themselves unconcerned with the mental state of the prisoner so long as justice, or at least due process, is seen to be done. This is nevertheless a core problem for law's force: if it is to be the force of law, not force *simpliciter*, punishment must be properly conjoined to its victims.

However, there need not be any strong metaphysical condition here. It would be excessive in a modern scheme of law, for example, to insist that the victim come to see himself as spiritually flawed or devil-marked in some fashion. It is sufficient that there be some track of mind that highlights the ordinary flaws that lead to a violation of the law: arrogance, ambition, temporary madness, akrasia, desperation, and the like. The important thing is that a link is established between the violator's state of mind at time T1 (when the case was in question) and at time T2 (after judgment and punishment have been handed down).

If skepticism remains about the need for this change of mind, consider the sort of case to which I believe it is best compared: the dyadic love-relation.

In a recent television series, *Jessica Jones*, based on a popular Marvel comic book, a demented mutant called Kilgrave (played with sinister-geek glee by David Tennant) has the ability to compel anyone to do his bidding. This is the result of a rogue experiment conducted on him by his scientist parents. Armed with this ability, life for Kilgrave becomes a series of ever more lurid episodes of getting his way. Every time he vocalizes a command, those who hear it have no choice but to obey. This has both comic and grotesque consequences, including Kilgrave's own sense of being burdened with this "gift" ("I have to painstakingly choose every word I say. I once told a man to go screw himself. Can you even imagine?") Kilgrave's whims and considered desires are alike impervious to disobedience. He is, in a sense, a man whose word is law, whether he likes it or not.

Enter Jessica Jones, an alcoholic downtown private eye with her own small portion of super-powers (extraordinary strength, modest flying ability). In the course of an ill-advised stint as a victim-saving hero, Jessica comes into contact with Kilgrave, who makes her into his love-slave. She barely escapes his clutches and begins a crusade to defeat him before he suborns more women to his will.

Kilgrave, for his part, becomes obsessed with Jessica and her incomplete devotion. "I promise that I won't touch you until I get your genuine consent," he tells her at one point, noting that he understands the idea of love: "I am new to love. But I know what it looks like. I do watch television." Unfortunately for him, his media-inflected notion of love combines the idea of consent with the toxic notion that, as critic Emily Nussbaum has put it, is "the ultimate in entitlement: he deserves Jessica because he desires her, which means that her own desires are just obstacles" (para. 6). He has already dominated Jessica with mind-control; now he needs her to submit to his domination without it. And this she refuses to do.

The scenario is all too familiar: the drama of seduction, the literally irresistible man who nevertheless desires genuine submission. "You can control her mind, but you cannot make a woman love you, when she loves another," a friend tells Count Cagliostro (Orson Welles) in the 1949 film *Black Magic* (directed by Gregory Ratoff, based on Alexandre Dumas' 1846 novel *Joseph Balsamo*). Every Casanova and Don Juan realizes that the dilemma of seduction, much like the dialectic of bondage of slavery in Hegel's *Phenomenology*, is predicated on a power struggle in which the apparently dominant player is in fact helpless. Mind-control is like ideological indoctrination or hypnotism: it can generate the outward results, but not the inner conversion. The seducer needs the seduced to be, paradoxically, a willing victim to his irresistible assault. The one thing even the most powerful law cannot compel is the agreement to be compelled.

And yet, we know that seduction does happen, and not always as a function of effective gaslighting or manipulation. It is surely an enduring and horrible male fantasy that desire should be its own unanswerable argument—she must love me *because* I love her—but it is also the case that, sometimes, a path is revealed leading from initial resistance to genuine regard. How is this possible? Simple: the initially resistant subject of seductive attention genuinely *comes to believe* in the appeal of the seducer. The hint of violence that remains in such a scenario is a useful reminder that the law, when it seeks to change minds, is also a patriarchal and self-serving construction. It desires our acknowledgment, but, failing that, it will settle fairly happily for mere obedience.

How, then, can I continue to speak of mind-change in this context? Well, consider again the notion of ego-decentered mind suggestion in the opening section. We mislead ourselves if we grant too great a role to the self-identifying "I" in mental states or their attendant actions. Desires and inner compulsions, often murky and ill-conceived, make up much of the individual's mental landscape. The narrative of passage from time T1 to time T2, whether the issue is one of crime-and-punishment or resistance-and-acceptance, is likely to be a patchwork of revisions and recursions, erasures and redactions, in the service of minimally acceptable coherence. It is all too plausible that I will tell myself a story in which I both identify with and reject the state of mind belonging to a previous version of myself. That narrative flexibility may be all that "changing one's mind" really means. The "I" is just tagging along for the ride.[1]

One of the many ironies of law's force is that, before the law, we are asked to reconstruct a mental narrative ("What was your motivation for that action at that time?"), which is antithetical to actual experience of the mental. In this, legal confrontation resembles a form of mental debriefing, as if our completed mind-missions were being examined by ranking officers with no direct experience, but lots of judgment about how things happen in the field.

This narrative flexibility, as I called it, is consistent not only with an ego-decentered conception of mind, but also with our self-reflexive recognition of the tension between freedom and necessity. Indeed, that recognition itself—that structural relationship between the self and its sense of self—is a good basic account of what mind is. Here, reflecting on the otherwise mysterious facts of choice and agency, we can acknowledge the limited but essential role of reason-giving in human life. Reasons are part of our narrative flexibility and are not at odds with it. They may curb wild excesses of choice, anticipating perhaps just the sort of debrief where we have to "explain ourselves." They also serve to guide choice, in the interests of coherence and, yes, submission to norms.

The complexity of these functions and relations can be explored in potentially infinite detail. For now, let us simply state that this conception of mind is also consistent with the possibility of changing one's mind under threat (or experience) of force. I can always submit to force; that is no more than categorical. But I can also come to see that the reasons for the threat of force, once external to me, are good reasons and, moreover, good ones for me. That is, I can come to see my mind as *rationally* changed, not just broken or subdued. This depends upon a rather narrow conception of "rational," to which we will now turn.

Essentially contested

I suggested earlier that "rational" ought to be counted among the essentially contested concepts (ECCs) that make up a large—some would say distressingly large—portion of certain fields of apparently reasoned dispute, such as art and politics. W.B. Gallie, in the landmark article outlining the notion of an ECC, sketches the logical conditions under which a concept may be so styled. These include (a) its appraisive character, (b) its complexity, (c) its variability, and (d) its openness. In addition, Gallie argues, and largely as a consequence of these first four features, the users of a given ECC recognize, at least in part, (e) that others are using the very same concept in ways divergent from their own without being insane, malicious, or disingenuous.

Thus, ECCs, "although not resolvable by argument of any kind, are nevertheless sustained by perfectly respectable arguments and evidence" (Gallie 169). This feature highlights the nub of the issue with such concepts. They are not merely hotly disputed or endlessly disputed; while they may indeed be both of these, their true essence is, at it were, their essentiality—it is in their nature to be disputed. In contrast to scientific disputes, even at the level of paradigm, let alone simple factual claim, there is no rational prospect of the dispute over these concepts coming to an end. This poses a particular challenge for philosophy's self-image: ECCs remind us that "there is to-day a widespread repudiation of the idea of philosophy as a kind of 'engine' of thought, that can be laid on to eliminate conceptual confusions wherever they may occur" (Gallie 168).

Gallie's own conclusions about ECCs were relatively modest, but like many a clever idea, the notion has cultivated a particularly virulent strain of academic kudzu, such that one is liable to find any concept that generates disagreement so described. This seems especially likely, for reasons I will suggest, in legal scholarship. Counterpunchers then step in to argue the contrary, characterizing this dispute or that as merely fiery, or prolonged, or founded on vagueness. The endgame suggested by such tit-for-tat proliferation might be—surely contrary to the author's own intentions—the sneaking suspicion that "essentially contested concept" is, itself, an essentially contested concept.

Let us avoid that grim outcome and instead note the enduring interest in Gallie's idea. To my mind, there are two points of interest: (a) that disputes about ECCs are (or can be) entirely rational; and (b) that this means we should not (perhaps cannot) discard such concepts on the basis of their essentially contested nature. We need the concept; we need the contestation.

My suggestion that "rational" falls under the ECC umbrella is therefore not intended as a version of the self-reference endgame mentioned above. On the contrary, I wish to suggest that the nature of any "rational" feature or action is precisely that they excite a dispute, impossible to settle, about the range and appropriateness of the adjectival extension. Indeed, it seems to me that "rational" is the ECC par excellence, just because it is implicated in the logical conditions of the category.

What do I mean? First of all, notice again Gallie's insistence that disagreement about ECCs is reason-based. In his ideal case (a neat thought-experiment concerning the nature of "the champions" in an imagined sport), the rival factions all employ the same concept *and* recognize that other factions are doing so without delusion or sinister intent. Hence, there is the essential logical possibility of a change of mind: adherence to a given faction is not a matter of overarching ideological blindness. There may be temptations to indulge indoctrination or various forms of coercion, but the most important, and subtle, weapon in the arsenal of the disputing factions is their *account of rightness* with respect to the concept.

The various supporters, Gallie says, "continue to regard and acclaim their favourite teams as 'the champions' and continue their efforts to convert others to their view, not through any vulgar wish to be the majority party, but because they believe their favoured team is playing the game best." He goes on: "There is, therefore, continuous competition between the contestant teams, not only for acknowledgment as champions, but for acceptance of (what each side and its supporters take to be) the proper criteria of championship" (171). One of the most telling moves in this continuous, multi-level effort is the execution of what Gallie calls "some shrewd appraisive comment" (189), which may succeed in getting a rival follower to see the criteria, and hence the game, in my (correct!) way. Such conversions are justifiable, and reveal the disputes as genuine: "we can distinguish more or less intellectually respectable conversions from those of a more purely emotional, or yet those of a more sinister kind" (Gallie 190).

We can see, I think, that rationality emerges on this account as a *relational function* enacted between adherence to a given way of seeing X and my ability to generate discourse that might cause another individual person to see X that way, against a presumed background of disagreement about X. Disputes about "rationality" are themselves the natural byproduct at a meta-level of the disputes carried on below, just to the extent that those first-order disputes generate the felt need for reasons.

The significant feature I want to highlight here is that not only is it possible to change our minds concerning a given ECC (X)—that much is built into Gallie's account—but also that this possibility raises the stakes of human interaction more generally. Our desire to persuade (and, prior to that, to believe) on the basis of reasons makes us vulnerable to endless meta-level disputes. But, far from forcing an acceptance of irrationalism or force at this meta-level, the vulnerability shows *at the very same time* the odd resiliency of self-reflexive notions of rationality. There is no universal reach, no reliable stopping-rule, no extra-human authority at the level of "rationality" any more than there is (or can be) at the level of X.

Nor can we save the category of "rational" by artful narrowing of its extension to the truths of mathematics, say, or the structure of scientific revolutions. Why not? This is, after all, a favorite move of philosophers: faced with a messy concept, they clean up the mess by, in effect, sweeping it under the carpet or into the closet. But Gallie is right to notice that this hygienic approach to concepts is unhelpful in far too many cases to remain unchallenged. This is especially so in our meta-case, since any commitment to rationality-as-mathematics or rationality-as-dominant-falsifiable-paradigm is itself just the call to a particular faction concerning the concept "rational."

Am I perhaps hoist on my own petard here? If these narrowing moves are not allowable knock-out punches, but instead forms of special pleading, then how does the claim that the concept "rational" is essentially contested differ from them? In other words, is the ECC claim not also a kind of narrowing exceptionalism, and thus self-limiting? Moreover, even if we were to accept the ECC view of things as best, and so to see the foundationalist rationality of the Platonic/Cartesian/Kantian tradition as an exceptionally strong faction, is the ECC view not then exposed as itself just a rival faction among others?

In truth, all of these accounts of "rational" stand as rival factions competing for adherence by attentive agents. The heart of my claim that "rational" is an ECC is that, by the logic of ECCs themselves, that claim is *not* exceptional. It does not stand outside the uses of "rational" as an external authority on how those uses should be organized and evaluated.

But, by the very same logic, nor do the other claims concerning "rational." There is no decisive outside authority, only the shrewd appraisive comment within the discourse. As before, this feature of "inside-only" use seems even more prominent in the case of "rational" than in the cases of "art," "democracy," or "social justice" (Gallie's real-world examples). You cannot rationally convince me about the superior nature of your account of rationality unless and until you appeal to reasons that I myself regard as good reasons. Gallie's remark about the failure of the hygienic model of dealing with conceptual confusion might obscure this, but by the end of his argument—while considering objections that the view is either obscurantist, or historicist, or both—matters are made clearer. "To find reasonableness in the pursuit of inevitably endless conflicts," Gallie notes, may be quixotic, but it is not a surrender to irrationalism (196). Appraisive concepts must be understood according to what a Gadamerian would call their *Wirkungsgeschichte*, or history of effects; this is all the more true for the conjunction of normativity and narrative that is the law.[2] There is no fallacious historicism and no obscurantism lurking here.

In sum, the fact of rational conversion even under conditions of essential contestation both confirms and destabilizes the status of rationality. It confirms it because we see that not all changes of mind are matters of obliterating bolts from the blue or the result of simple force, but it destabilizes it because we see the tenuousness of the very idea of authority. The force of reason is a matter of subtle discursive engagement and a shared willingness to engage. For all that, its force is surprisingly binding: when some shrewd appraisive comment allows me to see X in a new light, I genuinely see it that way—I am not deluded or compelled against my will. Instead, I am engaged in what might fairly be called a collective delusion, one whose compulsion is not contrary to will, but an emergent property of all our wills.

This brings us back to the specific issue of the *force of law*. The popularity of gesturing toward ECCs in legal scholarship is not, it seems to me, simply a matter of intellectual laziness or trend-surfing in the waters of legalese. Rather, the law's uncertain metaphysical status is an enduring source of confusion. This is especially so because of the law's status as force and not just a good idea. The exercise of force, contrary to most popular conceptions thereof, actually demands reasons. Thrasymachus is humiliated by Socrates because he allows a rational standard of advantage—one that is not simply reducible to strength—to creep into his discourse. Even a more perfected realist than Thrasymachus bespeaks his command of force as rightful in the very exercise of it. "Might makes right" is, after all, an explicable account of right.

Hannah Arendt, meanwhile, reminds us that proliferating death in political zones is not a sign of an emerging or established hegemony, but instead of power's desperate decline: "rule by sheer violence," she noted, "comes into play where power is being lost" (53). The persistent pathology of violence done in the name of the law is, despite formal exoneration, an insult to the law: white police officers shooting black teenagers and getting away with it or the financial sleight-of-hand of shady offshore tax dealing. The mechanisms of the law's oversight on its own enforcement are flawed to the point of outrage, but this violence does not, in itself, undermine legitimate enforcement. Indeed, the proper call here is for better enforcement of enforcement's implicit rightness. (Even terrorism, which might seem to flout this minimal notion of "rational" force, largely surrenders to the same logic of implied rightness: ISIS is evilly indiscriminate in the matter of particular victims, but evilly discriminate when it comes to general targets.)

Just as it may always be corrupt, even the legitimate law may always compel as a matter of brute fact, since it is in the nature of its force to do so, but what the law really demands is normative-narrative assent, not brute obedience. Consider a particularly vivid and brutal example. The dawning understanding of the tortured prisoners in Kafka's *Penal Colony*, subjected to the exquisite cruelty of the colony's slow-motion execution machine, illustrates the point—if rather nastily! It is not enough for the prisoners to suffer; they must know and, in some sense, acknowledge the reason for their suffering. That is why, strictly speaking, the execution of this punishment is not torture—though the methods are torturous enough to satisfy even the most bloodthirsty pain-merchant.

The Officer in charge of the Penal Colony's activities tells the visiting Explorer that the prisoners scheduled for punishment and execution experience, at about the six-hour mark of the full 12-hour duration on "the bed," a religious or mystical epiphany—a sort of conversion. We might better characterize it as a shrewd appraisive comment. It is, naturally, one which most of us would prefer to avoid! Or, to put it more accurately, it is one whose force we can perceive *and assent to* without the need of a penal machine to imprint the message upon our bodies. The interpersonal machine of the law's reasons is sufficient, and imprinting on our minds enough to make our bodies (mostly) willing servants of that authority.

However, the same story likewise contains a cautionary note concerning our allegiance to law's authority. The dedicated Officer, who wishes to continue the Colony's use of the machine against the views of the ailing Commandant, begs the Explorer to plead his case. When the Explorer demurs, the Office experiences a kind of fit of unreasoning commitment to ideas of crime and punishment. He frees the condemned prisoner and fixes the machine for his own execution, programming the torture bed to inscribe on his willing body the message "Be Just." But the worn and broken-down mechanism, creaking with overuse, malfunctions and instead of offering a delicious half-day of epiphanic violence, stabs him to death without further ado.

As with all of Kafka's parables, the final message is uncertain, but perhaps we can say, in the context of the current argument, that the Officer relied too readily on the rightness of the force of law. Perhaps, too, he was not sufficiently guilty of the specified charge. The law's reasons are not subject to our *particular* desires, only our shared discursive practices of sense-making and mind-changing.

Concluding remarks

The force of law does not rest on its alleged rationality as long as "rational" continues to be parsed as aspiration to universal authoritative reach. But nor does it rest purely on the state's monopoly on the legal ("justified") use of deadly or coercive force. Rather, the force of law consists in its latent ability to affect mind-change. This ability is realized through the looping effects set up between the possibility of force under the law and the play of reason within law's subjects. These subjects include the scofflaw, the outlaw, and the petty criminal, as well as the bulk of law-abiding citizens. Each of them orients and executes a series of self-perceived rational decisions based upon their relative proximity to the prospect of punishment by the mechanisms of the law. That is simply what their experience of "rational freedom" amounts to. You may evade the law's punishment, even unto death, but that is not the same as beating it.

It follows that the genuine authority of the law must not be (a) mystical, (b) blankly positivistic, or (c) harshly realist in Hobbesian fashion. Law retains authority just to the extent that it tracks—even as it enables—the looping effects of individuals exercising (what they understand to be) their reason. In this sense, the law is a form of collective delusion rather than a mind-independent fact. Like some other examples of such shared delusion, it is *necessary* from the perspective of reason as we each entertain it. We can change our minds about a lot of things, including about reason itself, but we cannot change our minds about that necessity without losing them.

You fought the law, but the law won. That's what it does and, in a minimally rational sense, that's what makes it the law.

Notes

1 An excellent account of this flexibility and decentering of mind can be found in Neil Levy, "Autonomy and Addiction." Levy's examination of the condition of addiction as compossible with a quite robust notion of personal autonomy reminds us that the notions of self-control and mind-control are far more complex than ordinary, and even some philosophical, usage would seem to allow.

2 Compare Robert Cover on the specific point of law's status within a normative order: "Law may be viewed as a system of tension or a bridge linking a concept of a reality to an imagined alternative—that is, as a connective between two states of affairs, both of which can be represented in their normative significance only through the devices of narrative." See Cover, "The Supreme Court, 1982 Term—Foreword," pp. 4–68.

References

All the President's Men. Directed by Alan J. Pakula, Wildwood Enterprises and Warner Bros., 1976.

Arendt, Hannah. *On Violence*. Harcourt Brace, 1970.

Black Magic. Directed by Gregory Ratoff, Edward Small Productions, 1949.

Cover, Robert. "The Supreme Court, 1982 Term—Foreword: Nomos and Narrative." *Harvard Law Review*, vol. 97, 1983, pp. 1–4.

——. "Violence and the Word." *Yale Law Journal*, vol. 95, no. 8, 1986, pp. 1601–1629.

Curtis, Sonny. "I Fought the Law." *In Style with the Crickets*, Coral Records, 1960.

Derrida, Jacques. "Force of Law: The 'Mystical Foundation of Authority'." In *Acts of Religion*. Edited by Gil Anidjar, Routledge, 2002, pp. 230–298.
Dumas, Alexandre. *Joseph Balsamo*. Vol. 1. Dufour, 1860.
Gallie, W.B. "Essentially Contested Concepts." *Proceedings of the Aristotelian Society*, New Series, vol. 56, 1955–1956, pp. 167–198.
Hegel, G.W.F. *Phenomenology of Spirit*. Trans. A.V. Miller. Motilal Banarsidass Publishing, 1998.
Inside Out. Directed by Pete Docter, Walt Disney Pictures and Pixar Animation Studios, 2015.
Kafka, Franz. *The Penal Colony*. Schocken Books, 1948.
Levy, Neil. "Autonomy and Addiction." *Canadian Journal of Philosophy*, vol. 36, no. 3, 2006, pp. 427–447.
Nussbaum, Emily. "Graphic, Novel." *New Yorker*, December 21/28, 2015, www.newyorker.com/magazine/2015/12/21/graphic-novel-on-television-emily-nussbaum.
Pascal. *Pensées*. Paris, 1852.
Rosenberg, Melissa, creator. *Jessica Jones*. Marvel Television, ABC Studios, and Tall Girls Productions, 2015.
Žižek, Slavoj. "Explaining the Panama Papers, or, Why Does a Dog Lick Himself?" *Newsweek*, April 7, 2016, http://newsweek.com/panama-papers-dogs-themselves-north-korea-vladimir-putin-444791.

Chapter 2

Cruel and thus not unusual

Jacques Derrida's seminar on the death penalty

Michael Naas

> *Le vocable cru, lui disputer ainsi le cru … le cru auquel je ne crois pas, et le mot cru laisse affluer en lui par le canal de l'oreille, une veine encore, la foi, la profession de foi ou la confession, la croyance, la crédulité … la cruauté surtout, encore le sang, cruor, confiteor, ce que le sang aura été pour moi.*
>
> Jacques Derrida ("Circonfession," 7–8)[1]

From the Eighth Amendment to the US Constitution prohibiting "cruel and unusual punishment" to the Universal Declaration of Human Rights "barring cruel, inhuman or degrading treatment or punishment," the common-sense assumption has been and continues to be that cruelty *can* be avoided and, when it comes to penal law, *should* be avoided and so prohibited. There are, it has been assumed, ways of treating criminals that are not only less cruel than others, but also ways that are not cruel at all. And that would seem to be common sense itself.

And yet, in his two-year seminar on *The Death Penalty* (over the academic years 1999–2000 and 2000–2001), Jacques Derrida seems to contest this common-sense assumption when he suggests that cruelty has no contrary, that there is no non-cruelty, and so no non-cruel punishment, and that it is, in fact, a dangerous illusion to think that there is.[2] Cruelty must therefore be rethought, he argues, according to a *differential* rather than an *oppositional* economy, a rethinking that will have all kinds of effects on our understanding not just of the death penalty, the explicit focus of his seminar, but of the justification and rationality for punishment itself.

In this chapter, I would like to follow Derrida's rethinking of cruelty over the course of the two years of his seminar, as well as in his 2000 essay "Psychoanalysis Searches the States of its Soul," a text written during the summer between the two years of the seminar.[3] In the course of these works, Derrida reads and questions many canonical discourses on the death penalty, both for and against, as well as the presuppositions and common-sense assumptions about cruelty that these discourses often share. Therefore, he does not simply oppose death penalty advocates and abolitionists, but tries to find what is common to their seemingly conflicting discourses. His strategy, as we will see, is to follow those two masters of suspicion, Nietzsche and Freud, in order to detect an interest behind or within every claim to disinterestedness and a cruelty behind every claim to non-cruelty—indeed, a cruelty even in, especially in, the law itself.

This strategy is initially rather surprising, for it could easily be thought that the difference between abolitionists and defenders of the death penalty translates rather straightforwardly into an opposition between those who are against cruelty and those who favor it or allow it, or who at least see it as necessary or unavoidable. And yet, Derrida demonstrates, this argument is flawed on almost every count. While it is tempting, for example, to think that advocates of the death penalty at the very least recognize the necessity of a certain cruelty in punishment as a deterrent to breaking the law, the most rigorous defenders of the death penalty have actually claimed, quite to the contrary, that they are the least cruel, if not altogether non-cruel. Kant, for example, whom Derrida considers the most rigorous of all the proponents of the death penalty, claims not just that the death penalty is not cruel but also that it is the only punishment capable of giving man his unique dignity. By excluding all psychological motives and practical considerations from both the justification of the death penalty and its application, the law would be, for Kant, absolutely disinterested and thus completely without cruelty. As Derrida phrases Kant, "the proper trait of a categorical imperative is to command beyond empirical or pathological interest ... and this should be true in particular of that categorical imperative of penal justice that ... the death penalty is, a death penalty that should then also be disinterested, according to Kant, pure of any calculation" (*DP1* 144/207).

To counter such claims, Derrida enlists the help of Nietzsche, who questions the supposed disinterestedness and lack of cruelty in proponents of the death penalty, and particularly in Kant. According to Derrida, Nietzsche in *On the Genealogy of Morals* attempts to "unmask an all-powerful interest hidden behind the discourse of disinterest of the Kantian type," an interest that in fact "conditions the legal doctrine of the death penalty" (*DP1* 147/211). But Nietzsche detects more than just interest in Kant's claim to disinterest; he also detects a certain cruelty, "a logic of cruelty," and, within or at the bottom of that cruelty, *blood* (*DP1* 147/211). Derrida writes that "Nietzsche is going to accuse Kant and the categorical imperative of cruelty (*Grausamkeit*), a cruelty that does not speak its name, a hypocritical cruelty that gives itself airs of keeping its hands clean, a cruelty ... that has the odor of blood and torture" (*DP1* 148/212).

It is not only interest, then, that Nietzsche detects behind Kant's supposed disinterest, and not only cruelty behind his supposedly non-cruel discourse, but blood (*cruor*), even though the German *grausam*, unlike the French *cruauté* or the English *cruelty*, is not etymologically related to *cruor* or to blood. As Derrida claims, still following Nietzsche:

> Nietzsche finds Kant "cruel" and ... he finds a certain wreak of cruelty, a certain odor of cruelty in the categorical imperative ... he smells blood, even if cruelty is not what Kant means to say, and even if the word *grausam* makes

> no reference, like *cruor*, *crudelis*, *crudelitas*, to blood, to flowing red blood (*cruor*) … Kant *stinks* (as one would say in English) of Christian cruelty.
> (*DP1* 158–159/225–226)

Kant's discourse is thus, for Nietzsche, interested *and* cruel *and* bloody, despite its claims or pretentions to the contrary.

But it is not just the proponents of the death penalty who are interested and cruel even as they claim they are not. It is also the critics of the death penalty, as Baudelaire and, before him, Voltaire, already suspected, abolitionists who oppose and criticize the death penalty not because it is cruel or too cruel, but, in essence, because it is not cruel enough. This would be the case of Beccaria, for whom, as Derrida paraphrases him, "the risk of a life sentence of hard labor will make the criminal suffer more and thus fear more than the threat of immediate death" (*DP1* 160/227). This is an argument that has not gone out of fashion and can still be heard today in many quarters of the US and no doubt elsewhere.

We thus see, in this relationship between Kant and the proponents of the death penalty, on the one side, and Beccaria and the abolitionists, on the other, not an opposition between those who "favor" cruelty and those who "oppose" it, but, in the end, two sides or two manifestations of the same cruelty drive, two sides of an "originary sadistic cruelty" that, according to Derrida, has no opposite or contrary (*DP1* 160/227). What Derrida diagnoses through Nietzsche is, in effect, "a cruelty that has no contrary because it is originary," such that "the phenomenon of non-cruelty, the appearance of non-cruelty, would be but a dissimulated cruelty, or even a bid to raise the level of cruelty" (*DP1* 159/226). As a result, Derrida concludes, "one no longer knows who is more cruel or more sadistic, Beccaria or Kant, the one who opposes the death penalty or the one who maintains its principle" (*DP1* 161/228). One does not know whether the proponent of the death penalty who disavows its cruelty is more or less cruel than the abolitionist who is against the death penalty because, as he willingly admits or as his rhetoric lets be heard, it is not cruel enough.

During the second year of his seminar on *The Death Penalty*, Derrida returns to many of these same arguments, but this time it is psychoanalysis, rather than philosophy, and Freud (along with Theodor Reik), rather than Nietzsche, that helps him to find cruelty there where it is easy to overlook or mistake it. Speaking of "Nietzsche's texts" as having "heralded a certain Freud … on the topic of sadism," Derrida recalls once again that cruelty "has no limit and no term but only an internal and qualitative differentiation" (*DP2* 3/21). Just as he pitted Kant against Beccaria during the first year of the seminar in order to conclude, rather surprisingly, that each could be thought to be more cruel than the other, so, during this second year, he pits Kant against Robespierre in order to come to a similar but even more surprising conclusion. He asks: "Who will have been the crueler of the two, Kant or Robespierre? And what if each were crueler than the other? And reciprocally? Each less cruel than the other? And what, then, would 'cruel' mean in this case?" (*DP2* 186/251).

Derrida introduces his comparison of these two seemingly incomparable figures by recalling Kant's mixed or divided feelings about the French Revolution and its cruelty, his "mix of horror and enthusiasm ... before the *signum* of the French Revolution that at once destroyed law, cruelly threw the foundation (*Grund*) of law into the abyss (*Abgrund*) by executing the sovereign and generating the Terror ... and established the law, killed and resuscitated it again, refounded and recalled it, the law of a free people and the rights of man" (*DP2* 204/273–274). It is Kant's respect for the law that leads to both his horror at the death of Louis XVI during the Revolution and his enthusiasm for the refounding of the law. Derrida goes on to suggest that "this mix of two contradictory feelings also divided Kant's view of Robespierre," contradictory feelings that "might have been shared by Robespierre, by Robespierre in his abolitionist phase when faced with Kant who was a cruel supporter of the death penalty, and then by the regicidal Robespierre when faced with Kant who was a reactionary and a pitiless judge of the simulacrum of revolutionary justice" (*DP2* 204/274). It was none other than Robespierre, Derrida recalls, who actually referred to the "*cruelty* of the death penalty," Robespierre who said that "everything argues in favor of moderate laws; everything conspires against cruel ones," with the death penalty being, for him, the cruelest of them all (*DP2* 194/262). As for Kant, one can always say, says Derrida, that "he was content to write about the death penalty, to write about it and to teach it," which would "seem less cruel" than Robespierre. Unless, of course, one can be *more* cruel by supporting something with one's writing and thinking while being unable or unwilling to *act* upon that thinking. All this leads Derrida to ask:

> if the death penalty is cruel, which of the two was more cruel, given that both were, each in his own way, supporters of the French Revolution and of the death penalty: the one, Robespierre, one type of actor, whose traits are recognizable as those of the actor, the man of action; the other, Kant, a thinker and thus an actor of another type?
>
> (*DP2* 196/264)

Derrida concludes: "If each appears crueler than the other, then the obscurity surrounding the question of knowing what cruelty is only increases" (*DP2* 204/274).

During the second year of *The Death Penalty* seminar, Derrida returns to many of the themes and questions of the first year, as one would expect, but with a much greater emphasis on psychoanalysis and particularly with regard to the question of cruelty. He suggests, for example, that "the psychoanalytic recourse to these words, *cruel, cruelty* ... is perhaps not adequate" and that a new concept of cruelty needs to be distinguished from "the confusion of its everyday usage" (*DP2* 204/274). But, during this second year, Derrida nonetheless seems to find in Freud, and in Theodor Reik, the disciple of Freud, some of the elements or at least the outline of just such a new concept of cruelty, a logic or law of "escalation" or "hyperbole" (as opposed to opposition), the notion of a cruelty that "has no contrary and no end, no termination or opposable term" (*DP2* 187/252). According to this logic, "one cruelty [can always be] more cruel than another, which also means that when we think we are less cruel, when we abstain from cruelty, we risk being even more cruel" (*DP2* 204/274).

This latter point is crucial and brings into even sharper relief the relationship between Kant and Robespierre in relation to cruelty. In *The Compulsion to Confess*, Theodor Reik actually "puts into causal relation the ideal and cruelty, idealism and cruelty, the inflexible law of ideal purity and cruelty." Rather than countering or combating cruelty, as we might think, "the ideal produces the cruel," according to Reik. In other words, it is "moral law that drives one to cruelty; it is the elevation of moral feelings, the elevation of moral demands that produces cruelty and vengeance, vindictive cruelty" (*DP2* 205/275). Hence, cruelty does not need blood or is no longer essentially related to blood. Indeed, it does better—it can become even more cruel—*without blood*. For Reik and, it seems, for Freud, one can put an end to bloody cruelty but not to cruelty itself, which, in the name of the ideal, as the ideal, can actually lead to an escalation of cruelty. As both Kant, in his advocacy for the death penalty, and Robespierre, in his pro-death penalty phase, would testify, it is not some outside of the law but "the inflexible law" itself that "produces cruelty" (*DP2* 206/277)—as well as terror.

To return to the question that Derrida asks throughout the second year of the seminar, who, then, is more cruel: Kant or Robespierre? Well, once again, each can be seen to be more cruel than the other:

> By being even more of an idealist than Robespierre, since he did not himself, in person and in actuality, cause heads to fall, Kant was in short crueler than Robespierre in this hyperbolic logic of cruel idealism or of the cruelty of idealism... Kant was more idealistic, consciously, in spirit (in his conscious or unconscious desire), thus even more cruel than Robespierre who was, in actuality, crueler than Kant, as if the act of cruelty, the acting out of cruelty, were less cruel than the desire, without action, for cruelty.
>
> (*DP2* 207/277–278)

The conclusion Derrida reached with regard to Kant and Beccaria is here even more striking and more troubling, and it calls even more clearly for a rethinking of the very concept of cruelty. For "what if Kant and Robespierre were each more cruel than the other?" (*DP2* 209/280) What if "man escapes cruelty only in the name of law or rights, and thus in the name of an even greater refinement in cruelty"? (*DP2* 209/280)

Now, as Derrida acknowledges, Freud and Reik articulated this other logic of cruelty with the aim of intervening within the current state of affairs and with the hope of "accelerating an evolution that is *less cruel*, more civilized," an intervention that, they hoped, "would not only abolish the death penalty but also substitute confession for punishment" (*DP2* 179/242, emphasis added). That is no doubt one of the reasons why Derrida turns to Freud and Reik in the first place. But another reason for doing so, and one even more important for my purposes here, is that psychoanalysis helps Derrida to think this bloodless cruelty of the ideal or of ideality, that is, it helps him to think *today's* bloodless cruelty, which, precisely because it is bloodless, can always *seem* to be less cruel or even not cruel at all. Derrida uses Nietzsche and Freud in order to move from the *cruor* of *cruauté* and *cruelty* to *Grausamkeit*, from bloody to bloodless cruelty, because that is precisely the "evolution" (or the mutation that passes for evolution) in cruelty and in the death penalty, and particularly in the US, over the last half-century. Derrida recalls that, since the eighteenth century, all the discourses on "euthanasia" or "anesthesia," all the debates surrounding the humanity of the guillotine, the electric chair, and, especially, since the 1970s, the lethal injection, have revolved around a putative elimination or reduction of pain and suffering, a reduction that is accompanied by an elimination of blood and, so it is thought, of cruelty. But has cruelty really been eliminated or has it just been displaced into other, bloodless forms?

Throughout the first year of *The Death Penalty* seminar, Derrida argues that beneath the opposition between proponents of the death penalty and abolitionists, there is interest, and cruelty, and blood. In this second year, he uses Freud to speak of a bloodless cruelty, a cruelty that breaks with blood. He does this because, he is claiming, we are today undergoing "a transformation of our experience in relation to blood in all of its registers: culture, religion but also medicine, genetics," and so on. In short, "our perception of blood is changing" (*DP2* 245/326), and this has been accompanied by what Derrida in "Psychoanalysis Searches the States of its Soul" calls a "mutation of cruelty itself—or at least new historical figures of an ageless cruelty, as old and no doubt older than man" ("PSS" 270/70). It is essential, therefore, to take this mutation into account if we are today going to think cruelty or the death penalty, or punishment more generally. Since punishments such as life imprisonment without parole could well be, as Beccaria himself actually suggested, even more cruel than the death penalty, though they would involve neither death—that is, what we call death—nor blood, a new conception of cruelty and of the transformation it is today undergoing is sorely needed.

Derrida explains this important transformation or mutation even more clearly in "Psychoanalysis Searches the States of its Soul," a work that dates from the summer of 2000, that is, right between the two years of his seminar on the death penalty. First delivered on July 10, 2000 at the Estates General of Psychoanalysis in Paris, "Psychoanalysis Searches the States of its Soul" is one of those texts that, like "Faith and Knowledge," initially appears to be just another "occasional" piece, in this case an address to a psychoanalytic institution, but that, upon closer inspection, turns out to be a major text in the Derridean corpus, an ambitious and wide-ranging work on a whole host of related topics. It is a text that not only summarizes much of Derrida's work before it, but also anticipates much that is to come, including, of course, the second year of *The Death Penalty* seminar, where, as we have seen, it is Freud rather than Nietzsche and psychoanalysis rather than philosophy that helps Derrida to rethink cruelty, and thus punishment, and thus the death penalty.

Derrida begins his address by exploring the tenuous difference between *making* suffer and *letting* suffer ("PSS" 238/9). Is the first, he asks, really opposed to the second as cruelty would be opposed to non-cruelty? Derrida has his doubts—just as he will in his seminar of the following year when he questions whether Robespierre was really, unequivocally, more cruel than Kant. Derrida suggests that this is perhaps simply a difference within cruelty itself, within a *psychic cruelty* where pleasure and cruelty cannot be radically distinguished ("PSS" 239/11). Psychoanalysis would therefore be a privileged discourse for addressing these issues, a privileged discourse for investigating the "radical evil" of making suffer for the sake of suffering and the pleasure that would be attached to this ("PSS" 240/13). As Derrida argues, "the only discourse that can claim the thing of psychical suffering as its own affair would indeed be what has been called, for about a century, psychoanalysis" ("PSS" 240/12). Since cruelty is not or is no longer related to blood, as both Freud and Nietzsche have shown, it would have no contrary not only in discourses or practices involving blood, but also in those that seem to have been purged of or purified of every hint or stain of blood ("PSS" 238–239/10). For were we one day able completely to stop or to staunch the flow of blood, there would still be psychical cruelty, an apparently bloodless cruelty, an *état d'âme*, so to speak, a state of the soul or the psyche ("PSS" 239/11).

For Freud, then, who believed that cruelty has no contrary, there is a kind of cruelty drive, related both to the death drive (the *Todestrieb*) ("PSS" 257/46) and to the drive for mastery (the *Bemächtigungstrieb*), an inherent and ineradicable cruelty in the power of sovereign mastery ("PSS" 241/14). Derrida goes on in "Psychoanalysis Searches the States of its Soul" to read the exchange between Freud and Einstein (published in 1933 under the title *Why War?*) in order to show that both thinkers believed there to be an irreducible cruelty drive and a drive for mastery ("PSS" 252/35). As a result, for both Freud and Einstein—and Derrida seems to be in agreement with them on this point—politics can only domesticate or deter, but never eradicate, such a drive ("PSS" 252/37).

These questions of cruelty in relation to sovereignty and mastery thus lead Derrida to questions of politics, the nation-state, the national and the international, questions about international organizations designed to regulate conflicts between nation-states (the League of Nations or the United Nations), but also to questions about the internationalization of psychoanalysis, its successes and its failures, and the "convulsive crisis" it is today undergoing.[4] Derrida asks, for example, what links psychoanalysis to the history of Greek, Jewish, and Christian Europe, and why psychoanalysis has never taken root in Arabo-Islamic cultures—or in the Far East ("PSS" 255/41–42). This question of the internationalization of psychoanalysis also leads to the question of the relationship between sovereignty and the exception and, finally, to the question of the US as an exception—an exception in its resistance to psychoanalysis today and in its maintenance and application of the death penalty. As Derrida recalls (in the summer of 2000), the US would be the last Western Christian nation to apply the death penalty, and to do so with a greater and greater cruelty and injustice ("PSS" 266/63). As such, it joins China and certain Arab-Muslin nations, Derrida reminds us, in its support of the death penalty ("PSS" 245/21), while Europe, for its part, would be a cradle of both abolitionism *and* psychoanalysis ("PSS" 263/56). By laying out these more or less incontestable matters of fact, Derrida is in effect suggesting that these two apparently unrelated things—the US's support of the death penalty and its resistance to psychoanalysis—need to be thought together. For both seem to suggest a common *resistance* to anything that threatens to erode the supposed sovereignty of the nation-state and its citizens.[5] Therefore, it is precisely psychoanalysis that must take up this question of the death penalty and of sovereignty in general, the supposed power or sovereignty of the state over the life and death of its citizens, and of the individual citizen over his or her supposedly free actions ("PSS" 262/54–55).

Law and politics must take psychoanalysis into account, and psychoanalysis must take politics and the history of law into account ("PSS" 273–274/77–78). It is in this spirit, it seems, and with this task in mind that Derrida recalls the four-year moratorium on the death penalty in the US, beginning in 1972 when the Supreme Court ruled that the death penalty was an arbitrary punishment that violated the Eighth Amendment's prohibition on "cruel and unusual" punishment. The moratorium officially ended in 1976, but then came to be supported and reinforced in 1977 with the invention of the lethal injection, a penalty that works by way of blood but does not spill blood, a penalty that would therefore be, in the eyes of the Supreme Court, without blood, without *cruor*, and so, when combined with a certain anesthesia, without cruelty ("PSS" 262–263/55–56).

But, again, Derrida renews his question "What is cruelty?" And how is it to be thought in relationship to what Derrida calls his triple question of "exception, sovereignty, cruelty" (*DP2* 3/22)? It is a question that seems particularly poignant when it comes to the American example or the American exception, the exception that America claims itself to be, the exception it claims for itself in terms of its sovereignty, and the exception it turns out to be when it comes to the death penalty. Derrida returns to Freud's belief—which also seems to be his own—regarding the ineradicable nature of the drives of hatred, destruction, and cruelty. Again, there is no non-cruelty, only differences of cruelty, differences in modality, quality, and intensity, activity or reactivity. The notion of eradicating cruelty is thus an illusion—a dangerous illusion, as we saw, that can always, in the name of the law or the ideal, actually intensify cruelty ("PSS" 271/72–73). One must thus cultivate a "differential transaction, an economy of detour and of différance," in short, an *indirect* route to combat the cruelty drive ("PSS" 271/72). Since cruelty (like Derridean violence, perhaps) has no contrary, since it is linked to life and will to power, it can be combated, Freud suggests, only indirectly ("PSS" 271/72), the cruel or destructive drives diverted or displaced in order to avoid their expression in war, Eros, or the love of life played against Thanatos or the Death Drive, without there being any pretense of eradicating this latter ("PSS" 271–272/73–75). The concept of *indirection* is thus crucial, for it involves being unable simply to *condemn* the cruelty drive or the sovereignty drive ("PSS" 272–273/76). It involves a recognition of the ineradicable nature of cruelty and it proposes a strategy for working with that cruelty in order to lessen or to temper it.

Indirection, then, is Freud's response to ineradicable cruelty, but it is not exactly Derrida's, or at least it is not Derrida's only gesture. Throughout "Psychoanalysis Searches the States of its Soul," Derrida asks whether there is a beyond of the drive for sovereign power, a beyond of the *Bemächtigungstrieb* or the drive for mastery (258/47)—and thus a beyond of cruelty (258/47). Since, as we have seen, Derrida argues *against* an oppositional logic of cruelty, this "beyond" obviously cannot be some place or some state of "non-cruelty." It will thus have to be of another order, an order that is heterogeneous to all powers and all principles. In the closing pages of "Psychoanalysis Searches the States of its Soul," Derrida characterizes this order, somewhat cryptically at first, in terms of an affirmation, namely, "the originary affirmation *from which*, and thus *beyond which* the death drive and the power, cruelty, and sovereignty drives determine themselves as 'beyond' the principles" ("PSS" 276/82–83). This "originary affirmation," he goes on to say, which "is not a principle, a princedom, a sovereignty," that is, something that can be *opposed* to power and, thus, to cruelty, comes:

> from a beyond the beyond, and thus from beyond the economy of the possible. It is attached to a life, certainly, but to a life other than that of the economy of the possible, an im-possible life no doubt, a sur-vival, not symbolizable, but the only one that *is worthy* of being lived, without alibi, once and for all, the only one from which to depart (notice I say from which *to depart*) for a possible thinking of life.
>
> ("PSS" 276/82–83)

Derrida suggests that this originary affirmation of this beyond of the beyond must be thought of in relation to an impossible unconditional, the kind he had thought of elsewhere under the names "hospitality," "gift," "pardon," or the "event." It is the experience of a "non-negative im-possible" ("PSS" 276/83) related to "the coming of the other in general, his or her or its arrival" ("PPS" 276/83), an impossible that is, for Derrida, the very origin of responsibility.

In the closing paragraphs of his essay—the closing moments, recall, of his address to the Estates General of Psychoanalysis—Derrida begins to lay out the entire "program," as it were, of much of his work of the preceding two decades, a thinking of the event as impossible and yet necessary ("PSS" 276/83). Derrida suggests that in order to understand this beyond of cruelty in relation to the event, we must think through the differences between three distinct orders: the constative, the performative, and the impossible itself ("PSS" 277/84). The first of these, the constative, is the order of theoretical knowledge (genetics, therapy, history, and so on) ("PSS" 277/84–85). The second, the performative, involves questions of the political and the juridical, "juridical performatives," as Derrida liked to call them, such as human rights, crimes against humanity, international law, and so on—attempts, in short, to invent or to bring about through language and conventions new juridical formations and the rights and responsibilities related to them ("PSS" 278/85).

Now, as Derrida underscores, there is between these two orders a *hiatus*, a discontinuity, a leap, a *saut*, since the "free responsibility [of the subject] will never be deduced from a simple act of knowledge" ("PSS" 278/86). Like the leap between *is* and *ought*, one will never be able simply to deduce anything like a right or a law or a responsibility from any state of affairs or from any knowledge about the way things are. The constative and the performative are thus heterogeneous orders with regard to one another. And yet both orders share something that makes them heterogeneous with regard to the third order, that is, the order of the impossible. Indeed, the orders of the constative and the performative are both orders of power and of the possible ("PSS" 278/86–87). In opposition, then, to these two orders of power and the possible would thus be what Derrida calls the "event." The event is what exceeds all power, whether in the form of constative knowledge or performativity; it is beyond all conventions, all mastery, all powers ("PSS" 254/39), all powers *of* or *as* the "I can" ("PSS" 276/82). It exceeds every horizon of expectations at the same time as it is neutralized by the power and mastery of the performative or the symbolic order ("PSS" 276–278/82–87). As such, the event, an event "worthy of the name" ("PSS" 254/40), as Derrida puts it, beyond the possible and beyond power, beyond mastery and sovereignty, would be the only place—the only place beyond place—for a beyond of cruelty:

> The unconditional coming of the other, its event without possible anticipation and without horizon, its death or death itself are irruptions that can and must put to rout the two orders of the constative and performative, of knowledge and the symbolic. Perhaps beyond any cruelty.
>
> ("PSS" 278/87)

Derrida says he does not quite *know*—and for good reasons—how to situate himself with regard to these questions of knowledge and power, the possible and the beyond of the possible ("PSS" 256–257/44–45). He does suggest, however, that it is psychoanalysis that can negotiate with this impossible and *calculate* with the unconditional ("PSS" 276–277/83), even if one must leave the field of psychoanalysis strictly speaking in order for a *decision* to take place ("PSS" 273/77). For the chance or the risk of any responsible decision must take place *beyond all knowledge*. Derrida insists that one must thus take psychoanalysis into account in law and politics without, however, reducing heterogeneity or the leap, the *saut*, into the undecidable ("PSS" 273/77). It is psychoanalysis—and, no doubt, deconstruction (the deconstruction that questions, for example, the supposedly airtight distinction or separation between conceptual couples such as cruel and non-cruel)—that must think something like an autonomous subject who is preceded and instituted by the other, beyond sovereignty and thus beyond cruelty. Derrida writes:

> How an authentic *auto-nomy* (egalitarian and democratic) institutes itself, and *must* do so, on the basis of a *hetero-nomy* that still survives what survives it, on the basis of a law of the other, as coming of the sur-viving other, this is one of the forms of the question "What is to be done?" that I would like to take, without alibi, beyond all possible sovereignty and all possible cruelty.
> ("PSSS" 264/58–59)

This rethinking of power, of sovereignty, and of cruelty, which is related, once again, to the living or the *sur-viving* of the other, is a matter not only of questions and of constative knowledge, of law and performatives, but also of an affirmation and a task. Derrida defines this latter in this way:

> The task, which is immense and remains entirely to be done, both for psychoanalysts and for whomever, citizen, citizen of the world, or mega-citizen, concerned with responsibility (in ethics, law, politics), is to organize this taking account of psychoanalytic reason without reducing the heterogeneity, the leap into the undecidable, the beyond of the possible, which is the object of psychoanalytic knowledge and economy, in particular, of its mythological discourse on the death drive and beyond the principle.
> ("PSS" 273/77)

The implications for cruelty are clear. If the orders of the performative and the constative are orders of power, and if power is always coextensive with cruelty, that is, with an irreducible and always differential cruelty, then there is perhaps something like a beyond of power and of cruelty only in this unconditional coming of the other, in an opening to the future that defines the life/death or surviving of this other.

At the end of his talk before the Estates General of Psychoanalysis, Derrida suggests that the psychoanalysts present at the gathering will have perhaps made the *leap* he has been talking about by welcoming him, as a foreigner, among them, thereby exposing themselves to risk—to what will have turned out to be an affirmation of their work and a questioning of it ("PSS" 279/87). That gesture, that invitation will have no doubt involved a certain calculation of risks and a certain use of power—various order of power—and yet it will have also required a leap, a hiatus, that cannot be calculated or counted on, but only *believed*.

By suggesting something beyond power and beyond cruelty, Derrida seems to suggest that the kind of "philosophical" abolitionism he is attempting to articulate will have to include not only knowledge (the order of the constative) and not only law and politics (the order of the performative), but also *belief*. For there is, perhaps, another dimension to the *cru* beyond *cruor*, blood, and cruelty. As my epigraph from Derrida's "Circumfession" reminds us, the vocable or syllable *cru* must be heard not only in or as the *cru* of crude (as opposed to refined) or raw (as opposed to cooked), or the *cru* of cruelty or of *cruor*, but the *cru* of *croire*, the past participle of the verb to believe. Cruelty and religion, cruelty and *croyance*, credit and credulity in religion: Derrida seems to suggest that these too need to be thought together. As he argued during the first year of *The Death Penalty* seminar:

> Since these two words hollowed into each other, *en creux*—belief [*croyance*] and cruelty, the credited [*cru*, also crude] and the cruel, whether or not there is blood involved—referred first of all … to Christian faith, in Kant and even in Sade, here we are again before the question of the death penalty and religion …
>
> (*DP1* 169/238–239)

Since the death penalty and religion, particularly Christianity, have both relied upon—since both will have in fact been—discourses of blood and cruelty, what is needed is "a reevaluation of both Christianity's and Kant's categorical imperative, of the bloody or bloodthirsty cruelty of the categorical imperative" (*DP1* 154/220). The death penalty and religion, blood (*cruor*) and belief (*cru*), must be thought together.

But, as Derrida suggests in "Faith and Knowledge" and elsewhere, there is another kind of belief, a kind of originary faith or belief that is *also* without contrary and that is the condition of every determinate belief, an originary belief that is, as Derrida defines it, "the ether of the address and relation to the utterly other" (§49). It is a belief (a *croyance*) that is not unlike the originary *affirmation* that Derrida speaks of in "Psychoanalysis Searches the States of its Soul," an affirmation, a belief, in the coming of the other.

En creux, then, the one inside the other, cruelty and belief, the one in the hollow of the other, the one at the bottom of the other: as if, just beyond cruelty, at the limit of cruelty, there were belief in the coming of the other, and, on this side of that limit, as soon as the other appears, an inescapable and ineradicable cruelty. Whereas the *cru* of *croire*, the *cru* of an originary faith or belief, opens up time, the *cru* of *cruor* and of cruelty, of a death penalty with or without blood, closes it down—or at least produces the phantasm of doing so. *Cru*—the syllable *cru*—would thus be the beginning and the end of cruelty. For if cruelty has no contrary, it would not be at all unusual; nothing, indeed, would be more common or less extraordinary. As soon as one crosses the threshold of *cru*, there is or there will have been cruelty—whether with or without blood. And yet, if we are to believe Derrida, the same goes for belief, which is what gives reason for hope in the future.

Notes

1 Geoffrey Bennington translates this impossible, untranslatable passage in this way: "The crude word, fight with him in this way over what's crude ... the crudeness I don't believe in, and the crude word lets flow into him through the channel of the ear, another vein, faith, profession of faith or confession, belief, credulity ... cruelty above all, blood again, *cruor*, *confiteor*, what blood will have been for me." ("Circumfession" 3–6.)

2 Jacques Derrida, *The Death Penalty, Vol. 1, Seminar of 1999–2000*; originally published as *La peine de mort, Vol. 1, 1999–2000* (hereinafter *DP1*). *The Death Penalty, Vol. 2, Seminar of 2000–2001*; originally published as *La peine de mort, Vol.* 2, *2000–2001* (hereinafter *DP2*).

3 Originally published as "États d'âme de la psychanalyse: L'impossible au-delà d'une souveraine cruauté" (hereinafter "PSS").

4 Derrida recalls Elisabeth Roudinesco, for example, saying that "Freud is dead in America" ("PSS" 261/54).

5 Other things too, such as religion, as we will see, must also be taken into account. Derrida cites *Future of an Illusion*, where the US is said to consider itself a country chosen by God the Father—"God's own country." Derrida says in passing that the death penalty is, in some sense, facilitated by a religion in which God punishes the evil and rewards the good (in the afterlife) ("PSS" 267/63–64).

References

Derrida, Jacques. "Circonfession." *Jacques Derrida*, Éditions du Seuil, 1991, pp. 7–8.

——. "Circumfession." *Jacques Derrida*. Translated by Geoffrey Bennington, University of Chicago Press, 1993, pp. 3–6.

——. *The Death Penalty, Vol. 1, Seminar of 1999–2000*. Translated by Peggy Kamuf, University of Chicago Press, 2014.

——. *The Death Penalty, Vol. 2, Seminar of 2000–2001*. Translated by Elizabeth Rottenberg, University of Chicago Press, 2016.

——. *États d'âme de la psychanalyse: L'impossible au-delà d'une souveraine cruauté*. Éditions Galilée, 2000.

——. "Faith and Knowledge: The Two Sources of 'Religion' at the Limits of Reason Alone." In *Acts of Religion*. Edited by Gil Anidjar, Routledge, 2002, pp. 40–101.

——. *La peine de mort, Vol. 1, 1999–2000*. Édition établie par Geoffrey Bennington, Marc Crépon, et Thomas Dutoit, Éditions Galilée, 2012.

——. *La peine de mort, Vol. 2, 2000–2001*. Édition établie par Geoffrey Bennington, Marc Crépon, et Thomas Dutoit, Éditions Galilée, 2015.

——. "Psychoanalysis Searches the States of its Soul: The Impossible Beyond of a Sovereign Cruelty." In *Without Alibi*. Edited and translated by Peggy Kamuf, Stanford University Press, 2002, pp. 238–280.

Einstein, Albert, and Sigmund Feud. *Why War?: The Correspondence between Albert Einstein and Sigmund Freud*. Chicago Institute for Psychoanalysis, 1933.

Reik, Theodor. *The Compulsion to Confess*. Farrar, Strauss and Cudahy, 1959.

Chapter 3

The violent rhetoric of accusation

Cicero and the Marcus Ameleus Scaurus case

George Pavlich

The Scaurus case

On 6 July 54 BCE, Marcus Ameleus Scaurus was formally accused of extortion while serving as the *praetor pro consule* of Sardinia (Asconius; Cicero and Dyck; Henderson). An antagonist by the name of M. Valerius Triarius spearheaded the prosecution, with two brothers (M and Q. Pacuvius Caldus) and L. Marius serving as assistants or *subscriptiones* (Alexander 100). This rather obscure group of accusers were probably seeking renown by accusing someone from a prominent family with political ambitions in that year's consular elections. And the family certainly was prominent: Scaurus' father had served as both consul and censor, while his mother, Caecilia Metelus Diadematus, remarried none other than Sulla after Scaurus senior's death. A successful prosecution before the calendar elections would discredit Scaurus junior as a viable candidate for consul, and this promised his accusers political and pecuniary gain (Alexander 105). Recognizing the stakes, Scaurus called upon six extremely well-known *patroni* (advocates) to mount his defense, including the famous Cicero.

From his analysis of remaining textual sources, Hendersen reveals Scaurus' flamboyant life. Having accumulated substantial wealth from service for Pompey in Syria, he returned to Rome to erect a massive home on the Palatine (for which he bought an adjoining property) and, once elected as *aedile*, built an impressive temporary theater for public games (decorated with no less than 360 massive columns and able to seat about 80,000 people!). Hendersen also notes that Scaurus' exploits give the "impression of rash scheming, ruthless ambition, and above all venality" (197). The profligacies for which he became known produced large debts, and his stint in Sardinia was to help defray these. While discontent with his actions as proconsul may have prompted the accusation, the actual trial played out in the context of consular politics at Rome (Alexander 100). Indeed, his accusers sought a verdict before the calendar consular elections could take place, no doubt hoping to disqualify him from running for office. They accused him of numerous offenses over and above extorting local Sardinians, including the use of violence, sexual transgression, and interfering with Rome's grain supply.

On one of the charges, Scaurus' accusers claimed he had a hand in the death of a Sardinian resident, Bostar, who had intended leaving the province before Scaurus' arrival. In the event, the man allegedly dined at his home, but died before Scaurus' "dinner was removed" (Cicero and Dyck 101). The prosecutors blamed him for Bostar's death, arguing that he intended to gain personally from the man's family estate. In his defense, Cicero rejected this story, suggesting instead that Bostar's mother poisoned her son to secure the family estate. In addition, the accusers blamed Scaurus for inciting the suicidal death of an unnamed woman. Seemingly her husband, Aris, had left for Rome without her and she had subsequently committed suicide. Scaurus' accusers alleged that she did so to avoid having to jeopardize her marital fidelity in the face of Scaurus' improper sexual advances. Again Cicero rejected the accusation, but this time a prejudiced dismissal that the "lady was not only supremely ugly but also in extreme old age" (Cicero and Dyck 103). He suggested instead that she either killed herself because of her husband's treachery or, indeed, that Aris had had her killed, making it look like suicide, so that he could marry—as he had since done—Bostar's mother (a witness in the case)! Moreover, the accusers indicted Scaurus for criminally speculating on the grain market and/or interfering with the grain supply. Cicero rejected this charge out of hand.

All in all, whatever the merits of the accusers' case, they seem neither to have investigated their indictments thoroughly, nor did they return to Sardinia for witness testimony, leading a commentator to this assessment: "It seems clear that the accusation of Scaurus was a political manoeuvre, intensified by a number of personal considerations, and designed to prevent Scaurus from campaigning" (Henderson 200). No doubt an unwanted intrusion into his election campaign for consul, Scaurus would stop at little to clear his family name.

Accusation, crime and standing courts in the late Roman Republic

As this case suggests, ideas and practices of accusation were basic to public law and "crime" of the late Roman Republic. However, it is worth mentioning that: "In republican Latin no words existed that can be literally translated as *murder, crime, criminal courts, or criminal law*" (Gaughan 2). Even if what we call homicidal acts evoked communal disquiet, their general framing as "crime" was absent (Gaughan). So, as Riggsby (*Crime*) points out, in contrast to our emphasis on crime, Roman culture was indifferent to abstracted notions of criminality. It focused instead on individual instances of wrongdoing, the precise status of which was worked out via its "public" law. That said, certain acts, like extortion, were framed under the heading of *crimen* (which referred to accusation) and were defined publicly through accusatory processes (Riggsby, *Crime*).

In other words, accusation was integral to defining public or communal wrongdoing (Harries). The criminalization of events and subjects was legally initiated through specific accusations, and no crime or criminal was recorded without an accuser bringing the matter to light. If this underscored the significance of accusation to the appearance of crime in this society, it also highlighted the value of examining how accusers and the accused's defense initiated, structured, shaped, and fed Roman patterns of criminalization. Such accusations did not simply operate through pre-trial procedures, for which there are scant extant sources; accusations and counter-accusations continued as integral elements of late republican court process. In other words, throughout a jury trial, criminal wrongdoing was claimed and countered, defined and redefined, just as specific accusations were made or displaced and calumny was asserted. Such accusatorial processes, which were considered to have a distinct nature, often also took place within a wider politics of the day (Gruen, *Roman Politics*; Marshall).

In his related analysis of Roman punishment over the course of the first century BCE, Bauman (*Crime*) points to the changing organization of public (criminal) courts within which accusations of a crime-like nature could be enunciated. Compared with Roman society's elaborately formal civil law (Tellegen-Couperus 53ff; Versteeg) or, indeed, its use of restitution through delict, public law was rather underdeveloped (Bauman, *Crime*; Powell and Paterson). Even so, actions considered as harmful to broader Roman society were gradually brought forward as "public" legal measures in "courts" of the *iudicium populi* ("judgment of the people"—see Harries 14). Though varied, these "courts" usually operated under the auspices of the "tribune of the plebs," who summoned suspects to appear for an enquiry known as the *anquisitio* (Bauman, *Crime* 7–10).[1]

In the changing political climate of the second century BCE, a species of "courts" were established as special senate commissions (*quaestiones perpetuae*) to investigate particular circumstances. Governing as a dictator (that perhaps set the precedent for Caesar's later one), Sulla instituted multiple legal reforms including the introduction of standing courts:

> ... within the framework of his political reforms Sulla reorganized the permanent courts and increased their number. Thereafter there were six courts: for murder and poisoning, for forgery of wills and other documents, for high treason, for bribery during elections, for extortion in the provinces and finally for embezzlement of public funds.
>
> (Tellegen-Couperus 52)

These standing courts, *iudicia publica* ("public courts"), became important sites for criminal accusation before authorized state agents, rendering them "analogous" to criminal courts nowadays (Riggsby, *Crime* i). They developed around specific crimes, identifying four as especially prominent during Cicero's time: "*ambitus* (electoral bribery), *de sicariis et veneficis* (murder), *vis* (assault, riot), and *repetundae* (extortion by provincial administrators)" (see Harries 3; Riggsby, *Roman Law* 198ff; and Riggsby, *Crime* i). Headed by magistrates, including those who dealt with "foreign" matters (e.g., *praetor peregrines*), the courts superseded the rituals of popular assemblies and targeted specific offenses (Bauman, *Crime* 17; Riggsby, *Roman Law* 196ff). From an annually drafted list of jurors, the praetor chose between 50 and 75 jurors (*iudicum*) by lot; both accused and accuser were given an opportunity to reject a limited number of jurors. And it was in these courts that "the public as a whole" could try to find amends for communal wrongs (Riggsby, *Crime* xii).

Against this background, the accusations against Scaurus were made to a *quaestio de repetundis* (extortion court, or literally "the court about [funds] to be recovered" (Cicero and Dyck 2)), which was established in 149 BCE through Sulla's *Lex Culpurnia*: "The court was to consist of a panel of assessors ... presided over by a praetor charged with handling disputes between Romans and foreigners (*praetor peregrinis*)" (Cicero and Dyck 2). Caesar's later reforms also allowed juries to include non-senators, but the court's procedure was only overhauled by Augustus' Principate of 27 BC and later simplified as *cognitio extraordinaria* (Bauman, *Crime*; Versteeg 126ff). In any case, the drama of Scaurus' case unfolded where specific "criminal accusations" were solicited, authorized, and used as the basis for calibrating whether subjects could be considered guilty of crimes. The setting, the rules, and the processes did not simply reflect preexisting identities; rather, they were active criminalization mechanisms, involved in creating criminals and leading toward coordinated (state) responses to wrongdoing.

Criminal accusation in action

Standing criminal courts of the late republic were accusatorial rather than inquisitional in the sense that "no action could be initiated unless the citizen laid a formal accusation (*accusatio*) against another and thereby undertook to prosecute at the trial" (Mousourakis 80). To initiate an accusation, adult male citizens of "good repute" (Bauman, *Crime* 17) could lay an information (*nominis delatio*) before the *praetor* or magistrate of a relevant standing court, requesting permission to instigate charges (*postulatio*; Harries 18ff).

Once permission was granted, the accuser was required to present a written statement about the purported offense in front of the accused (Cicero and Dyck 6ff). The accuser and those supporting the claim (*subscriptores*) signed the document outlining the accusation (*inscriptio*), and the accuser then "had to swear an oath that he did not issue a false accusation out of malice (*calumnia*)," or in collusion with the accused (Mousourakis 80ff). Magistrates were supposed to determine (*legibus interrogatio*) impartially whether the case was permissible under the laws relevant to the court (Alexander 8). Here one might note that in so doing, the magistrates were in effect determining whether the accusation, as framed, was legible and understandable to an authorized legal authority. With such formalities out of the way, the accuser was then given time to prepare the case—usually 10 days, but possibly more in extortion cases, to allow prosecutors time to visit provinces in search of evidence (Harries 18). Accusers could also request that the court summon up to 48 witnesses (*testes*)—a number subsequently expanded to 120 (Cicero and Dyck 6).

The actual criminal trial started with the accusers' opening speeches, the defenses' reply, and then an examination of witnesses (Powell and Paterson 32). Harries describes the process thus:

> Speeches setting out the facts of the case and the lines of argument were made, first by the prosecution *patronus* (advocate) and then by the defence, both of whom were subject to time limits. Both sides then engaged in cross-questioning or interrogating the other (skill at which the quick-witted Cicero excelled) before moving to the calling of witnesses.
>
> (19)

At Scaurus' trial, one could expect a noisy court convened in an open forum where jurors, if bored, "might walk about, chat with each other or in groups, send a slave to find out the time, or ask the president of the court for an adjournment" (Lintott, "Legal Procedure" 63–64). The setting had "something of a free-for-all" quality (Powell and Paterson 36), since its rendition of justice was "both public and rowdy and there was little sense that the jurors might require a period of quiet reflection" (Harries 19). Indeed, after witness examination, the jury members were expected to decide forthwith on ballots marked either " 'A' for acquittal and 'C' for condemnation" or could vote that there was insufficient evidence (Harries 19). There were no summary statements and no formal jury deliberation (indeed, their votes were supposed to be independently cast).

Even so, justice here demanded that participants play recognized roles—accuser, accused, jury member, magistrate, witness, spectator, etc. Certain rhetorical rudiments were also viewed as fundamental to the very nature of accusation and to rendering events intelligible to legal scrutiny. By implication, if accusers or defenders of the accused did not use the appropriate rhetorical forms, the legitimacy of accusatorial forms of law was potentially undermined. But this, in turn, suggested that accusation was distinguishable from its perversions, and so could be said to harbor an essential nature. Rutledge frames the point in this way:

> There was something inherent in accusation, according to Roman rhetoricians, which was either violent by nature or which could easily lead to such an impression. Recognition of this fact led them to develop what was tantamount to a theory of accusation.
>
> ("Delatores" 562)

In other words, accusation could be discerned through a distinctive rhetorical practice; that this was a "violent" nature underscored a recognition of the damaging potential for participants' lives,—their names, reputations, and socioeconomic standing. At the same time, there were differences in how this "nature" played out in the rhetoric of accusers as opposed to the accused's defense. Let us now deal with each separately.

The accuser's "violent" oratory

As noted above, accusers in the late republic were neither government officials nor public (state-sponsored) prosecutors. They were supposed to be men of "good standing" within the general citizenry who, for various reasons, launched accusations. When initiating a charge, the accuser had to swear an oath before a magistrate indicating that the indictment was free from both "*calumnia*, launching a prosecution that one knows to be unfounded; and *praevaricatio*, collusion with the defendant for the defendant's benefit" (Alexander 7). Since the very integrity of public law rested on "truthful" accusations, severe punishments faced violators of either offense. On this note, Foucault's helpful lectures on avowal—truth telling across changing juridical forms—call attention to the importance of "governing the truth" and how avowers were governed as accusatorially sanctioned truth tellers. This work also alerts us to the danger of assuming in advance that such identities as "accuser" or the "accused" exist *a priori*; on the contrary, it suggests that the way in which law requires subjects to avow truths in juridical contexts is part of the means by which they come to be constituted as subjects of that law. That is, the very requirements, processes, and kinds of truthful narratives of accusation considered historically acceptable recursively shape the subjects at hand.

But what prompted people to avow truths as accusers? From Cicero's writings, as suggested, subjects tended to do so for various reasons: making a name for themselves; serving the public good; continuing a family feud; and representing people in the provinces in extortion cases (Alexander 7). In addition, accusers were often enticed by the prospect of economic enrichment as spoils could be directed to those most responsible for securing a conviction (Cowles). Others used legal processes to further political ambitions, such as in the Scaurus case, where the prosecution seemingly leveled accusations (in part) to prevent him from running in the consular elections (Gruen, *Roman Politics*).

Whatever the reason, accusing someone of a crime—especially in cases of extortion—involved considerable rhetorical and logistic aptitude: "Extortion cases, involving as they did large—often huge—sums of money and witnesses from a foreign, often distant part of Rome's empire, required the greatest organizational effort from the prosecutor" (Alexander 245). Increasingly, with the development of standing courts, accusations were managed by practiced rhetoricians: "the actual pleading of cases became a matter for professional orators" (Lintott, "Delator" 105). In other words, the courts offered new opportunities for occupations that today might be considered "prosecutorial" in form. Indeed, Lintott ("Delator") describes the rise of the professional *accusator* as a product of such changes, and indeed this was accompanied by the rise of the *index* or informer, who provided material for the former. Although not much survives about late republic informers, Rutledge surmises that they foreshadowed the Principate's prominent use of professional *delatores* (Rutledge, *Imperial Inquisitions*). But, during Cicero's time, it would seem that the informer's status was generally considered as less than salutary: "Accuser (*accusator*) is the neutral term; informer (*index*) implies somebody on the fringes of the crime he denounces. Hence our earliest references to accusers who were not themselves victims are already pejorative" (Robinson, *The Role* 207). Even if held in negative regard, informers did serve as key aids to accusers, helping to stock and sharpen their rhetorical arsenals—'digging up dirt' as it were in efforts to persuade juries of an accusers' denunciations (Lintott, "Delator"; Robinson, *The Criminal Law*; "The Role").

Yet, it was not only the index whose morality was questioned. In any case, Robinson points out that out that the moral status of accusers, who prosecuted others of crime, required justification: "Criminal prosecution, even apart from the rewards, and the temptation of calumny, was thus morally dubious, rather than neutral. It could be justified, but it needed justification" ("The Role" 211). Cicero largely agreed with this assessment and even wrote a kind of apology for participating in an earlier prosecution of *Verres* (Cowles). At the same time, however, he thought that, like the geese and dogs that stood guard at the Emperor's palace, criminal accusation served to deter crime by virtue of a persistent threat:

> It is a useful thing that there should be a number of accusers in the state, so that audacity may be held in check by fear … This is the reason why we are all ready to allow that there should be as many accusers as possible, because an innocent man, if he is accused, can be acquitted, but one who is guilty, unless he is accused, cannot be condemned. For it is more expedient that an innocent man should be acquitted, than that a guilty man should not be brought to trial.
> (Quoted in Robinson, "The Role" 209)

Regardless of its moral ambiguity, Cicero and other rhetoricians like Quintilian and the unknown author of *Rhetorica ad Herennium* described accusation as having a distinctive rhetorical style that reflected how *properly* to accuse another person of crime. In his analysis of effective orators who admirably accused others, Cicero (2006) construed a rhetorical style properly suited to successful accusations. Rutledge's review of surviving texts that describe how to accuse or prosecute effectively leads him to the view that making an accusation was premised on *a priori* knowledge of proper ways to accuse. Specifically, he argues that: "Terror, treachery, and singularity of purpose were the foundation blocks of the *accusor*, whose task was to excite … [hatred, anger and envy] … in his audience by drawing a caricature of the accused based on innuendo and probability" (Rutledge, "Delatores" 563). As a result, he argues that the rhetoric of accusation appeared as innately "vehement," acerbic, emotive, hard-hitting, and even "violent" in its attempts to annihilate the accused's character and reputation. Additionally, for Quintillian, the nature of the accusation was premised on a basic objective: "By the accuser nothing more is to be kept in view than that he must prove that something was done; that a particular thing was done; that it was done wrongfully; and that he brings his action according to law" (Quintilian Book 3, Chapter 6: 85).

To achieve this (see Quintillian Book 3, Chapter 6), the accuser had to take full advantage of the element of surprise available to him as the first to speak—whether at initial indictments or at trial. This advantage, which he thought made accusing easier than defending, provided accusers with unique opportunities to prepare and plan a rhetorical strategy to reach a clearly defined end (whereas the accused is always left in a position of reacting to charges). So, the accuser might use this advantage slyly by putting gentle, even irrelevant questions to the accused before suddenly shifting to very direct accusations designed to throw the accused on the back foot (Quintillian, Book 3, Chapter 5: 717–718). This open ing perfidy provided a way for accusers to disarm the accused and clear the way to a full-frontal attack on his character.

The rhetorical use of caricature and character assassination as techniques was especially important to the rhetoric of both accuser and accused. Accusers, however, as Rutledge ("Delatores") indicates, were expected to caricature the accused in the worst possible light, trying to assign a character that contemporary Romans would have expected to commit the alleged crimes—thus, the murderer might be cast as rash, the thief as greedy, and so on. If they could not pin such character traits on the accused, then a "fallback" position was to allege that there must always be a first time (Quintilian, Book 7, Chapter 2: 33). Such rhetorical techniques seemed to tap a pervasive sense that people's characters are more or less "fixed" throughout adult life, and that a close, but incomplete, link exists between character and action (Riggsby, *The Rhetoric* 169–170). Sometimes people acted "out of character" or concealed their true characters, but in general they acted in line with past "character"; as a result, Riggsby notes that: "Accounts of a person's character (most commonly but not necessarily that of the defendant) clearly count as evidence of guilt or innocence in a Roman court" (*The Rhetoric* 177).

The aim of referencing character was thus, in part, to amplify the savageness of person able to commit an atrocious crime, and doing so in as emotive a way as possible (Quintillian, Book 6, Chapter 2: 27–28). The able accuser was also expected to direct attention to the motives anticipated of the caricature ascribed to the accused, and if no such motives can be found, he was to declare the crime all the more atrocious for not having one (Quintillian Book 7, Chapter 2: 35–36).

Reflecting on the wider significance of strategic character battles, one might note that a successful accusation constituted the very basis for declaring wrongdoing in context:

> Whether the orator will prevail or not depends not on the crime itself, but on how the prosecution represents it. The character of the accused must be represented in such a way that it corresponds to the type of crime that the defendant is accused of having committed.
>
> (Rutledge, "Delatores" 563)

Even with limited sources indicating the precise *modus operandi* of Scaurus' accusers (although see Alexander; Asconius), one might infer that they sought to impugn his character by alluding to recurring accusations against his father (this is perhaps why Cicero opened and closed with a defense of the father and the family's contributions to Rome). Here, "facts" could be considered as secondary to effective argument. Indeed, a proper accusation demanded well-developed rhetorical strategies to convince jurors that: a "crime" had actually taken place; it was committed by the accused whose character either motivated the offense, or did not disqualify him from so doing; and that all the accusations were made in accordance with law and the nature of accusation. Accusers were encouraged to speak indirectly, casting "facts" in a suspicious light and making copious use of innuendo to appeal to jurors' emotions, and even flattering them with charms about their age and social status (Quintilian, Book 4, Chapter 2: 81). A basic aim was to incite feelings of anger, hatred, outrage, and fury toward the accused. And in that quest, the accuser was to be "remorseless and unrelenting, driving away all sympathy from the accused"; he "must, in short, make the defendant's crime appear as savage as possible" (Rutledge, "Delatores" 564). With this in mind, we might note why accusing could be cast as a "violent" affair, for successful prosecutions made use of rhetoric to "Aggressive parody of the defendant's character" and to incite "anger or hatred to manipulate the audience" (Rutledge, "Delatores" 566). It is not hard to see why prosecutors created "antagonism," since their trade was plied on anyone and could bring about "total ruin for a convicted defendant" (Alexander 14).

Accusations also often fed and could affect the politics of the day. From the timing of the accusation, and the accusers' eagerness to prosecute him as expeditiously as possible—even declining to visit Sardinia in search of witnesses (Cicero and Dyck)—one might infer political overtones to Scaurus' prosecution. Indeed, Alexander argues that:

> Scaurus' prosecutors clearly wanted to finish their trial before the calendar elections, in the hope that they would be able to convict Scaurus by then and that, therefore, he would not be able to stand for office as a matter of law, he would not be a viable candidate as a matter of practical politics, or both. (105)

From this, one might note that the rhetorical nature of accusation was not simply a legal matter; it formed part of wider Roman politics (Gruen, *Roman Politics*; *The Last Generation*; Stein). It was especially influential in a politics of recognition where statuses were made and broken, and where vehement rhetorical practices sought to liquidate political characters through allegations of criminal activity. Regardless, it is worth pausing for a moment to consider the sorts of accusing subjects that such practices generated; namely, in order to be successful, accusers had to be unflinching in their ruthless, violent rhetoric designed to destroy the characters and past lives of those they accused. Behind this lies a bordering and ordering politics that generated accusers as subjects who rendered events legible as crimes to legal authority, force, and framing political (sovereign) contexts.

The accused and the "nature" of accusation

Extending Rutledge's important insights about the nature of accusation generally, one might argue that Cicero's rhetorical strategies followed what he believed to be essential elements of an effective defense for the accused. This was especially pertinent when considering that the law had already cast the accused as an increasingly silent witness to legal procedures, delegating "representation" to specialist orators with knowledge of how to defend those accused of wrongdoing. In Scaurus' case, esteemed defense orators were hired to speak on his behalf; this platform was used to define his identity. Their orations rejected the accusers' accounts (often by alleging calumny) in attempts to convince juries of his innocence. They drew on accepted knowledge that detailed the multi-faceted nature of accusation, and specifically how to defend an accused party. Cicero's counsel, for instance, followed his enunciations of effective of defense oratory; he had written about the topic by examining the styles and techniques of successful orators like Crassus, Antonius, etc. (Cicero and Watson). In effect, Cicero here enunciated knowledge of how to defend against accusations, and so added a dimension to the overall "nature" of accusation. He argued that defensive rhetoric certainly operated in realms of opinion, but viewed it as founded on an art of how to persuade people; knowledge of this art was to be discovered by carefully studying past successes (Solmsen). By extrapolation, Cicero's defense of Scaurus tapped what he considered to be essential to defending an accusation.

In the fragmentary remains of his defense, Cicero referenced Roman versions of an ancient Greek tradition of practicing "forensic oratory" (Powell and Paterson), and so opened with an *exordium*. The aim of this opening was to secure the jury's and other listeners' attention, and to curry their favor (Lintott, *Cicero*; Powell and Paterson). In the rhetoric of the defense he offered, Cicero framed himself as an impartial truth teller, one who avowed entirely in accordance with the law, as might be expected of a great Roman leader. His exordium respectfully but frankly engaged the jury, recursively marking him as a fair peer amongst equals—someone who could be trusted as an insider. Although courteous, his tone was unapologetic, pleading that Scaurus hoped—as any juror might—to "without giving offence or causing distress, hold on to the standing of his line, his family, and his name, which is what he was always particularly eager to do" (Cicero and Dyck 101). Here, as elsewhere, his approach appeared to take the jury into his confidence, enabling him to claim to have a secret truth that he was prepared to share with peers.

His basic approach was to portray Scaurus as an unassailably good character from a good family, before showing the duplicitous and devious motives of the accusers' bad characters. So, he took time to share the Scaurus family's longstanding contributions to Rome. Acknowledging—to prove his commitment to truth—that Scaurus senior had over the years been accused of various things, Cicero was quick to point out that none stuck and all were products of devious accusers seeking to feather their own nests. He thus confronted the prosecutors' negative attacks on the Scaurus family, while simultaneously contrasting the family's communal standing with a history of false accusations. This allowed him to mount a brief attack on the current accusers, framing their prosecution as disorganized and based on the dubious assertions of scoundrel witnesses wishing only to benefit from, and thereby reduce, the fortunes of that family.

Cicero then summarized the main arguments that would comprise his defense, signaling that he would contest the very kind of accusation presented, challenge the character of Sardinian witnesses upon which the persecution rested, and contrast this with the debt the Sardinians owed Scaurus, who—it had to be said—never disrupted the grain supply. Through his defense, Cicero seamlessly cast the accused in a favorable light, using structured assertions, digressions, and arguments to present a character faithful to Roman law and to portray Scaurus as entirely deserving of the social standing that he currently enjoyed. Magnifying a view of the accused as an undeserving victim of calumny from ungrateful and greedy accusers, Cicero emphasized his impartiality on the matter. He claimed to be happy to yield to the prosecution case if it were based on reliable and truthful claims that could be backed up by unassailable evidence:

> The argument appropriate to the matter—nothing else can truly be called an argument—is the voice of the facts, the footprint of nature, the mark of truth; whatever it is, it must remain immutable; it is not invented but taken by the speaker. Therefore if I am bested in a prosecution of this kind, I would yield and give way; for I would be defeated by the facts, by the case, by the truth.
> (Cicero and Dyck 104)

Cicero's defense here engages a specific idea of truth as descending from the "voice of facts." In context, this would require accusers to support all claims with unimpeachable witness testimony that immutably declares the truth. This rhetorical move allowed Cicero to reject the strategy of refuting specific accusations; he argued instead that all their accusations were so vague and amorphously construed as to render them impossible to support.

Cicero's implication here was no doubt clear to his contemporaries: the accusers had violated the proper or inherent nature of accusation. They inexcusably had misrepresented the "facts." For example, as already referenced, he challenged the accusers' account of the events surrounding Aris' wife's death. She did not commit suicide, according to him, because of Scaurus' supposed advances, but because she had to face the shame of her husband's adulterous relations with Bostar's mother in Rome. In his version, Aris' wife was:

> upset by the disgrace of adultery; when she heard that Aris had gone to Rome with his beloved pretending to flee in fear—so not only had there previously been a relationship between them but they would even be joined in matrimony—she flared up with a woman's rage and preferred to die rather than endure it.
>
> (Cicero and Dyck 103)

Cicero here presented an evocative, emotive, and patriarchal interpretation of "facts" in a lexicon designed to tap into jurors' prejudices in an effort to portray Scaurus as a maligned victim of false accusations.

Moreover, Cicero contested the actual "type" (nature) of the accusation leveled against Scaurus in two ways. First, he claimed that the accusations were scandalously slapdash and disorganized; they were so blatantly political that the accusers did not even bother to visit Sardinia to investigate the charges or to produce reliable witnesses to support their allegations. Because of this complete lack of expected diligence, Cicero called on jurors to:

> resist the entire type of prosecution in which you see nothing has been undertaken in the customary way, moderately, with deliberation, with integrity, on the contrary everything has been undertaken in a base, disorderly, hasty, rapid way by collusion, command, authority, hope, and threats.
>
> (Cicero and Dyck 108)

In other words, the prosecutors had mounted an improper kind of accusation that neither reflected integrity nor followed "customary" ways of doing things. Corrupt accusers masked their political motives and, indeed, coerced, threatened, and cajoled witnesses to support their vague accusations. The overall implication was that the entire case presented fell short of the customary thresholds that would have allowed it to be described as a proper accusation.

Second, Cicero noted that the accusers had failed to investigate their claims in Sardinia, and so could not provide reliable witness testimony. This allowed him to cast their claims as "savage" because they could have crushing effects on Scaurus and his family. Consequently, he rhetorically asked of Triarius, the chief prosecutor:

> What manner of accusation is this, Triarius, that, in the first place, you have not gone to investigate? What was the basis of that confidence? So savage, so assured, that you could crush my client?
>
> (Cicero and Dyck 105)

Cicero framed the "type" of accusation at hand as so disorganized, incompetent, and without merit that one might ponder why it was presented at all. This astute rhetorical move allowed him to attribute devious political and pecuniary motives to Triarius. His accusations were not driven, as they should have been, by a public concern for truth; they were attempts to achieve political gain in the race for Consul. Indeed, Cicero pointed out, had he actually visited Sardinia, he would have discovered the true, positive "state of opinion" about Scaurus.

Having thus discredited the general type of accusation presented and the character of a main accuser, Cicero's defense circled back to a previous claim: that the prosecution's case rested ultimately on the credibility of witness testimony that it could not supply. Here he challenged the very foundations of the case, eliminating the need for detailed refutations of more specific claims. A considerable portion of his speech sought to discredit Sardinian witnesses by prejudicially ascribing to them a "general type" of character; namely, as descendants of "nations" whose "vices" were, as enemies of the Punic wars, at odds with Roman interests. From here, he imputed an even more bigoted version of character:

> When I speak of a people's vices, I certainly make exceptions. But I have to discuss the general type; within it, by their character and culture, some may have conquered the vices of their line itself and their people. The facts themselves show clearly that the majority is without credibility, without partner-1ship and bond with our nation.
>
> (Cicero and Dyck 109)

This paved the way for another extraordinary claim; namely, that Sardinians "not only lack all credibility and authority but do not even have the appearance or semblance of witness," and that their "credibility is destroyed by their very unanimity," which amounts to a "conspiratorial pact" (Cicero and Dyck 108). As if such imperial bigotry were not enough, he went on to allege that their participation was prompted by "well-known greed" and the "hope and promise of rewards," implying a mendacious people who claimed a "licence to tell lies." However astonishing such assertions may now appear, Cicero imputed these character traits on the assumption that they were widely held and to collapse the prosecution's case around the testimony of its discredited witnesses.

Cicero then moved to his conclusion, or *peroration*, leaving the jurors with a positive account of the Scaurus family's achievements: their tangible contributions to Rome were abundantly evident in many buildings in striking distance of the court (the Senate house, the Temple of Castor and Pollux, etc.). He described the accused as a humble representative of a great family who wished no more than to continue the family line, a reasonable desire threatened by the accusers' avarice and false accusations. As Dyck notes, this appeal to pity was invited by "a standard part of Roman judicial 'theatre' for the defendant and family to dress in squalid clothing in order to appeal to the jurors' pity in the peroration" (Cicero and Dyck 161).

Cicero concluded his defense with a basic question: "By now, jurors, surely no residue of suspicion lingers in these charges does it?" (Cicero and Dyck 104). Based on this and the other five defense orations, the jury acquitted Scaurus of the accusations, and several members even moved a motion to pursue calumny charges against the accusers. In the event, this motion was rejected, but from the above we get a sense of how the accused identity was shaped through by defense arguments and how these might have been weighed by the jury to render a verdict with considerable consequences. Scaurus did eventually run for the consulship, which appears to have led to all the candidates, including him, being accused of bribery. Confirming the political tenor of the charges, this time he was convicted, even with Cicero's defense. It is perhaps not irrelevant that he no longer enjoyed Pompey's favor after marrying Pompey's ex-wife Mucia. In any case, Scaurus was seemingly exiled from Rome (Cicero and Dyck).

Concluding musings

From the above analysis, one gleans that the late Roman Republic framed images of wrongdoing from communal strictures about perceived threats to its well-being. It developed legal rituals to deal with "crime" that descended from public law institutions—more or less organized peoples' assemblies, leading to standing courts headed by magistrates (often *praetors*) with large juries (Harries; Riggsby, *Crime*) and directed to individual offenses. The latter were fundamentally dependent upon initiating accusatorial processes, the course of which determined how to define and then deal with given circumstances thought to challenge community order (Riggsby, *Crime* Chapter 6). If this cemented the importance of accusation to an emerging criminal law and consequent conceptions of crime, it also shows how late republican thinking understood rituals of accusation as constituting a distinctive rhetorical field, necessary to the very possibility of regulating crime, and framing persons as "criminals." This realization has several important implications for understanding criminal justice then, and potentially today too.

First, as we have seen, accusation was presented as having a distinct and intrinsic rhetorical nature that could be detected on its own terms. Although recognized as an art dealing with opinions, the field of accusation was also deemed capable of yielding knowledge of how properly to accuse someone of wrongdoing (crime), and how to mount an apposite defense against such accusations. In many ways, Roman thinking suggested that its rhetorical essence could be discovered by studying examples of successful orators and the technologies they employed either to accuse people of crime, or defend those so accused. Accusation could then be designated as a discrete rhetorical field with an intrinsic set of qualities to further the authority of emerging legal structures. It was thereby tied to the foundation, even constitution, of public law and the development of ideas around crime as an offense against the entire community that required initiating public responses. Accusation became, in short, the starting point for criminalizing processes that might produce a criminal identity.

Second, the rhetoric of "proper" accusations depended on accepted techniques of persuasion, even though their format depended on whether one was accusing or being accused. We have isolated and analyzed several techniques in relation to the specifics of the Scaurus case. To begin with, we saw how accusers and the accused, through the process deemed proper to accusation, tried to contest the facts as presented by opponents. Accusers had the advantage of offering their narratives of events and participants first, while defenders of the accused were left to react and respond to what was alleged to have happened. An accused person was expected to use cunning methods to catch the accused off guard and to use any rhetorical advantage to maximal effect. The accused might have been left to react to accusers, but their defense was expected to be equally unremitting in its challenges and attempts to attribute dubious or deliberately misleading intentions to accusers, or using emotive devices to make the accusations appear to be false or, worse, deliberate calumnies.

Another technique concerned the use of terror and treachery to destabilize the assurance with which accusations were declared or denied. One of the more enduring techniques in this respect, used by both accusers and accused, revolved around the ascription of character or the promulgation of pithy caricatures. As noted above, the close relationship between character and action was generally upheld in the courts and allowed accusers to evoke past indications of character as a way to explain why one might have expected the accused to commit the criminal actions in question. Similarly, the accused was to discredit the character of the accusers, or witnesses supporting the accusers' case, in order to question the credibility of the people responsible for enunciating and solidifying a particular criminalizing narratives. So, as we have seen, allegations of calumny might be attributed to politically ambitious characters, just as extraordinary extravagance might be attributed to someone accused of extortion. Such characterizations and counter-characterizations were to become critical features of a tango between accusers and the accused, accusation and counter-accusation. We also referenced the technique of repudiating witness testimony, especially by the accused, that in the Scaurus case had Cicero claiming that the prosecution's case rested entirely on the presentation of witnesses whose character he impugned via a prejudiced attack on an entire "nation"—the Sardinians—as being incapable of reliable testimony.

Third, accusation was deemed to involve an essentially violent rhetorical nature, for it involved the decimation of people's everyday lives; the designation of criminal or false accuser stood as potential effects of its socially destructive force. Either way, people's lives and reputations were shattered through single-minded and intentional rhetorical attempts to cast people as worthy of being stripped of their social standing. Its violent rhetoric lay at the heart of legal designations that would later be called crime. Accusation provided a way to bring matters to the court that pitted accusers against the accused, with state authorities (*praetors*) as mere arbiters for accepted court procedures. In this respect, Roman formulations of accusation provided us with a helpful way to understanding the roots of an adjudicative justice approach that called upon accusers and the accused. Local identities were mutually constituted out of criminal accusation processes, and so too the overseeing authorities and the sovereign orders in whose name prosecutions proceeded. One might say that the rhetorical form of accusation was then more than simply a way to accuse pre-existing subjects; its "nature" was also to mold the identities of participants to its processes, and at the same time buttress the orders in whose name the accusations and their consequences proceeded.

Fourth, it is important to note that accusation was very much involved in what eventually materialized as a "crime" and who was designated as "criminal." As Harries points out, what was then taken to be criminal in the later republic was not a function of previously established criminal codes. Rather, there was a decidedly "after the fact" quality to what appeared as criminality, starting with specific accusations that might eventually be identified as "criminal" or "an offense against the public good," for, as Harries suggests, because "it was up to the community to decide not only on guilt but also on the nature of criminality itself, it was not necessary that a statute should be in place to outlaw wrongdoing" (15).

The courts did not then work off general laws, beyond a magistrate deciding whether a given accusation could be tried in the court to which application was made. Instead, as reflected in the concept *crimen* (meaning "reproach," "charge," or the manner of "calling subjects to account" for wrongdoing through accusation (Ayto), procedures of accusation did not so much claim to "discover" crime as to formulate its presence in given instances. Its role was in fashioning narratives on the legal facts of events and framing particular act as wrongs against the public with specific individuals as criminals. This placed accusation at the heart of emerging criminalization processes. It is worth quoting Harries at length on this:

> The law on "crime" was defined in terms not of a hierarchy of offences but of the nature of the accusations that could be brought and the procedural and penal consequences of so doing for both accuser and accused. The Romans therefore did have a vocabulary for what might be termed "crime" in a moral sense but there was no one word for "crime" in Roman law. Instead, the procedure, through public accusation, served as a signal as to the nature of the offence. The "accuser" asked the public, through its courts, to hold the accused to account. (5)

From this passage we might note that through the rhetorical nature ascribed to accusation, it served as a foundation for defining crime, criminal wrongdoing, and criminal persons through criminal trials.

Finally, aside from an internal politics of recognizing specific participants as accusers, the accused, and so on, criminal accusation also contributed to the political life of the republic. It was framed around specific offenses defined as threats to the Roman public; which actions it was possible to enunciate as criminal was bound to the political consolidations of a sovereign order that was partially defined by the court decisions made in its name. But one might here echo the observation that:

> Roman criminal trials were political not because they were co-opted by politicians; politics is in a strong sense at the very heart of the definition of offences tried in the *iudicia publica.* At Rome there were no crimes that were not political crimes. The courts existed not for the sake of justice in the abstract ... But for the good of the Roman people as a whole ... The public courts are those where the community protects itself, its property and its rights. This idea, if not always in the front of the minds of the jurors is one they could be led to accept. Hence a higher political good may on occasion be used to preempt the issue of guilt or innocence.
>
> (Riggsby, *Crime* 157–158)

Gruen reiterates the point by showing how the rise of standing courts provided a venue for various sorts of political struggle, from "personal rivalries" to important constitutional matters that hinged on "the outcome of a prosecution"; in short, criminal trials provided a mechanism "for struggles within the governing class, or indeed a means whereby to attack that class itself" (*Roman Politics* 6–7). In various ways, then, criminal accusation was used as "political weapon," so much so that "the business of politics" was frequently conducted in courts (Gruen, *Roman Politics* 6). For example, the "governing class" often took accusations in criminal trials as offering the prospect of permanently neutralizing political opponents, affirming, as with the Scaurus case, a means to wage "political warfare" decisively (Gruen, *Last Generation* 260). Indeed, "electoral defeat was only temporary embarrassment," whereas "conviction on a criminal charge might entail permanent exclusion from the public scene" (Gruen, *Last Generation* 260).

From the above, one glimpses the constitutive role accusation, understood as having an intrinsic if vehement rhetorical nature, played in the development of crime as an idea of general public wrong, and criminals as wrongdoers against a wider "public." Although much more can be said about this, it is perhaps important to reiterate criminology's big mistake: its decision to study crime *sui generis* when its etymology suggests that it might have examined the idea of *crimen* as a calling to account through accusation. This would have turned it away from abstracted notions of crime and its causes to the accusations that gave rise to concepts of wrongdoing in the first place.

Note

1 This early enquiry process played out over three different days where the guilt of the accused was affirmed and suitable penalties devised (Bauman, *Crime* 7–10). In these contexts, spectators shouted out comments, allowing the Tribune to gauge public opinion, but the decision rested with the Tribune unless the accused did not

confess. In the latter instance, the matter would be referred to a formal assembly, usually of the *Commitia Centuriata*, for a vote without discussion (Mousourakis 37ff). Another version of this early court dealt with market related offences under the auspices of specific *aediles* (Bauman, "Criminal Prosecutions").

References

Alexander, M.C. *The Case for the Prosecution in the Ciceronian Era*. University of Michigan Press, 2003.
Asconius, P.Q. *Commentaries on Speeches of Cicero*. Edited by A.C. Clark, J. Harries, and R.G. Lewis, Oxford University Press, 2006.
Ayto, J. *Dictionary of Word Origins*. Arcade Publishing, 1991.
Bauman, R.A. *Crime and Punishment in Ancient Rome*. Routledge, 1996.
——. "Criminal Prosecutions by the Aediles." *Latomus*, vol. 33, no. 2, 1974, pp. 245–264.
Cicero, M.T. *Cicero's Brutus or History of Famous Orators*. Translated by E. Jones, 2006. *Project Gutenberg*, www.gutenberg.org/ebooks/9776.
Cicero, M.T. and A.R. Dyck. *Marcus Tullius Cicero: Speeches on Behalf of Marcus Fonteius and Marcus Aemilius Scaurus: Translated with Introduction and Commentary*. Oxford University Press, 2012.
Cicero, M.T. and J.S. Watson. *Cicero on Oratory and Orators*. SIU Press, 1986.
Cowles, F.H. "Cicero's Debut as a Prosecutor." *The Classical Journal*, vol. 24, no. 6, 1929, pp. 429–448.
Foucault, M. *Wrong-Doing, Truth-Telling: The Function of Avowal in Justice*. Translated by Stephen W. Sawyer, edited by F. Brion and B.E. Harcourt. University of Chicago Press, 2014.
Gaughan, J.E. *Murder was Not a Crime: Homicide and Power in the Roman Republic*. University of Texas Press, 2010.
Gruen, E.S. *The Last Generation of the Roman Republic*. University of California Press, 1974.
——. *Roman Politics and the Criminal Courts, 149–78 B.C.* Harvard University Press, 1968.
Harries, J. *Law and Crime in the Roman World*. Cambridge University Press, 2007.
Henderson, C. "The Career of the Younger M. Aemilius Scaurus." *Classical Association of the Middle West and South*, vol. 53, no. 5, 1958, pp. 194–206.
Lintott, A. *Cicero as Evidence: A Historian's Companion*. Oxford University Press, 2008.
——. "Delator and Index: Informers and Accusers from the Republic to the Early Principate." *Accordia Research Papers*, vol. 9, 2001, pp. 105–122.
——. "Legal Procedure in Cicero's Time." In *Cicero the Advocate*. Edited by J. Powell and J. Paterson, Oxford University Press, 2004, pp. 61–78.
Marshall, B. "Two Court Cases in the Late Second Century B.C." *American Journal of Philology*, vol. 98, no. 4, 1977, pp. 417–423.
Mousourakis, G. *A Legal History of Rome*. Routledge, 2007.
Powell, J. and J. Paterson, J. (eds.). *Cicero the Advocate*. Oxford University Press, 2004.
Quintilian. *Institutes of Oratory*. Lee Honeycutt, 2010.

Riggsby, A.M. *Crime and Community in Ciceronian Rome.* University of Texas Press, 1999.
——. "The Rhetoric of Character in the Roman Courts." In *Cicero the Advocate.* Edited by J. Powell and J. Paterson, Oxford: Oxford University Press, 2004, pp. 165–186.
——. *Roman Law and the Legal World of the Romans.* Cambridge University Press, 2010.
Robinson, O.F. *The Criminal Law of Ancient Rome.* Johns Hopkins University Press, 2000.
——. "The Role of Delators." In *Beyond Dogmatics: Law and Society in the Roman World.* Edited by J.W. Cairns and P.J. du Plessis, Edinburgh University Press, 2007, pp. 206–221.
Rutledge, S.H. "Delatores and the Tradition of Violence in Roman Oratory." *American Journal of Philology*, vol. 120, no. 4, 1999, pp. 555–573.
——. *Imperial Inquisitions: Prosecutors and Informants from Tiberius to Domitian.* Routledge, 2001.
Solmsen, F. "Cicero's First Speeches: A Rhetorical Analysis." *Transactions and Proceedings of the American Philological Association*, vol. 69, 1938, pp. 542–556.
Stein, P. *Roman Law in European History.* Cambridge University Press, 1999.
Tellegen-Couperus, O. *A Short History of Roman Law.* Routledge, 1993.
Versteeg, R. *Essentials of Greek and Roman Law.* Carolina Academic Press, 2009.

Chapter 4

The colonialism of incarceration

Robert Nichols

Despite common perception to the contrary, the Canadian prison population is disproportionately large relative to other comparable societies, the result of a dramatic increase over the past 25 years. In the 1990s alone, federal prison populations increased by 25% and provincial prison populations by a further 15%. The number of young people in the country's correctional institutions has increased by nearly 30% since 1986 (Dauvergne; Perreault).[1] A large omnibus crime bill recently passed into law by the Conservative government, which promotes further ideologically driven yet demonstrably dysfunctional "tough on crime" policies, ensures that these trends will only expand and compound over time.[2]

This reality has been somewhat obscured by the hyperbolic violence of prison expansion and carceral power in the US. Nevertheless, just as is true of the US case, prison expansion north of the border has been highly racialized, especially targeting indigenous peoples. In 2010/2011, Aboriginal peoples comprised 27% of the total adult population in provincial or territorial custody and 20% in federal custody in Canada (Juristat). Since Aboriginal peoples account for only 3–4% of the total Canadian population, this incarceration rate is seven to eight times higher than the general average. This discrepancy is particularly striking when considered in conjunction with a gendered analysis: Aboriginal women make up the single fastest-growing imprisoned population and now account for 33.6% of all federally sentenced women in Canada (Government of Canada). Additionally, Aboriginal inmates are subject to what the head Federal Correctional Investigator refers to, rather euphemistically, as "routine over-classification." This means that indigenous peoples are commonly classified as higher risk and are more likely to reoffend; thus, they are released later in their sentences and are more often subjected to highly intense forms of incarceration, such as maximum security prisons and "administrative segregation" (otherwise known as solitary confinement). Partially as a result of this intensification, Aboriginal peoples are more likely to be involved in incidents involving harm to self or others while in custody, including 45% of all documented cases of self-injury (Government of Canada 30). Significant discrepancies between indigenous and non-indigenous incarceration rates can be found consistently across all provincial and territorial jurisdictions in Canada, but the degree of disproportion increases significantly in the

West (e.g., Alberta, Manitoba, and Saskatchewan) and in the Territories of the North. Moreover, just as with the US case, racial disproportionality is increasing over time. As the Office of the Correctional Investigator recently put the matter: "Aboriginal over-representation has grown in recent years: between 1998 and 2008, the federal Aboriginal population increased by 19.7%. Moreover, the number of federally sentenced Aboriginal women increased by a staggering 131% over this period" (Office of the Correctional Investigator 6).[3]

Critical prison studies—and the various forms of radical, grounded praxis out of which it has emerged, been transformed, and subsequently reinvigorated with conceptual and practical tools—has insufficiently attended to the centrality of colonialism to the origins, scope, scale, and legitimation techniques of carceral power in North America and, as a result, it has by and large deprived itself of the energy and force of indigenous critique. With the aim of contributing to a positive interjection and reinvigoration of the *decolonizing* possibilities latent within this field, then, this chapter seeks to expand and refocus this framework. I argue that although the incarceration of indigenous peoples is closely related to the experience of other racialized populations in North America (especially African Americans) with regard to its *causes*, it is importantly distinct with respect to the *normative foundation* of its critique. Indigenous critique is (1) first and foremost a political critique, related but not reducible to causal explanations rooted in economic and sociological developments. It is a form of critique that (2) challenges the prevailing paradigm of "over-representation" in critical prison studies by calling into question the biopolitical category of "racialized population" itself, (3) challenges the ideological distinction between the logic of war and the logic of social pacification upon which carceral expansion depends, (4) situates critical prison studies within the broader horizon of settler colonialism and territorialized sovereignty, and (5) offers alternative normative grounds from which to launch a general critique of these processes.

I

The single most important set of tools available to any contemporary critical prison analysis in North America comes to us from decades of work in African-American and women of color feminism, broadly defined. Academic/activists such as Angela Davis and Ruth Gilmore are central to this debate, but so are organizations such as *Incite! Women of Colour against Violence*, *Critical Resistance* and the *Sylvia Rivera Law Project*.[4] Since these thinkers and organizations are building their analysis and critical praxis out of the US experience, they have been particularly focused on the centrality of anti-Black racism to understanding prison expansion in that country.[5] This has taken the form of drawing a line of continuity between the contemporary prison system and the long history of slavery, either by way of a causal link or via argument by analogy. The former attempts to demonstrate how the proliferation of Black Codes in the wake of formal abolition was directly and causally responsible for the turn to incarceration as a primary mechanism of social control over racialized populations (but especially African Americans). However, such causal explanations have been difficult to establish with sufficient certainty and can tend toward reductive, "single variable" forms of analysis that may improperly bracket out alternative explanations. Of late, then, critical prison studies in the US has tended toward a looser analogizing structure of argumentation, making the case that contemporary forms of imprisonment are *functionally equivalent* to Antebellum slavery or Jim Crow legislation in the post-Reconstruction era, even if not causally determined by these antecedents.[6]

Any critique of indigenous incarceration will have to grapple with a similar ambiguity whenever it links imprisonment to colonialism, and in this we can no doubt learn from Critical Race Theory, women of color feminism, and their related domains. However, we will as fundamentally require some departure from them. For just as any properly grounded critical praxis would be, these other fields are rooted in a historical experience that, while intersecting with settler colonialism and indigenous struggles, also diverges from them in relevant ways. Although some important literature exists that focuses on the specificity of indigenous incarceration—most notably, work by Patricia Monture and Luana Ross—to date, this dimension of the field remains relatively occluded from view.[7]

One feature of prevailing discourses on prisons that serves to propagate a certain occlusion of its colonial dimension is the persistent language of "over-representation" and "racial disproportion," an idiom one can find even in the most critical camps. In this framework, empirical evidence is presented just as has been given here (above). The standard narrative structure begins with a recitation of statistical evidence pertaining to demographics, specifically comparing the racial organization of society at large versus that of the incarceration population. Any incongruity or discrepancy between the two is noted, commonly named as over-representation, and then employed to offer tacit or overt condemnation of the system. This rhetorical strategy is, not surprisingly, most evident in mainstream organizations and academic research, but it is also startlingly widespread in more critical or radical literature as well. To offer but one influential example of the former, in April 2011 the National Association for the Advancement of Colored People (NAACP) released a major report entitled *Misplaced Priorities: Over Incarcerate, Under Educate*. This meticulously detailed report documents the rapid growth of racialized incarceration in the US with a particular focus on its impacts on African-American communities, and the detrimental effects this is having on state capacities in other areas of investment and service delivery (especially education). Nevertheless, the primary critical thrust of this work rests with the idea of *disproportionality* or the *over-representation* of racialized populations. As the title attests, it is primarily about *over*-incarceration, not imprisonment per se.

Over-representation is a highly ambiguous and malleable idiom, susceptible to multiple interpretations and easily rendered into diverse programs for action. For instance, disproportion may be construed as the result of economic or social pathologies exogenous to the criminal justice system itself. In this formulation, the over-representation of racialized populations in prisons merely *makes visible* broader social pathologies, albeit in a highly dramatic way. For instance, criminality is correlated to poverty, which in turn is correlated to racialization and marginalization. Thus, the over-representation of certain populations in penal institutions may be thought a function of racism, but only in a highly mediated manner. On a different reading, however, we also know that the judicial system *itself* is rife with racialized violence and injustice. Such relatively unmediated mechanisms of racism operate endogenously to the system and have also been found to directly contribute to over-representation, for instance, in the manner in which racial bias operates at various stages of interaction with criminal justice officials, from being stopped for routine infractions (especially "stop and frisk" policies), through to sentencing and treatment by prison officers. Returning to the Canadian context, then, both of these (external and internal) factors have been central to understanding the expansion of indigenous incarceration. To cite but one example, a 2004 study found that Aboriginal women in maximum security institutions were involved in security incidences at a rate (28.6%) comparable to female inmates in minimum and medium security institutions (26.8%), and the correlation between the Security Risk Score (based on previous criminal history) and involvement in such incidences was found to be practically zero: 0.01 for violent incidences and 0.05 for non-violent incidences. The report drew the following conclusion from this evidence: "Aboriginal women are thus more routinely placed into tighter security settings despite the fact that their *criminal history has no predictive value* for whether they are genuinely a risk to other inmates or staff" (Milward 43). In other words, racial bias is demonstrably impacting internal prison operations, a key factor in understanding divergence between Aboriginal and non-Aboriginal experiences of incarceration (in terms of scope, scale, and intensity).

Analysis of the racism both exogenous and endogenous to the criminal justice system is clearly indispensable to a comprehensive analysis of imprisonment. It therefore remains the focus of much critical prison studies, as analysts seek to provide causal explanations for recent carceral expansion. However, this focus has its limits. While discriminatory implementation is undoubtedly important to the overall operation of penal power in North America, it is limited as an explanatory device in relation to prison expansion. For racial discrimination to serve this explanatory function, one would need to demonstrate not merely its contemporary extent and operation, but also its dramatic *increase* since the 1970s. However racist the operation of the criminal justice system today may be (and no credible position can deny this generally), it is another thing altogether to suggest that the system prior to the 1970s was significantly *less* so.[8]

Thus, as numerous works have documented, understanding the expansion of prisons in North America requires not merely a *social* analysis—that is, one rooted in the sociology of criminal justice officials in their interactions with targeted populations—but also a *political* one. This is to say that carceral mutation and expansion is explainable principally as a political strategy, one that links up with a variety of social and economic transformations taking place over the last few decades (especially neoliberal economic "adjustments," and deregulation and dissolution of social welfare networks) without being entirely reducible to these other factors.[9] In other words, while these social and economic forces produced the relevant context, multiple responses to these transformations were nevertheless possible. Carceral expansion was not so much then the necessary, automated effect of these various causes: it was (and is) a political choice adopted from within a range of possible responses. This point is punctuated by the fact, made repeatedly in the literature, that carceral expansion is not a function of increased crime. In fact, as volumes of work attest, there is little connection between crime and punishment in North America: technologies of punishment (and their ideological justifications) grow and morph quite independently of changes in crime trends.[10] Nor are such punitive transformations a function of economic demands in any simple, straightforward manner. Despite a continued emphasis in activist literature on privatization, for-profit motives, prisoners-as-surplus-labor, or even the somewhat misleading "prison industrial complex" neologism, prisons remain overwhelmingly public institutions and carceral expansion a function of state imperatives. So the growth of prisons is not straightforwardly a function of either an increase in crime or unmediated profit motives. This is not to say that privatization has not increased or that it is not a central component of many contemporary prison systems in the Western world. However, such phenomena are more properly understood as the effects of prison expansion rather than its causes.[11] As such, this indicates that prison expansion is a distinctly *political* phenomenon.

Ruth Gilmore theorizes the politics of carceral expansion in terms of "surplus state capacity," which she defines as a "quality that can emerge over time as a result of the difference between what states can do *technically* and what they can do *politically*" (Gilmore 113). Thus, while the surplus state capacity mobilized toward carceral expansion is about technical power, it equally pertains to and has its roots in discourses of legitimation, namely social pacification and managerial democracy. Political elites push "law and order" ideologies and carceral expansion because they recognize that these work to solidify hierarchical chains of authority and control over of the state apparatus, and this functions primarily because large swaths of middle-class white people, driven by fear and racist fantasies, support such policies even in the face of overwhelming evidence that they do not operate to reduce crime. By bringing forward this political circuit of violence and legitimation, we can thus break from the kind of social critique proffered by the prototypical exasperated criminologist who throws up her hands in frustration that governments continue to pursue legal reforms that are not only ineffective, but actively counterproductive (i.e., they fail to reduce crime rates and may actual increase them). For, unlike this naïve approach, we can see that such policies may not be designed to reduce crime in the first place. They can only be viewed as failures if one adopts the view that they are primarily enacted in order to make communities safer. Once we see that this is not the case—once we realize that such policies are first and foremost devised to maintain a system of state violence, racialized hierarchy, and, as I will argue, continuous colonial reterritorialization—then we must confront how effective and successful they truly are.

Thus, carceral expansion as a *political formation* has been increasingly grasped as a function of the emergence and consolidation of a new "penal ethos" in North America over the last 20–30 years.[12] This entails the deliberate dismantling of the social welfare state (however inadequate and uneven its institutions were), a corresponding growth and glorification of the penal state, and an internal transcription of the very terms of the penal state toward an increasingly moralized, punitive approach that prioritizes the isolation, segregation, and politically symbolic (though functionally ineffective) performance of castigating criminals (overwhelmingly the racialized poor). In other words, it is not merely that the state punishes *more*, but that it does so *differently*, with a new penology that emphasizes highly intense sociospatial isolation.[13] As Loïc Wacquant reminds us: "The expansive and expensive penal system is not just a consequence of neoliberalism ... but an *integral component of the neoliberal state itself*" (Wacquant 175–176). The ritualized morality of punishment has ensured that even those remnants of the social welfare state that persevere have been effectively integrated into and subordinated to carceral rhetoric and imperatives, for instance in so-called "workfare" programs.[14] The horizontal spread of carceral governmentality thus exceeds its limited institutional manifestation in the prison itself, confirming yet exceeding one of Foucault's central insights from *Discipline and Punish.*

II

Much of the survey above is known. Although the general trajectory of critical prison studies has been driving toward the kind of distinctly *political* critique of carceral expansion outlined above, the field nevertheless still remains fixated primarily upon causal explanations. To be clear, I am not suggesting that explicating the sociological causes of prison growth over the last 30 years or so is unworthy of time and attention. However, no causal explanation, however complex and nuanced, can satisfy our need for a normative critique. And in this regard, historically and in the present, the indigenous peoples of North America provided indispensable tools since their critical praxis (decolonization) has always *primarily* focused on a robust normative critique of state sovereignty *as such*, and only secondarily upon its racist implementations. The focus of indigenous peoples' struggles has always been the imposition of the Euro-American state apparatus itself. This critique imports a broader perspective, one that activists from various other traditions (indigenous and non-indigenous) can learn from and must contend with.

In light of this perspective, sociological and demographic analysis of racialized incarcerated populations is inadequate when thinking about the political form of carceral power in North America. The colonial violence of carceral power in North America is not exclusively, or even predominately, a function of the *number* or *proportion* of racialized bodies within institutions. Moreover, framing the matter in this way may exacerbate the problem. When the critique of incarceration rests upon the over-representation of racialized bodies within penal institutions, this tacitly renders carcerality as a *dehistoricized* tool of state power—even if distorted by the pathological effects of a racist society—displacing an account of the continuity and links between carcerality, state formation, and territorialized sovereignty.

As indigenous scholars such as Taiaiake Alfred, Joanne Barker, Glen Coulthard, and Audra Simpson (*inter alia*) have consistently argued, unlike other racialized populations in North America, indigenous peoples constituted self-governing political communities prior to the imposition of European state and market forms.[15] Thus, their *continued* sovereign presence on the North American continent attests not only to the failure of a series of projects of racial population management, but also fundamentally calls into question the very legitimacy of Euro-American states themselves. The central role of policing, prisons, and the criminal justice system in the maintenance and reproduction of the state form is therefore challenged in a manner that exceeds the paradigm of over-representation. Moving beyond the over-representation model thus means asking after the political function of the carceral system as a whole beyond that of racialized bodies within. In so doing, we confront a series of new questions: how can we analyze carceral power in the context of an ongoing denial of indigenous peoples not merely as individuals, or even as "populations," but as self-organizing, self-governing political collectivities? How are we to apprehend the cataloging and deploying of statistical evidence itself in this situation, especially when the evidentiary record is itself so indebted to a state apparatus of monitoring, tracking, and documenting indigenous bodies?[16] How do we draw upon such statistical evidence while recognizing that these numbers constitute bodies as "populations" in a context of a depoliticizing biopolitics of surplus humanity and human management?[17]

Returning once more to the Canadian case then, indigenous peoples do not merely represent racialized bodies produced by a biopolitics of population management. Rather—and this is the radical actuality that must always be held at bay by the state—they constitute alternative political, economic, ecological, and spiritual systems of ordering, governing, and relating. In the context of ongoing occupation, usurpation, dispossession, and ecological devastation, *no* level of representation in one of the central apparatuses of state control and formalized violence would be proportionate. Instead, indigenous sovereignty itself calls forth an alternative normativity that challenges the very *existence* of the carceral system, let alone its internal organization and operation.

III

Before turning more centrally to the question of alternative normativities, consider how indigenous critique recasts another, related theme currently circulating in activist-academic literature, namely, the contemporary concern over a collapse between military and police operations. We are repeatedly reminded that, at present, foreign policy objectives described explicitly in terms of "war" are advanced not through the traditional confrontation of armed combatants, but through police-like operations over a globe envisioned as one large domestic space of surveillance and pacification. As we repeatedly hear from critics and defenders alike, U.S.-led empire functions as a "global policeman." The corollary development is the increased militarization of traditional, domestic policing. Policing is thought to be militarized either when (1) it begins to employ certain technologies of intense violence normally not deployed against civilian citizenry (the use of armed personal carriers, drones, aerial surveillance, etc.) or (2) when it begins to serve overtly political aims, exceeding its traditional mandate to "serve and protect" the citizenry.[18] In such situations, the police risk being viewed as a force imposed externally by a government that the subjugated population does not recognize, authorize, and/or does not have effective participation within.[19] Criminal control bleeds into war.

Assertions that the logic of war and that of social pacification can still be effectively disentangled are belied by our reality. In the current climate, no attempt to fully insulate these two logics from one another can succeed. Yet, while recent commentators have expressed great dismay at the nakedly fluid boundary between military and policing operations today, viewed from the vantage point of settler colonialism and indigenous critique, there is nothing new about this permeability. In the history of Anglo-American settler colonialism, for instance, the extension of criminal jurisdiction has long been central to the subjugation and displacement of indigenous polities.[20] Existing in the "third space of sovereignty," indigenous nations have always subverted foreign/domestic distinctions, as well as attempts to distinguish war decisively from crime management (Bruyneel). The largest and most important domestic policing organization in Canada, the Royal Canadian Mounted Police (RCMP), emerged from its predecessor organization, the North-West Mounted Police (NWMP). The latter was modeled upon the Royal Irish Constabulary (RIC) and was expressly intended to function as a paramilitary organization, meant simultaneously to defeat indigenous resistance politically and pacify it criminally (Harring; Macleod). In the US as well, although the Office of Indian Affairs, created in 1824, was very symbolically relocated from the War Department to the Department of the Interior in 1849, from this point forward, including Wounded Knee and the complex and tense relationship between American Indians and the FBI, indigenous peoples have always been doubly subjected to these two logics of violence and control.[21] As a result, they are well positioned to observe that these are not, and never have been, fixed and parallel logics, but have always intersected one another. Indigenous critique thereby discloses the oscillation of these forms of state violence as *constitutive* of territorialized sovereignty in a colonial context rather than extraneous and novel.

However, the deep challenge posed by indigenous peoples does not merely consist in their doubly subjected position here. Rather, it resides in the delegitimizing of the war/crime dichotomy in the first place, for indigenous peoples in North America are in precisely the position mentioned above: experiencing policing itself as a force imposed externally by a government that the subjugated population does not recognize, authorize, and/or does not have effective participation within.[22] In short, the *state itself* is apprehended as the primary vehicle for the collective organization of violence upon indigenous peoples, historically and in the present. Indigenous politics is founded upon this existential challenge. As indigenous (Mohawk) scholar Patricia Monture-Angus points out, in the Canadian context, study after study has demonstrated that "Aboriginal people do not view the criminal justice system as a system that represents or respects them," and, as a result, "the perceptions of Aboriginal peoples (while keeping in mind their diversity) thus thoroughly challenge the perspective of those who regard Canada to be a free and democratic state" ("The Need for Radical Change" 244). In this context, reforming the penal system to produce less "disproportionality" in racial demographics (between inside and outside the prison walls) will continue to fail to take into account Aboriginal justice traditions themselves, which are "a clear component of the inherent right to self-government" (Monture-Angus, "The Need for Radical Change" 240).[23] While indigeneity consistently avoids reduction to any fixed or determinate content, the condition of possibility for continued creative reinvention and reproduction of culture, tradition, spirituality, and life itself *as* indigenous peoples has meant a persistent refusal to acknowledge the dehistoricized naturalization of domestic/foreign distinctions meant to legitimize state violence.

Although this has a centuries-long history, what has changed is that, unlike previous eras (unlike even the 1970s, e.g., Pine Ridge) the incarceration of indigenous peoples is increasingly dehistoricized—and thus depoliticized—through its representation as the general extension of racialized criminality. Even though far more indigenous peoples are incarcerated today than, say, when Lenard Pelltier was convicted in 1977, today this is more effectively and smoothly enacted because it has been routinized, bureaucratized, and detached from the longer colonial history of the state itself. By attending to the colonial function of carceral expansion today, we are thus cautioned against too hastily accepting the supposed radical novelty of the present, not to mention the story of neoliberalism's hollowed-out states or empire's virtuality. Indeed, we are even cautioned against too hastily accepting one of indigenous studies' prevailing narratives today, namely, that North American settler states have moved from openly coercive and violent relations with indigenous communities toward a more flexible, docile, politics of recognition and assimilation—a move away from the "hard infrastructure" of military operations and residential schools to the "soft infrastructure" of public apologies and cultural accommodation. While this transition to soft tactics has certainly occurred in some fields of governance, it is coeval with the growth of a whole shadow system of hard infrastructure that is every bit as material, physical, and coercive as ever. The settler colonial state has not gone away at all, or even become less of a physical, material presence—it has merely shifted its site of operation, perhaps most symbolically from the residential school to the prison. Read against this larger backdrop, then, we can begin to read the vast network of prisons in North America in terms of its ideological function relative to settler colonialism—that is, the manner in which it functions strenuously to depoliticize this ongoing material violence and erect a strict separation between *criminal control* and *conquest* despite indigenous societies' continued insistence that externally imposed coercive control over their members (for whatever reason) is an affront to the inherent right to self-government.

IV

Ruth Gilmore has persuasively argued that if we are to understand and properly subject carceral power to an effective critique, then we must not only "develop complex understandings of how prisoners became so massively available as carceral objects"—a matter surely deeply rooted in processes of racialization—but we must also "figure out how the ground the prisons stand on becomes available for such a purpose" (Gilmore 130). In thinking about how this ground becomes available, Gilmore has in mind the manner in which a permanent crisis in the workfare-welfare state has been literally displaced onto the landscape of relatively low-density, rural communities, which has produced new opportunities and demands for land grabbing. However, highlighting the colonialism of incarceration further draws our attention to the territorial foundation of prison expansion in a deeper and longer history. It forces consideration of the politics of territoriality in North America in a variety of forms, including the ways in which territorialized sovereignty aspires to impose an exclusivity and singularity of command and control that obliterates alternative normative orders beneath and beyond its aegis.

At the most immediately level, criminalized capture by the state is about management of "disorderly populations" through isolation. As Allen Feldman famously put it: "Arrest is the political art of individualizing disorder" (235). Of course, isolation and sequester are always already geospatial and are thus implicated in territoriality in a general sense. Prisons are a spatial and territorialized matrix of punishment and control inasmuch as they attempt to provide geographic solutions to socioeconomic and political contradictions (in the form of cages, walls, and other technologies of isolation and segregation). As Gilmore forcefully put this point:

> Incapacitation doesn't pretend to change anything about people except where they are. It is in a simple-minded way, then, a geographical solution that purports to solve social problems by extensively and repeatedly removing people from disordered, deindustrialized milieus and depositing them somewhere else.
>
> (Gilmore 14)

Prisons certainly operate through geospatial media in this general sense, sharing a certain continuity with other technologies of spatial control such as "ghettoization." As a result, there is overlap here with other importance experiences of, for instance, African-American subjugation and control. Prisons, ghettos, and other tools of capture and separation exhibit a revealing morphological continuity.[24] However, attending to the historical experience of indigenous peoples, these general geospatial formations are refocused through another lens of territoriality—settler colonialism and land acquisition—reframing Gilmore's considerations on the territorial foundation of the prison apparatus.

Indigenous (Dene) political theorist Glen Coulthard provides a succinct and precise definition from which we may begin to bring the colonial-territorial politics to the fore here. He designates a "colonial relationship" in terms of the distinct form of domination it engenders. Colonialism is:

> A relationship where power—in this case, interrelated discursive and non-discursive facets of economic, gendered, racial, and state power—has been structured into a relatively secure or sedimented set of hierarchical social relations that continue to facilitate the *dispossession* of Indigenous peoples of our lands and self-determining authority. In this respect, Canada is no different than any other settler-colonial power: in the Canadian context, colonial domination continues to be structurally oriented around the state's longstanding commitment to maintain—through force, fraud, and more recently, so-called "negotiations"—ongoing access to the land that contradictorily provides the material and spiritual sustenance of Indigenous societies and the foundation of colonial state-formation, settlement and capitalist development.
>
> (Coulthard, "From Wards" 57–58)

Coupling Coulthard's work with the emergent field of settler colonial studies brings into focus the extent to which state and market formation in North America has always been intimately bound up with *land acquisition* and *resettlement*, and that these have called forth distinct ideologies rooted in notions of agrarianism, territorial possession, and improvement. The defining feature of this particular political formation is not the appropriation of labor or the subjugation of indigenous self-governing powers (although these are both also present). Rather, as James Tully reminds us, "the ground of the relation is the appropriation of the land, resources, and jurisdiction of indigenous peoples, not only for the sake of resettlement and exploitation ... but *for the territorial foundations of the dominant society itself*" (Tully 39, emphasis added). Or as Patrick Wolfe states rather more bluntly: "Territoriality is settler colonialism's specific, irreducible element" (388).

Contemporary critical theory has largely evaded an analysis of territoriality and its relationship with classical colonial formations, often staking much on a supposed movement toward a decentered, deterritorialized, virtual, or "postmodern" empire thought to have succeeded the older, land-based form of colonial power that held sway over an era now imagined as distant to us.[25] However, viewed from the vantage point of indigenous struggles, settler colonialism and—our focus here—carceral power as it is subtended by colonialism, predictions of a neoliberal hollowed-out state and/or a deterritorialized Empire appear not merely premature, but also inattentive to the dialectical inversion of these tendencies, that is, to the processes of concretization and the persistence of *fixity*, *rigidity*, and *territoriality*. Thinking through carceral power and indigenous incarceration, we can here instead ask after the continuation of classical state building practices, including its hard infrastructure, as well as classical colonial relationships to land acquisition and dispossession that have provided the literal terrain upon which biopolitical population management techniques as segregation and sequester rest, observing not only that these remain central to the global organization of capital and biopower, but also that such forces are in fact advancing rather than melting away.

Work by political theorist Wendy Brown stands as an exception to this general occlusion inasmuch as she has attended to the paradoxes of the territoriality of contemporary sovereignty by highlighting the continuing importance of walls, fences, borders, and barriers to the organization of political space. Brown notes that what we have come to call "globalization" in fact:

> harbors fundamental tensions between opening and barricading, fusion and partition, erasure and reinscription. These tensions materialize as increasingly liberalized borders, on the one hand, and the devotion of unprecendented funds, energies, and technologies to border fortification, on the other.
> (Brown 7–8)

In other words, while capital and military technology is increasingly deterritorialized and fluid, it is so only through the reassertion of rigidity, fixity, and territorial segmentation for certain populations. And, quite rightly, Brown draws a line of continuity between the contemporary resurgence of concrete barriers and the historical lineage of settler colonialism and land appropriations. In this way, she provides tools for understanding how the regulation of political space is not merely about the construction (or removal) of any specific walls, fences, or cages, but more properly "a technology of separation and domination in a complex context of settler colonialism and occupation" (Brown 30).

In so-called "Indian Country," there is nothing new about this paradoxical relationship of segregation and fluidity. Indigenous peoples are well acquainted with what Ann Laura Stoler has termed (following and building upon Foucault) the carceral archipelago of empire, which has always combined spatial isolation and confinement with links and connectivity—in this particular case, highlighted most dramatically by the circuit many indigenous peoples traverse today between the reserve or reservation and the prison, two sites of physical and spatial containment that are intertwined in one other (Stoler).[26] In settler colonial societies today, however, this reality is obscured not only by the ideological depoliticization of carceral expansion in general, but also by the delinking of prison abolitionism from decolonialism and the "land question" specifically. To speak of the colonial violence of carceral power in North America is precisely to focus attention on how incarceration facilitates dispossession, in this time, in this place.

In the final analysis, then, indigenous critique launches its evaluation of carceral power by attending to the ways in which this apparatus of capture operates as one armature of territorialized colonial sovereignty, a continuous process of dispossession that (always imperfectly) undermines indigenous practices of self-government by severing peoples from their historical relationship to the land. As such, this critique already speaks of alternative normative relationships of governance, sociality, and ecology.

Consider again the work of Patricia Monture-Angus. Drawing upon extensive work with Aboriginal women's associations across Canada, Monture-Angus points us directly to the ultimate normative foundation of the critique proffered here. In 1989, the Aboriginal Women's Caucus submitted a brief to the Solicitor General of Canada, making clear the status of indigenous women as both (1) multiply subjected by sexist, racist, and colonial forms of governance, and yet (2) firmly rooted in an alternative ethic that precludes their legitimate incorporation into the criminal justice system, whatever their "level of representation" therein. They wrote:

> All Aboriginal, First Nations citizens are in conflict with the law. We are First Peoples with an inherent right to exercise our own systems of justice and the values these systems represent. The issue of Aboriginal women and the criminal justice system is merely the most blatant example of the oppression of First Nations People under a system of laws to which we have never consented.
>
> (Correctional Service Canada 23)[27]

Reflecting on this and other examples, the conclusion Monture-Angus draws is that "the foundational ideas of current correctional philosophy"—namely, punitive power and risk management—are "incompatible with Aboriginal cultures, law and tradition" ("Aboriginal Women" 56).[28] This therefore presents a unique and important challenge to the new penal ethos, since it cannot be easily resolved even through a "de-racialization" process or the reorganization of demographics. Even attempts to incorporate the alternative ethical systems of indigenous peoples will fall short under such conditions. The inclusion of Healing Lodges and other Aboriginal-centered correctional facilities cannot conceal the fact that these institutions remain "within the legal and bureaucratic structure of the Canadian prison system ... no matter how much Aboriginal culture and tradition inspires their contour, shape and form" (Monture-Angus, "Aboriginal Women" 53).[29] As such, whereas "racialization" approaches tend to focus on the racist operation of correctional institutions, indigenous critique focuses attention on the normative critique of carceral power within a broader horizon, but especially insofar as it functions as a principle apparatus of colonial-state power. This deep, territoriality grounded normative vision is not reducible to the more prevalent anti-racist analysis of critical prison studies (however indispensable the latter remains) and cannot be overlooked or ignored.

V

Theorizing and interrupting indigenous incarceration means attending to more than the over-representation of racialized bodies.[30] It calls instead for an analysis of the colonial function of the carceral form in the here and now. To recapitulate: the concern here is not with a general notion that all imprisonment, regardless of time and place, is inherently colonial merely due to its form or mode of operation. Rather, it is with the fact that, in *this* context, carceral power takes on a colonial function as a result of its central role in manifesting and managing the territorialized violence of *these* states.[31] If sovereignty can be said to comprise the continual practice of asserting the singularity of political control in a given territorial space—thus combining exclusion and absolute decision—colonialism is the practical mediation of the external/internal boundaries of this process. It is the means by which sovereignty extends outward and is then reterritorialized through continual internal reorganization, hence the association of colonization as an outward expansive force and an internal reorganization through containment, capture, and divisive social organization. In the contemporary Anglo-American world, this colonization is predicated by its *settler* form, as so many important interventions in Native American studies have demonstrated.

Settler colonialism is a distinctive ideological and material formation, and it should be clear here that the prison industrial complex in North America is one technique in its operation today. Set alongside that other archipelago of spatial containment—the Indian reservation and reserve system—the contemporary carceral system colonizes and recolonizes in a classical sense: by providing a solution to that which exceeds and destabilizes sovereignty via a spatial reorganization of populations and a depoliticization of that process. While this apparatus is currently situated within empire and manifests itself in fully racialized terms of articulation today, it cannot be reduced to these other formations. For settler colonialism aims not primarily at exogenous domination or the extraction of surplus value from an enslaved and subjugated population, but, first and foremost, at the acquisition and maintenance of territorialized sovereignty through continual spatial containment, reorganization, and pacification—a process that both undermines and is continually challenged by the plurality of indigenous normative worlds. Thus, the rise of carceral power in the Anglo-American world cannot be told without attending to the history of settler colonialism, and it is only on the basis of this reframing that prison abolition can properly announce itself as decolonization.

Notes

1 Unless otherwise indicated, statistical information on Aboriginal incarceration in Canada is drawn from Dauvergne and Perreault. The majority of statistical evidence on indigenous incarceration in Canada derives from *Juristat*, a periodical published by Statistics Canada, which advertises itself as "of interest to all those who plan, establish, administer and evaluate justice programs and projects, as well as to anyone who has an interest in Canada's justice system" (Statistics Canada).

2 The controversial bill, traveling under the equally bloated and mangled title *Bill C-10: An Act to Enact the Justice for Victims of Terrorism Act and to Amend the State Immunity Act, the Criminal Code, the Controlled Drugs and Substances Act, the Corrections and Conditional Release Act, the Youth Criminal Justice Act, the Immigration and Refugee Protection Act and Other Acts* (Abbreviated title: *Safe Streets and Communities Act*), passed into law in September 2013. See www.parl.gc.ca/LEGISInfo/BillDetails.aspx?Mode=1&billId=5120829&Language=E.

3 For a study on the imprisonment of women in Canada (but with little specific attention to Aboriginal women and no mention of colonialism), see Hannah-Moffat.

4 Two of the most frequently cited works in contemporary critical prison studies include Davis and Gilmore.

5 In the section that follows, I will be speaking frequently of "racism" and "racialization." My specific understanding of these terms is highly indebted to Ruth Gilmore's definition of racism as "state-sanctioned or extralegal production and exploitation of group-differentiated vulnerability to premature death" (28).

6 For example, see Alexander.

7 See also Dickson-Gilmore and La Prairie; Green; and Monture-Okanee and Turpel. On incarceration as a theme in indigenous literature, see Rymhs.

8 As Loïc Wacquant puts this point: "True, discrimination in sentencing remains a reality at the final stage of the criminal justice process … but discrimination clearly has not *increased* since the mid 1970s and so it cannot account for the spectacular worsening of 'racial disproportionality' in prison administration in the recent period" (156).

9 See further Soss et al.

10 E.g., in the same year that the Conservative government of Canada announced sweeping new "tough on crime" laws, Statistics Canada reported that the crime rate was the lowest in decades. See "Canada's Crime Rate Lowest since 1972."

11 For criticism of the "new slavery" arguments and the idea that capitalist labour exploitation is the primary driver of prison expansion, see Gilmore 21; and Kilgore.

12 Loïc Wacquant has meticulously documented how this new "penal common sense" has been actively exported by the US to Western Europe (and beyond) through neoliberal think tanks, policy experts, and lobby groups. It is reasonable to expect that the appearance of many of the same trends in Canada can be attributed to the adoption of this new kind of "Washington Consensus." See Wacquant 54.

13 For a powerful political-phenomenological critique of solitary confinement, see Guenther.

14 See Soss et al.

15 See Alfred, *Wasáse: Indigenous Pathways* and *Peace, Power, Righteousness*; Barker; Coulthard, *Red Skin, White Masks*; and Simpson.

16 For instance, consider the role of *Juristat* in the Canadian context (Statistics Canada).

17 Statistical evidence of over-representation is neither irrelevant nor a useless as a tool of argumentation. However, due to the inherent ambiguities of "over-representation," it has never been sufficient tool for a robust normative critique of carceral power itself. Consider that between 1967 and 1991, there were 30 major studies commissioned on Aboriginal peoples and justice in Canada that, on some accounts, have resulted in some 1,800 recommendations for reforming the Canadian justice system. In 1996, the Report of the Royal Commission on Aboriginal Peoples (RCAP) included a separate volume on Indigenous peoples and criminal justice, *Bridging the Cultural Divide*, which provided 15 major new findings on the matter and 17 additional recommendations. Almost none of these has been implemented and, in the time since the RCAP was released, the problem has only grown (Monture-Angus, "The Need for Radical Change" 239).

18 For examples from mainstream and journalistic work of spreading fear related to the former development (but which completely overlooks the colonial and racial dimensions of these questions), see Balko; Rizer and Hartman; and Stillman.

19 See Wacquant 19.

20 For historical work documenting this fluidity, see Harring.

21 The FBI shares jurisdiction with the Bureau of Indian Affairs, Office of Justice Services (BIA-OJS) and has primary law enforcement responsibility on nearly 200 Indian reservations. The Department of Justice traces its authority over law enforcement to treaty responsibilities established in *Cherokee Nation v. Georgia*, 30 U.S. (5 Pet.) 1, 17 (1831), which set out the US government's duty to "protect" Indian tribes as "domestic dependent nations." See https://fbi.gov/investigate/violent-crime/indian-country-crime and www.justice.gov/otj. Perhaps the locale most symbolically associated with the overlap of military and policing powers as they relate to American Indians is Alcatraz, which initially functioned as a military prison where indigenous political opposition was routinely incarcerated and, as a result, was later the target of indigenous (re)occupation from 1969 to 1971 by the United Indians of All Tribes. See Smith and Warrior.

22 This chapter does not attempt to extend the comparison beyond Canada and the US to include other Anglo-settler polities, such as Australia and New Zealand. No doubt, however, such comparative work is possible and needed. For an example of such analysis, see Ford.

23 See also RCAP 289.

24 See Wacquant 82.

25 Important exceptions to this rule include Foucault, *Security, Territory, Population*, and the work of Stuart Elden, especially *The Birth of Territory*.

26 Stoler is building upon, while critically provincializing and decentering Foucault's classic genealogy of carceral power in *Discipline and Punish*, but especially the symbolic function of the Mettray institution. While Foucault employs the opening of the Mettray penal colony in January of 1840 to "fix the date of the completion of the carceral system," Stoler rightly points out that the institution was in fact part of a global, imperial formation that "connected strategies of confinement from metropole to colony and across the imperial world" (Stoler 131). See also Foucault, *Discipline and Punish*.

27 The Aboriginal Women's Caucus was a group of Aboriginal Women working in the Canadian criminal justice system.

28 She goes on to elaborate: "People (or any 'thing' with a spirit) were not intended to be managed but rather respected. The conclusion is that one of the foundational ideas of current correctional philosophy is, in my opinion, incompatible with Aboriginal cultures, law and tradition" (Monture-Angus, "Aboriginal Women" 56).

29 This principled, deep normative critique of prisons as institutions of violence displaces and eclipses work whose primary aim is to diagnose the manner in which carceral expansion is "antagonistic to democratic participation" and "inspires negative orientations toward government" (Weaver and Lerman 1).
30 For work that carefully avoids the generalized "racialization" framework in favor of a rich historical analysis of the intertwining of anti-Black racism and settler colonialism, see Jackson.
31 This leaves open the question of how to relate the specificity of the carceral-colonial link in North America to other Anglo-settler colonies or other occupied lands (which is beyond the scope of this particular chapter).

References

Alexander, Michelle. *The New Jim Crow: Mass Incarceration in the Age of Colorblindness.* The New Press, 2012.

Alfred, Taiaiake. *Peace, Power, Righteousness: An Indigenous Manifesto.* Oxford University Press, 1999.

——. *Wasáse: Indigenous Pathways of Action and Freedom.* Broadview Press, 2005.

Balko, Radley. *The Rise of the Warrior Cop: The Militarization of America's Police Forces.* Public Affairs, 2013.

Barker, Joanne, ed. *Sovereignty Matters.* University of Nebraska Press, 2005.

Bill C-10. An Act to Enact the Justice for Victims of Terrorism Act and to Amend the State Immunity Act, the Criminal Code, the Controlled Drugs and Substances Act, the Corrections and Conditional Release Act, the Youth Criminal Justice Act, the Immigration and Refugee Protection Act and Other Acts (Safe Streets and Communities Act). 41st Parl., 1st session. Parliament of Canada, 2013.

Brown, Wendy. *Walled States, Waning Sovereignty.* Zone Books, 2010.

Bruyneel, Kevin. *The Third Space of Sovereignty.* University of Minnesota Press, 2007.

"Canada's Crime Rate Lowest since 1972." *The Canadian Press*, July 25, 2013, www.cbc.ca/news/canada/canada-s-crime-rate-lowest-since-1972-1.1334090.

Cherokee Nation v. Georgia, 30 U.S. (5 Pet.) 1, 17 (1831).

Correctional Service Canada. *Creating Choices: Report of the Task Force on Federally Sentenced Women.* Government of Canada, 1990.

Coulthard, Glen. *Red Skin, White Masks.* University of Minnesota Press, 2014.

——. "From Wards of the State to Subjects of Recognition? Marx, Indigenous Peoples, and the Politics of Dispossession in Denendeh." In *Theorizing Native Studies.* Edited by A. Smith and A. Simpson. Duke University Press, 2014, pp. 56–98.

Dauvergne, Mia. "Adult Correctional Statistics in Canada, 2010–2011." *Juristat*, October 11, 2012.

Davis, Angela *Are Prisons Obsolete?* Seven Stories Press, 2003.

Dickson-Gilmore, J. and Carole La Prairie, eds. *Will the Circle Be Unbroken?: Aboriginal Communities, Restorative Justice, and the Challenges of Conflict and Change.* University of Toronto Press, 2005.

Elden, Stuart. *The Birth of Territory.* University of Chicago Press, 2013.

Feldman, Allen. *Forations of Violence.* University of Chicago Press, 1991.

Ford, Lisa. *Settler Sovereignty: Jurisdiction and Indigenous Peoples in America and Australia, 1788–1836.* Harvard University Press, 2010.

Foucault, Michel. *Security, Territory, Population.* Palgrave Macmillan, 2007.

——. *Discipline and Punish*, 2nd edn. Vintage, 1995.

Gilmore, Ruth W. *Golden Gulag: Prisons, Surplus, Crisis, and Opposition in Globalizing California*. University of California Press, 2007.

Government of Canada. *Annual Report of the Office of the Correctional Investigator (2012–13)*, 2013, www.oci-bec.gc.ca/cnt/rpt/annrpt/annrpt20122013-eng.aspx.

Green, Joyce. "From Stonechild to Social Cohesion." *Canadian Journal of Political Science*, vol. 39, no. 1, 2006, pp. 507–527.

Guenther, Lisa. *Solitary Confinement*. University of Minnesota Press, 2013.

Hannah-Moffat, Kelly. *Punishment in Disguise: Penal Governance and Federal Imprisonment of Women in Canada*. University of Toronto Press, 2001.

Harring, Sydney. *White Man's Justice: Native People in 19th Century Canadian Jurisprudence*. University of Toronto Press, 1998.

Jackson, Shona. *Creole Indigeneity: Between Myth and Nation in the Caribbean*. University of Minnesota Press, 2012.

Kilgore, James. "The Myth of Slave Labor Camps in the U.S." *Counterpunch: Tells the Facts and Names the Names*, August 11–13, 2013, pp. 9–11.

Macleod, R.C. "Canadianizing the West: The North-West Mounted Police as Agents of the National Policy, 1873–1905." In *The Prairie West: Historical Readings*. Edited by. R. Douglas Francis and Howard Palmer, Pica Pica Press, 1992, pp. 225–238.

Milward, David. "Sweating it Out: Facilitating Corrections and Parole in Canada through Aboriginal Spiritual Healing." *Windsor Yearbook of Access to Justice*, vol. 29, no. 1, 2011, pp. 27–72.

Monture-Angus, Patricia A. "Aboriginal Women and Correctional Practice: Reflections on the Task Force on Federally Sentenced Women." In *An Ideal Prison?: Critical Essays on Women's Imprisonment in Canada*. Edited by Kelly Hannah-Moffat and Margaret Shaw, Fernwood Publishing, 2000, pp. 52–60.

——. "The Need for Radical Change in the Canadian Criminal Justice System: Applying a Human Rights Framework." In *Visions of the Heart: Canadian Aboriginal Issues*. Edited by David Long and Olive Patricia Dickason, Oxford University Press, 2011, pp. 238–257.

Monture-Okanee, Patricia and Mary Ellen Turpel. "Aboriginal Peoples and Canadian Criminal Law: Rethinking Justice" *University of British Columbia Law Review* (Special Edition), vol. 26, 1992, pp. 239–277.

National Association for the Advancement of Colored People (NAACP). *Misplaced Priorities: Over Incarcerate, Under Educate*. 2011, http://naacp.3cdn.net/ecea56adeef3d84a28_azsm639wz.pdf.

Office of the Correctional Investigator. *Good Intentions, Disappointing Results: A Progress Report on Federal Aboriginal Corrections*, Government of Canada, 2009, www.oci-bec.gc.ca/cnt/rpt/pdf/oth-aut/oth-aut20091113-eng.pdf.

Perreault, Samuel. "The Incarceration of Aboriginal People in Adult Correctional Services." *Juristat*, July 2009.

Rizer, Arthur and Joseph Hartman. "How the War on Terror Has Militarized the Police." *The Atlantic*, November 7, 2011, www.theatlantic.com/national/archive/2011/11/how-the-war-on-terror-has-militarized-the-police/248047.

Ross, Luana. *Inventing the Savage: The Social Construction of Native American Criminality*. University of Texas Press, 1998.

Royal Commission on Aboriginal Peoples (RCAP). *Bridging the Cultural Divide: A Report on Aboriginal People and Criminal Justice in Canada*. Minister of Supply and Services, 1996.

Rymhs, Deena, ed. *From the Iron House: Imprisonment in First Nations Writing*. Wilfred Laurier University Press, 2008.

Simpson, Audra. *Mohawk Interruptus*. Duke University Press, 2014.

Smith, Paul Chaat and Robert Warrior. *Like a Hurricane: The American Indian Movement from Alcatraz to Wounded Knee*. New Press, 1997.

Soss, Joe et al. *Disciplining the Poor: Neoliberal Paternalism and the Persistent Power of Race*. University of Chicago Press, 2011.

Statistics Canada. *Juristat*, Minister of Industry, Government of Canada, 2013, www.statcan.gc.ca/pub/85-002-x/index-eng.htm.

Stillman, Sarah. "Swat Team Nation." *New Yorker*, August 8, 2013, www.newyorker.com/online/blogs/comment/2013/08/swat-team-nation.html.

Stoler, Ann Laura. *Along the Archival Grain: Epistemic Anxieties and Colonial Common Sense*. Princeton University Press, 2009.

Tully, James. "The Struggles of Indigenous Peoples for and of Freedom." In *Political Theory and the Rights of Indigenous Peoples*. Edited by D. Ivison, P. Patton and W. Sanders, Cambridge University Press, 2000, pp. 36–59.

Wacquant, Loïc. *Prisons of Poverty*. University of Minnesota Press, 2009.

Weaver, Vesla M. and Amy E. Lerman. "Political Consequences of the Carceral State." *American Political Science Review*, November 2010, pp. 1–17.

Wolfe, Patrick. "Settler Colonialism and the Elimination of the Native."' *Journal of Genocide Research*, vol. 8, no. 4, pp. 38–409.

Chapter 5

"Ran away from her master … a negroe girl named Thursday"

Examining evidence of punishment, isolation, and trauma in Nova Scotia and Quebec fugitive slave advertisements

Charmaine A. Nelson

> The sound of the whip is so common in the field, that *one gets to hear it as a matter of course, and that without any particular observation or feeling*. Hence many persons, after a residence of a few years in the colonies, fall into the idea, that the slaves are, on the whole, mildly treated, and that there is really no necessity for making any material alteration in their circumstances.
>
> (Cooper 53, emphasis added)

> Jamaican slaves lived in a world of *radical uncertainty*, always vulnerable to the depredations of whites and fellow slaves. Unprotected by law, subject to a harsh work discipline, and forced to submit to the wills of often unpredictable masters or else suffer horrific punishments, slaves were cast adrift in a hostile and uncertain sea.
>
> (Burnard 165, emphasis added)

As the nineteenth-century observer of slavery Thomas Cooper explained, corporal punishment was such a common aspect of Jamaican slavery that it seemed perfectly normal to the island's ruling white minority. However, as Trevor Burnard suggests, the ubiquity of corporal punishment led to dire consequences for the enslaved majority population, both physical and psychological. Transatlantic slavery was premised upon the strategic dehumanization and animalization of enslaved Africans as a way to "break" or "season" a population that was deemed, by Western pseudo-sciences and popular thought alike, to be uniquely fit for servitude due to their supposed brutishness and insentience (Wood). In the early modern world, slavery and the conceptualization of Africans as sub-human allowed Europeans to export forms of corporal punishment to their colonies, which were deemed to be too cruel and inhumane for the punishment of whites. The physical dehumanization of the enslaved went hand in hand with strategic material deprivation, cultural prohibitions, and social humiliation. A part of this process necessarily involved the regularized use of corporal punishment.

While much is known about the commonality of abuse and torture within Caribbean and southern American plantation regimes, a significant body of scholarship on the white use of violence to control, punish, and torment the enslaved in the northern territories that became Canada has yet to be produced. But this lack of knowledge is not necessarily about deficits in the archives, but rather about the lack of scholars of Canadian slavery asking such questions and the disorganization of Canadian archives in ways that suppress histories of Canadian slavery. This chapter seeks to redress this scholarly void by examining the use of corporal punishment in the eighteenth and nineteenth centuries within the practice of British Canadian slavery (Halifax, Montreal, and Quebec City) and to distinguish it from Jamaica, a tropical British plantation regime. Using the ubiquity and refinement of violence in the slave-holding territory of British Jamaica as a point of contrast, I will examine the un(der)explored archive of Canadian fugitive slave advertisements to provide evidence of the various types of cruel and unusual punishment which were employed by white slave owners in Nova Scotia and Quebec. Specifically, by reading fugitive slave advertisements as "portraits" (however dubious) of the runaways, I will attempt to recuperate the visual signs of physical trauma inflicted upon enslaved populations to argue that slavery obliterated the line between legal violence and "cruel and unusual punishment," by rendering the latter a part of the former.

Content, function, and circulation: reading fugitive slave advertisements

Fugitive or runaway slave advertisements are full of resistive promise. The promise was at least twofold. First, the fact that such advertisements existed across the Americas is a testament to the consistent resistance of Africans to slavery. But the function of the advertisements—to recuperate property—also resulted in an uncommonly "honest" archive being produced. Second, in comparison to slave sale advertisements through which the slave, as product, was presented almost always without defect (physical or moral), fugitive advertisements functioned through the description of corporeal detail which consistently pointed out the lie of the supposed homogeneity, inhumanity, inferiority, dependency, and lack of civility of the enslaved population. Indeed, the desire to recuperate their lost property was so great that white slave owners took great pains to detail all manner of characteristics, attributes, traits, mannerisms, and skills of their missing "property," details which arguably individualized and humanized the enslaved.

The process of slave escape, often deliberately revealed in such advertisements, also inadvertently exposed the forethought, intellect, and sophisticated reasoning of the enslaved that involved the intimate knowledge of their owners' lifestyles, the customs of the colony, and regional knowledge of the governing racial, class, religious, and political orders. For instance, when Cloe, described as "a NEGRO WENCH." fled from the Jewish merchant Judah Joseph of Berthier, Quebec,

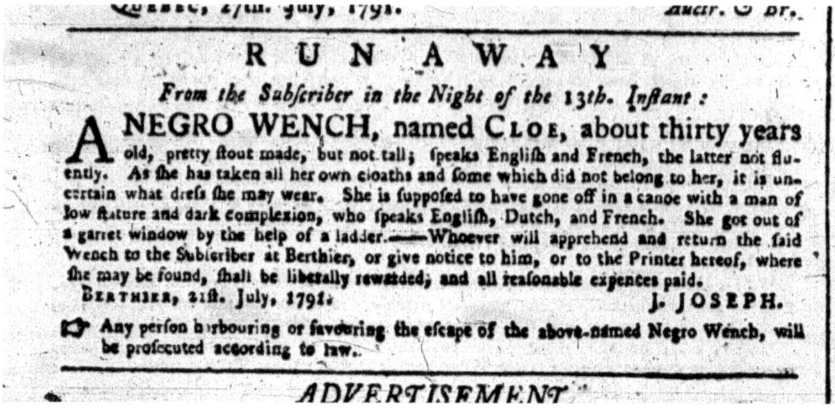

RUN AWAY

From the Subscriber in the Night of the 13th. Instant:

A NEGRO WENCH, named CLOE, about thirty years old, pretty stout made, but not tall; speaks English and French, the latter not fluently. As she has taken all her own cloaths and some which did not belong to her, it is uncertain what dress she may wear. She is supposed to have gone off in a canoe with a man of low stature and dark complexion, who speaks English, Dutch, and French. She got out of a garret window by the help of a ladder.——Whoever will apprehend and return the said Wench to the Subscriber at Berthier, or give notice to him, or to the Printer hereof, where she may be found, shall be liberally rewarded; and all reasonable expences paid.

BERTHIER, 21st. July, 1791.

J. JOSEPH.

☞ Any person harbouring or favouring the escape of the above-named Negro Wench, will be prosecuted according to law.

Figure 5.1 J. Joseph, "RUN AWAY From the Subscriber in the Night of the 13th Instant." *Quebec Gazette*, July 28, 1791, vol. 1358, p. 4; Bibliothèque et Archives nationales du Québec, Montreal

Joseph's (1791) advertisement disclosed that "She got out of a garret window by the help of a ladder" (334, 540, note 58) and subsequently departed in a canoe with an unidentified man.

In another example, when the 26-year-old enslaved black female named Cash escaped from the Quebec City-based tailor Hugh Ritchie on October 24, 1779, she did so with:

> a large bundle of wearing apparel belonging to herself, consisting of a black sattin Cloak, Caps, Bonnets, Ruffles, Ribbons, six of seven Petticoats, a pair of old Stays, and many other articles of values which cannot be ascertained, *it is likely she may change her dress.*
>
> (Ritchie 323, 536, note 34, emphasis added)

Clearly the process of attempting to recapture one's slave through the textual order of print culture required slave owners to disclose details about the runaway which were unhelpful to the idea of slaves as controlled, idle, unintelligent property. Thus, while the American (North, South, Central and Caribbean) archive of fugitive slave advertisements points out the failure of slavery to fully disrupt the individual and collective agency of Africans, slave owners attempted to reframe such failure as the individual fault of morally corrupt and ungrateful slaves.

Printers fundamentally reinforced slavery and its racial hierarchy by facilitating the rights of slave owners to reduce certain humans to property. The arrogance of the slave-owning class can often be deduced in the tone of the notices which, when the enslaved made a habit of escape, became more aggressive. For instance, while upon her first (documented) escape on August 18, 1778, the enslaved female Bell was described by her owner George Hipps (*RAN AWAY*) as a "Mulatto Negress" (321), when she again fled on October

29, 1778, he referred to her instead as a "Mulatto *wench*" (*RUN-AWAY* 321, emphasis added).[1] The fact that Hipps' second notice combined the description of Bell as both wench and a girl is indicative of the imposition of an abject sexuality upon black females at a young age by white colonialists.[2] The Montreal baker and slave owner John Saul's arrogance was arguably revealed not through aggression, but through humor. When the enslaved Negro man named Tight escaped on August 12, 1784 with another enslaved male named Snow (also described as a Negro, but belonging to Capt. René Hippolyte Laforce), Saul's notice read: "Whoever will apprehend the first mentioned Negro named Tight, and secure him so tightly that his master may have him again, shall have *Forty Shillings* reward, and all reasonable charges" (326–327, 332, 537 note 41).

Fugitive slave advertisements circulated widely due to the cheapness and reproducible nature of the print medium. This circulation was also calculated to match the distances across which fleeing slaves traveled and slavers sometimes blanketed a region with simultaneous advertisements in multiple papers. In one case, John Holt, a native of Virginia and the former Mayor of Williamsburg, placed fugitive slave advertisements in New York and Philadelphia papers, seeking to recapture Charles Roberts (Waldstreicher 253). While broadsides were printed for strategic public display, slave owners also begged their readers to assist them in the cropping and display of newspaper advertisements in public spaces (Waldstreicher 269). For instance, Holt placed multiple advertisements in his own *New York Gazette; or, the Weekly Post-Boy* and the other two New York newspapers in his desire to recapture Roberts (Waldstreicher 265–267). As the consummate go-betweens, printers informed against fleeing servants and slaves at the same time as they often guarded the anonymity of the slave owners (Waldstreicher 269).[3] Print became the means through which slave owners sought to inscribe and legitimize their role as property owners, the mainly white men, women, and children who owned "people-commodities" (Waldstreicher 249).

Pushing back against this practice, the enslaved attempted to refashion themselves through what David Waldstreicher calls "acts of cultural hybridization" in order to transform how others, mainly whites, perceived them. But what was an enslaved person's access to such self-fashioning and how was it achieved? While the flight of the runaway, and their often-premeditated acts of redefinition and passing, sought to unbind the runaway from the category of slave, the advertisements worked not only to reconstitute this connection, but also to naturalize it. Thus, the slave-owning class sought to criminalize demonstrations of agency by the "self-motivated" (Waldstreicher 248) people who were enslaved, to code running away as what Marcus Wood has termed "an act of theft, albeit a paradoxical self-theft" (79). Against this colonial act of dehumanization, I would like to position the fugitives not as criminals, but as freedom-seekers, and the act of running away as a defiant and extremely perilous act of self-(re)definition.[4]

Grappling with a colonial archive

Fugitive slave advertisements were also a primary source with prescribed limits. The limit of the slave advertisement is that it confirms only that someone, socially deemed to be a slave, ran away from the person who claimed to own the runaway. Such advertisements also confirm that the runaway was valuable enough to be pursued. The advertisements provide a window into the lives and worlds of the enslaved because each example was about the recapture of an individual or individuals who had fled, and as such required that their owners share details that illuminated what made the runaways unique, both in manner and appearance. As such, these advertisements, ubiquitous across the Americas, are repositories of data on enslaved populations, recording all manner of visual characteristics, skills, and oral attributes of the runaways. Amongst the visual characteristics most commonly recited were the condition of the bodies of the enslaved. While such details included scarification and hairstyles created by the enslaved person and their communities, they also described bruising, lacerations, branding scars, and other marks of owner-imposed violence, torture, and corporal punishment.

While, as described above, the corporal punishment and torture of the enslaved was ubiquitous and "normal" in Jamaica, did the proximity of the enslaved to their owners in the urban spaces of Halifax, Montreal, and Quebec City and the "heavy burdens of continual surveillance" change the way in which white slave owners used material deprivation, physical violence, and psychological manipulation to control the enslaved (Berlin 283)?

Fugitive slave advertisements are what Shane White and Graham White have referred to as "the most detailed descriptions of the bodies of enslaved African Americans available" (49). I would argue that their contention also applies to most regions of the Americas in general, particularly places where abolition predated the development of photography.[5] Displaced from their homelands and forced to take up the role of unfree labour in the Americas, the enslavement of Africans severely impeded their ability to remember their histories and practice their cultures. This was strategic on the part of the white colonialists and slave-owning classes and was evident in the immediate implementation of slave practices,[6] like branding and renaming, that were meant to break the enslaved from their sense of individuality, family, and ancestry.[7]

Furthermore, ruling-class whites deliberately developed the colonial archive to allow Africans to enter as partial and incomplete entries; the objects or "stock" owned by another. This disturbing fact—that the most detailed representations of the enslaved were produced by their owners—provokes a confrontation with the archive, not as an objective or neutral container of facts and information, but as a site through which the elite secured their power through determinations on who could be represented and in what fashion. The colonial archives of European empires were defined by the effacement or the strategic partial representation of the enslaved African. As such, as Ann Laura Stoler has explained, we are left to sort out "what was 'unwritten' because it could go without saying and 'everyone knew it,' what was unwritten because it could not yet be articulated, and what was unwritten because it could not be said" (3).

The callousness of slavery wherein whites sought to demarcate and preserve their supposed racial difference and superiority was also enshrined through sale advertisements in what Aimé Césaire called a process of "thingification" (42).[8] This strategic racial hierarchy was the same in Canada as it was in more southern, tropical colonies. To my point, the March 23, 1773 advertisement "To be SOLD, By PUBLIC AUCTION" in the *Nova Scotia Gazette and Weekly Chronicle* listed amongst the items to be auctioned at the late Joseph Pierpont's Wharf: "Three Gondolaes, three small Boats, a quantity of Salt in Barrels, a quantity of empty Barrels, *a Negro Man*, three Horses, three Seines, Salmon Nets, a Parcel of Iron, a large Canoe, Carts and Cart wheels, &c" ("To be SOLD" 4, emphasis added).

Sandwiched between local and international wares, materials, and animals, the black man's dehumanization was advanced by his listing as merely one of a variety of goods for sale.

Similarly, in Quebec, an advertisement placed in the *Quebec Gazette* on August 21, 1788 by Melvin and Burns included "a likely healthy NEGRO Man named Caesar" for public auction, along with "ABOUT twenty-five pipes and hogsheads of Old Madeira Wine, from fifteen to twenty pipes and hogsheads Port ditto, both of which are of the finest quality and truly genuine" (331).

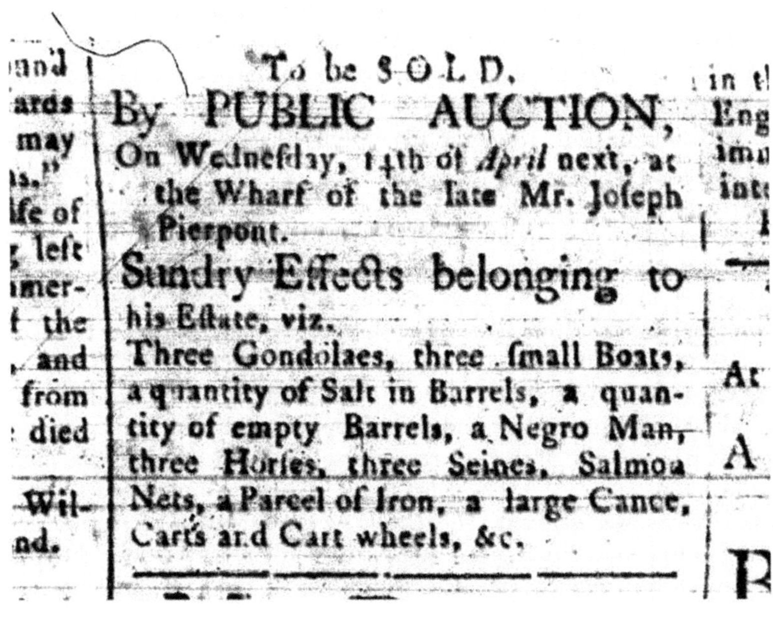

To be SOLD,
By PUBLIC AUCTION,
On Wednesday, 14th of *April* next, at the Wharf of the late Mr. Joſeph Pierpont.
Sundry Effects belonging to his Eſtate, viz.
Three Gondolaes, three ſmall Boats, a quantity of Salt in Barrels, a quantity of empty Barrels, a Negro Man, three Horſes, three Seines, Salmon Nets, a Parcel of Iron, a large Canoe, Carts and Cart wheels, &c.

Figure 5.2 Anonymous, "To be SOLD, By PUBLIC AUCTION." *Nova Scotia Gazette and Weekly Chronicle*, Tuesday, March 23, 1773, vol. 3, no. 134, p. 4; NSA Newspaper Collection, reel 8155. Nova Scotia Archives and Records Management, Halifax, Nova Scotia

Furthermore, in Quebec, the enslaved were not just sold with imported or Caribbean goods. An auction notice in the April 14, 1791 *Quebec Gazette* offered "A young NEGRO LAD about 18 or 19 years of age," along with various household furniture and other domestic items, including "A Compleat sett of hand organs, half a dozen mahogany chairs, one elegant four post mahogany bedstead, several other bedsteads, beds and bedding, tables, a clock, looking glasses, a quantity of porter in hogsheads, also a quantity of kitchen furniture" ([sic] "ADVERTISEMENT" 334).

Following Stoler's insight above, I would add to her list what was unwritten because to do so would further humanize the enslaved. As such, I want to suggest that the representation of the enslaved by white slave owners and their surrogates was intended as a *strategy of erasure*. To this end, the colonial archive of which fugitive slave advertisements were a significant part was an attempt at the mastery of an ever-changing world and the conflation of Africans with the status of slave.

An infrastructure of violence: print technology and gaols (jails)

As Waldstreicher has noted, fugitive slave advertisements were generally premised on four categories, "clothing, trades or skills, linguistic ability or usage, and ethnic or racial identity" (249), the manipulation of which could alter the perception of one's class and race. Advertisements are a form of print technology that is both potently problematic and full of potential promise. The biggest problem of using such an archive stems from its source, the white slave owners who produced them while conspiring with a host of other whites, like the printers that published the advertisements and the populace that conspired to spot and recapture the runaway, often for a reward. Given this context, I would argue that fugitive slave advertisements were an essential part of what Steve Martinot has termed the colonial "machinery of whiteness and white supremacy" (10).

Fugitive slave advertisements were undeniably biased toward the maintenance of white supremacy through the ownership and dehumanization of enslaved Africans. Furthermore, the durability of the print technology of the fugitive slave advertisement must be understood as both the continuity across centuries and empires, but also as regards their undeniable appeal to the slave owners themselves, whose repeated use of them, across their lifetimes and through the multiple printings for the escapees they failed to catch, speaks to their belief in the usefulness of such advertisements. The usefulness was as a way to recapture and re-enslave fugitives, but also as a mechanism to re-instate their power through the racial order which aligned whiteness with the social, political, and economic power of ownership. At a fundamental level, I would like to argue, following Martinot, that the advertisements became a key site where: "In the hierarchy of 'race,' one group racializes another by thrusting them down to subordinate levels in a dehumanizing process" (Martinot 11). As such, following Steve Garner, the fugitive slave advertisement was a technology wherein the enslaved were "devalued merely for existing" (Garner 33).

Indeed, colonial print culture and slavery were arguably fundamentally linked. Newspapers placed slave owners in contact with other owners, and their surrogates, like jailers across vast territory (Waldstreicher 269). Slave owners ably exploited this fact by placing fugitive notices in newspapers both local and further afield. As a case in point, when the enslaved "Negro Man" Ireland escaped with the white indentured servant Francis Freeland on September 18, 1777 from their owner and employer William Gilliland of Willsborough, New York, Gilliland placed an advertisement in the *Quebec Gazette* the following day (318). The public was directed to apply for all or half of the six-dollar reward to Gilliland or "Moses Hazen, Esq, at *St John's*, Mr John McCord, Merchant in *Quebec*, Mr Thomas McCord, Merchant in *Montreal*" (Gilliland 318, emphasis added).

While workhouses were the penal institution of choice in which slave owners requested that escaped slaves be lodged in Jamaica, in the slave minority contexts of Nova Scotia and Quebec, the common gaol (jail) sufficed. When the African-born pressman known as Joe fled the first four of five times (between 1777 and 1779) from the Quebec printer William Brown, he did so directly from the printing office in Quebec City (Brown, *November* 319; Brown, *January* 320; Brown,

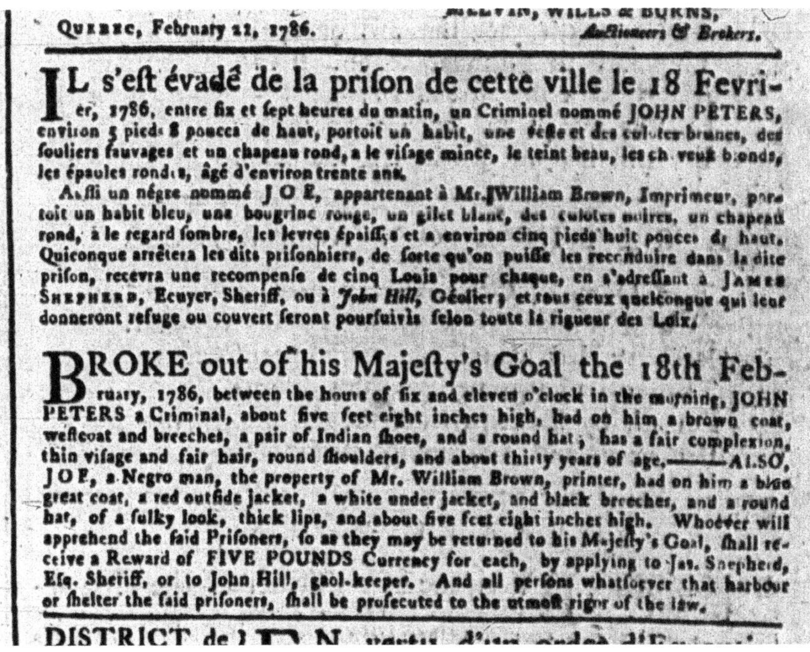

QUEBEC, February 22, 1786. — Auctioneers & Brokers.

IL s'eſt évadé de la priſon de cette ville le 18 Fevrier, 1786, entre ſix et ſept heures du matin, un Criminel nommé JOHN PETERS, environ 5 pieds 8 pouces de haut, portoit un habit, une veſte et des culotes brunes, des ſouliers ſauvages et un chapeau rond, a le viſage mince, le teint beau, les cheveux blonds, les épaules rondes, âgé d'environ trente ans.

Auſſi un négre nommé JOE, appartenant à Mr. William Brown, Imprimeur, portoit un habit bleu, une bougrine rouge, un gilet blanc, des culotes noires, un chapeau rond, a le regard ſombre, les levres épaiſſes et a environ cinq pieds huit pouces de haut. Quiconque arrêtera les dits priſonniers, de ſorte qu'on puiſſe les reconduire dans la dite priſon, recevra une recompenſe de cinq Louis pour chaque, en s'adreſſant à JAMES SHEPHERD, Ecuyer, Sheriff, ou à *John Hill*, Géolier; et tous ceux quelconque qui leur donneront refuge ou couvert ſeront pourſuivis ſelon toute la rigueur des Loix.

BROKE out of his Majeſty's Goal the 18th February, 1786, between the hours of ſix and eleven o'clock in the morning, JOHN PETERS a Criminal, about five feet eight inches high, had on him a brown coat, weſtcoat and breeches, a pair of Indian ſhoes, and a round hat; has a fair complexion, thin viſage and fair hair, round ſhoulders, and about thirty years of age.——ALSO, JOE, a Negro man, the property of Mr. William Brown, printer, had on him a blue great coat, a red outſide jacket, a white under jacket, and black breeches, and a round hat, of a ſulky look, thick lips, and about five feet eight inches high. Whoever will apprehend the ſaid Priſoners, ſo as they may be returned to his Majeſty's Goal, ſhall receive a Reward of FIVE POUNDS Currency for each, by applying to Jas. Shepherd, Eſq. Sheriff, or to John Hill, gaol-keeper. And all perſons whatſoever that harbour or ſhelter the ſaid priſoners, ſhall be proſecuted to the utmoſt rigour of the law.

DISTRICT de

Figure 5.3 Jas. Shepherd, Esq., "BROKE out of his Majesty's Goal." *Quebec Gazette*, February 23, 1786, vol. 1071, p. 3; Bibliothèque et Archives nationales du Québec, Montreal

December 321; Brown, *September* 322). However, the two notices for his fifth attempt claimed that he had broken out of "his Majesty's Goal" on February 18, 1786 with the help of the white criminal John Peters ([sic] Shepherd; Brown, *BROKE* 328–329).

There is some indication too that jails were, like workhouses, used deliberately as a means to punish and abuse the enslaved (Cooper 27, 57–58). Frank Mackey has deduced that Archibald and Elizabeth McNiell had an enslaved man, "John a Nagor Man," imprisoned in 1780 "for Misbehaving to his Master Mr Archibald McNiel" ([sic] Mackey 538 note 45).[9] Significantly, according to a calendar of prisoners in the Quebec jail in the summer of 1780, John had been committed the previous March 6 (Mackey 538 note 45). There is a possibility, then, that the McNiells abandoned him there over a period of months.

Jails were routinely used in the northern settlements to lodge the enslaved so that their owners could reclaim them. When Charles, described as a Negro man, fled from New Richmond in the district of Gaspé on April 29, 1794 to escape Azariah Pritchard, the notice placed on May 22 of the same year requested that the public "confine him in any of the jails or prisons in the province of Lower Canada, and notify the Subscriber by the earliest opportunity" (Pritchard 337). Similarly, when "a Negro man called *Bruce*" who was suspected of stealing "a great quantity of Liquors, Soap, Sugar and other effects" from the cellar of John Jones on Saint Paul Street, Quebec City, the Captains of militia and other peace Officers were directed to apprehend Bruce and "send him in safe custody to the Goal [sic] of Montreal" (Gray 319). In Quebec, slave owners called for female fugitives to be treated in the same way, asking that they be "apprehended and secured."[10]

Fugitive slaves in the Halifax Work House, 1790

Nova Scotia fugitive slave advertisements also include owners' requests for the public to use the local jails to imprison enslaved runaways. When Abel Michener placed five notices for the return of a "NEGRO MAN" named James who had fled from Falmouth on July 26, 1786, Michener offered to provide a 40-shilling reward and pay all reasonable charges to "whoever will apprehend said Negro and return him to his Master, or secure him in any of his Majesty's Goals [sic]" (Michener 3).

But northern British colonies like Nova Scotia also had workhouses which functioned in the same respect. Besides shedding light on the sex and racial makeup of prisoners, the duration of their imprisonment, and the circumstances of their criminal status, the annual ledger of the work house or house of correction of Halifax for the year 1790 allows for an analysis of its role as a site for the criminalization of fugitive slaves and servants ("Account of Persons Committed to the Work House"). Although the ledger lists 42 names corresponding to those who were locked up between January 1 and December 31, 1790 (inclusive), in reality a total of 35 people, both men and women, were incarcerated since two prisoners were imprisoned multiple times ("Account of Persons Committed to the Work House").[11] In the first case, a man, presumably white, named William Wilson was imprisoned seven times ("Account of Persons Committed to the Work House").[12] The second prisoner who seemed to make more than one appearance in the work house was Joe. Listed as prisoner #16 and #18, Joe was incarcerated from June 7 to June 13 and from June 25 to June 28 respectively.

Of these 35 prisoners, 16 or 17 were women, a fact that can be discerned not because the sex of the prisoner was specified, but because of the gender implications of the prisoners' first names.[13] Much like the sex of the prisoners, the race of certain prisoners can also be ascertained, but not because of the specified categories of the ledger. The ledger was organized across two pages with the following columns: number, names, when committed, by whom committed, when discharged, by whom discharged, number of days in the house, paid for, and remarks. However, racial categorizations were written into the ledger after the names of certain individuals.

Crucially for my arguments, it was people of African descent only that were highlighted in the ledger with the terms "black" and "Negro." Of the 42 names listed, seven specify black subjects: #6 Peter (a black man), #16 Joe (a black man), #18 Mary (a black woman), #23 Joe (a black man), #32 Jane (a Negro wench), #38 Geo' Love (a black man), and #40 Belfast (a black man).[14] Therefore, of the 35 prisoners, since the man listed twice as Joe (#16 and #23) was likely the same person, at least six black people seem to have been imprisoned in the Halifax work house in 1790.

While Hugh Kelly, the keeper of the work house, unfortunately did not see fit to include a column for the prisoners' crimes, a remark inscribed in red ink provides a means of ascertaining the most likely "crime" of some of the prisoners ("Account of Persons Committed to the Work House").[15] Kelly wrote that "those marked in red figures have been paid for by *their masters*" ("Account of Persons Committed to the Work House," emphasis added). Although the word "masters" does not distinguish between the employer of an indentured servant and the owner of a slave, the addition of racial identifiers makes it very likely that at least some of the black prisoners were fugitive slaves. While the fines paid range between 1 and 14, no currency was specified. However, since Kelly's tally of annual costs on the third page was provided in pounds, shillings, and pence (25.3.6), the "paid for" column likely adhered to the same currency.[16] Of the 42 entries, nine included the red-inked fine: #7 Walter Edwards, #12 Joseph Alexander, #18 Mary (a black woman), #29 Richard Allicate, #32 Jane (a Negro wench), #35 William Lucas, #38 Geo' Love (a black man), #39 William Watson, and #40 Belfast (a black man).

While Edwards, Alexander, Allicate, Lucas, and Watson were most likely white fugitives who were indentured servants, Mary, Jane, Geo', and Belfast were almost definitely fugitive slaves whose owners collected them from the Halifax work house after their capture. Further evidence exists that suggests Belfast's slave status. A fugitive slave advertisement initially dated February 8, 1794 placed by Michael Wallace in the *Weekly Chronicle* of Halifax described the escape of "a

Negro Man Servant, property of the Subscriber, named BELFAST" (Wallace, February 8, 1; Wallace, February 15, 1; Wallace, February 22, 1; Wallace, March, 1).[17] The dates of the two documents (the work house list of 1790 and the fugitive slave advertisement of 1794 respectively) and the uncommonness of the enslaved man's name (Belfast) make it likely that the man listed in the work house in 1790 was the same man who escaped from Wallace in 1794. Although the black man Joe, listed twice in the work house list, was not amongst those who was claimed by a master who paid his releases, the combination of his race, the lack of a family name, and the date of the ledger makes it extremely likely that he too was enslaved. That the ledger listed last names for the racially unspecified prisoners, something that only one of the black people possesses (Love), is further evidence of the unfree status of the black prisoners.

Fugitive slave advertisements as evidence of corporal punishment and psychic abuse

While fugitive slave advertisements noted forms of bodily manipulation like scarification that were the choice of the enslaved and their communities, they also registered the transformation inflicted by white owners and their surrogates through violent acts like branding and whipping. The dangers of slave labor in Jamaica where sugar cultivation was the norm were many. Shoeless slaves often worked with machetes to cut the tough stalks of the full-grown cane, and processing the plant into sugar, rum, and molasses meant dangerous mill and distillery work, the latter in extreme heat (Nelson 253–254, 304). The workers who were tasked with "feeding" the mill at crop time faced the ever-present threat of the loss of fingers or limbs. Even two visiting white women to nineteenth-century Jamaica, Eliza Chadwick Roberts and Maria Nugent, recounted being schooled on the frequency and necessity of the amputations of hands and limbs, performed by overseers with hatchets, when slaves got fingers drawn into working mills (Klepp and McDonald 650).

The disfigurement of the enslaved was a common outcome of their work regimes and the ferocity of the planters, and their surrogates, the overseer and drivers who induced the slaves to labor beyond natural human limits, and produced the extreme fatigue, which led to disabling accidents. For the field slave, labor was always incentivized by force with the whip or other implements of torture. And the vengeance of the disciplinary regime was not reserved for male or adult slaves (Cooper 16).[18] Indeed, the enslaved black men who the Jamaican planter Matthew Lewis referred to as "governors" or "chief governors" (Terry xxii) (otherwise known as drivers) were described by some like the observer of Jamaican slavery, the Reverend Bickell, as "ignorant and revengeful" slaves (Bickell 13). That the whips that were commonly used on horses, mules, and cattle were normatively also applied to enslaved Africans in Jamaica, allows for an understanding of the extent to which not only scars, but also nerve damage on various parts of the body (particularly the back and buttocks) would have been common causes of ongoing suffering and shame. As Marcus Wood has argued of fugitive notices:

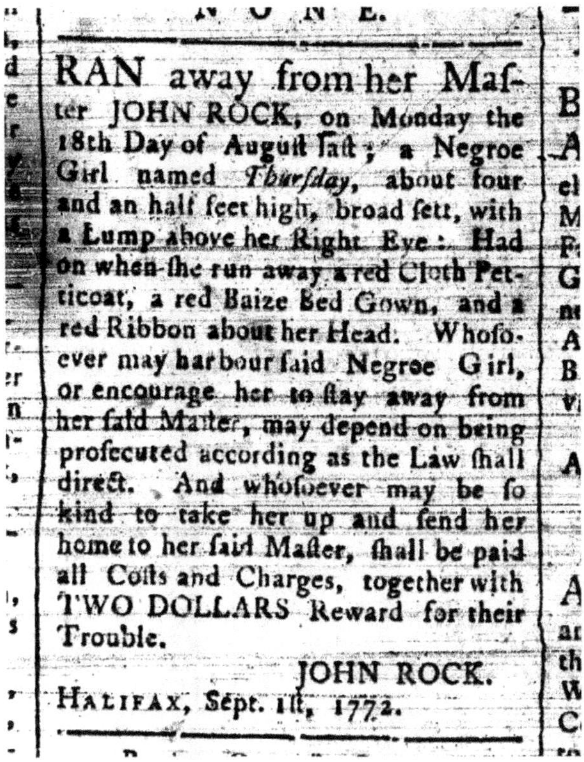

RAN away from her Maſter JOHN ROCK, on Monday the 18th Day of Auguſt laſt; a Negroe Girl named *Thurſday*, about four and an half feet high, broad ſett, with a Lump above her Right Eye: Had on when ſhe run away a red Cloth Petticoat, a red Baize Bed Gown, and a red Ribbon about her Head. Whoſoever may harbour ſaid Negroe Girl, or encourage her to ſtay away from her ſaid Maſter, may depend on being proſecuted according as the Law ſhall direct. And whoſoever may be ſo kind to take her up and ſend her home to her ſaid Maſter, ſhall be paid all Coſts and Charges, together with TWO DOLLARS Reward for their Trouble.

JOHN ROCK.

HALIFAX, Sept. 1ſt, 1772.

Figure 5.4 John Rock, "Ran away from her Master John Rock." *Nova Scotia Gazette and Weekly Chronicle*, Tuesday, September 1, 1772, vol. 3, no. 105, p. 3; (repeated September 8, 22, 1772); Nova Scotia Archives and Records Management (1772–1774), Halifax, Nova Scotia: PANS MFM #8155, reel 0155

> The scars and deformities listed recreated the slave's body as a living and moving text. The advertisements constituted a perpetual catalogue of the abuse of the slave body and as such had the potential to be subverted by antislavery authors. (81)

Although it is unclear if branding was a uniform slave practice in parts of Nova Scotia or Quebec, certainly some enslaved people in those sites would have had brand marks, if not from their time in Canada, then from their previous residences. However, runaway slave advertisements from Nova Scotia do reveal signs of abuse in their descriptions of the bodies of the enslaved. An advertisement placed by John Rock on Tuesday September 1, 1772 recounted the flight of a black female known as Thursday. While the demeaning and comical name paralleled the practice of naming the enslaved after their day of birth in other regions (Ohri),[19] Thursday's description as a girl is also alarming (Rock, *Ran Away*, September 1, 3).

The advertisement describes her as a "Negroe *Girl* … about four and a half feet high, broad sett," and upon John Rock's death, Thursday was also listed in

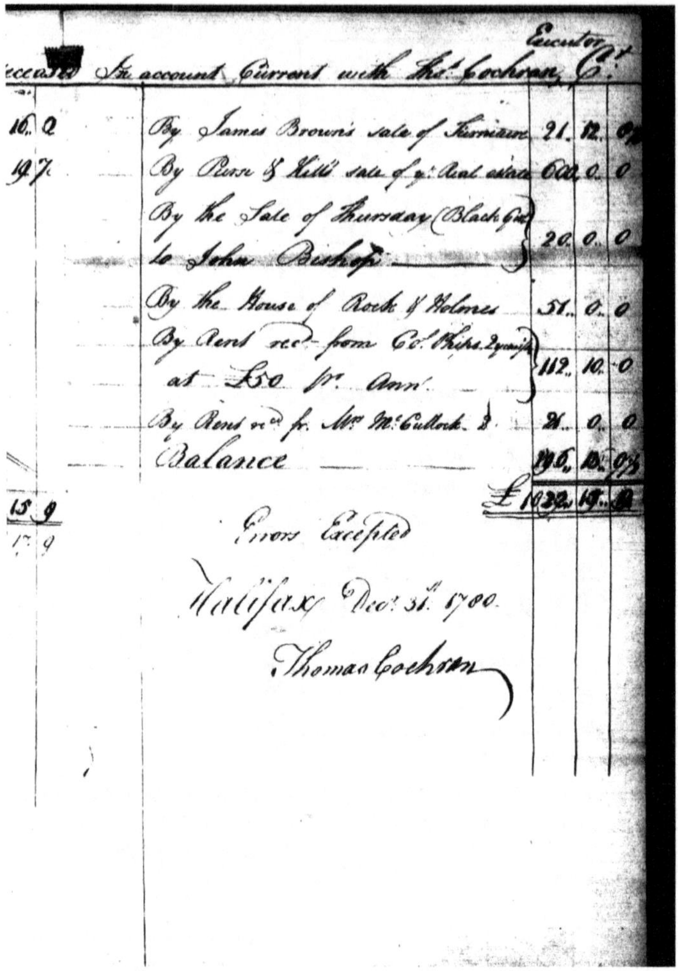
In account Current with Thos. Cochran, Executor, Cr.

By James Brown's sale of Furniture 21. 12. 0½
By Perse & Hill's sale of ye Real estate 600. 0. 0
By the Sale of Thursday (Black Girl) to John Bishop 20. 0. 0
By the House of Rock & Holmes 51. 0. 0
By Rent recd. from Col. Phips 2 years at £50 pr. Ann. 112. 10. 0
By Rent recd. fr. Mr. McCulloch 21. 0. 0
Balance 196. 15. 0½
£ 1032. 19.
Errors Excepted
Halifax Decr. 31st. 1780
Thomas Cochran

Figure 5.5 John Rock, Estate Inventory, 25 September 1776, PANS MFM #(19)420, RG48 Reel 420, #61 (Halifax), NSARM. The estate inventory is 17 pages in length. On page 7 on the third and fourth lines under the title, it reads "by the sale of Thursday (Black Girl) to John Bishop—20.0.0."

his estate inventory as a "Black *Girl*" when she was sold to John Bishop for £20 (Rock, Estate Inventory, emphasis added).[20]

The duplication of this description, along with the fact that the drive to infantilize slaves was more commonly directed at males, would seem to indicate that Thursday truly was, by eighteenth-century standards, a child. Based upon the use of the term "woman" in a seventeenth-century Montreal notice for the sale of an enslaved female named Louison, aged 17, this likely meant that Thursday had not reached the age of 16.[21] While Rock did not mention if Thursday was branded, he did describe her body in a way that signaled the possibility of corporal punishment. The notice describes Thursday as having "a Lump above her Right Eye" (Rock, *Ran Away*, September 1). While the lump may have been caused by an accident, illness, or birth defect, which had nothing to do with Rock, there also exists a distinct possibility that the lump was a mark of violence inflicted by Rock as a punishment of some kind. If so, the fact that the "lump" was still visible and the protuberance had not healed sufficiently to deprive Rock of this further means of describing Thursday's body, may indicate that a physical assault against Thursday had immediately precipitated her flight.

The impact of the isolation of enslaved Africans in temperate colonies where owners tended to possess far fewer slaves must not be underestimated. While the sexual violation of enslaved women in tropical colonies was ubiquitous, similar acts of sexual coercion and terror were surely employed in temperate colonies with impunity since the lack of a significant slave community within the same residence or property meant that white male sexual predators would have been faced with little to no immediate resistance from other enslaved people, like slave "husbands," and therefore likely felt less constrained in their actions.[22] This would have been particularly true in cases where the male slave owner was unmarried.

Similarly, the isolation and living arrangements of enslaved people in places like Nova Scotia and Quebec left them open to various forms of corporal punishment and torture. Many fugitive slave notices hint at the effects of such physical abuse. Reuben Tucker's advertisement for the 28-year-old "NEGRO MAN, named FRANCES ZEBB" disclosed that Zebb had "lost all the Toes off one of his Feet, and walks somewhat lame" (Tucker 3). Similarly, Andrews Reynolds' fugitive notice of September 7, 1790 described "a Negro Boy Slave Named DICK" as having "lost the first joint of his great Toe of the left Foot" (Reynolds 1). While Zebb's and Dick's missing toes could have been caused by frostbite or labor accidents, another equally plausible explanation was corporal punishment.

When a slave owner named Richardson offered four guineas for the return of two black men, he described the older, Bon Porter, as about 30 years old, "stout and well made; nearly Five Feet Six Inches high," but also as "lame in one Foot, and limps much in his Walk" (Richardson 3).[23] While Porter's limp may have been the result of a birth defect or an accident, it could just as easily have been the outcome of corporal punishment.

Quebec fugitive notices also yield evidence of physical hardship and abuse. While the 23-year-old Andrew of Maryland was described by his owner James Crofton as having crooked fingers, 25-year-old Fortune was noted as having "lost the toes off his right Foot," and 20-year-old Charles as having "a white mark on the right side of his forehead" ("RUN-AWAY, from *James Crofton*" 315; "RANAWAY from Carleton-Island" 323; Geurout 325). Described by Elizabeth McNiell as "A NEGRO MAN" (327–28), Cuff also had "some scars on his temples, and a scar on one of his hands" ("BROKE" 328–329), the printer William Brown's enslaved pressman Joe had "several scars on his legs," John Sargent's enslaved "Mulatto fellow named PASCAL PURO" had "a scar under one of his ears" (Freeman 331), Azariah Pritchard Sr.'s enslaved "NEGRO MAN" Isaac had

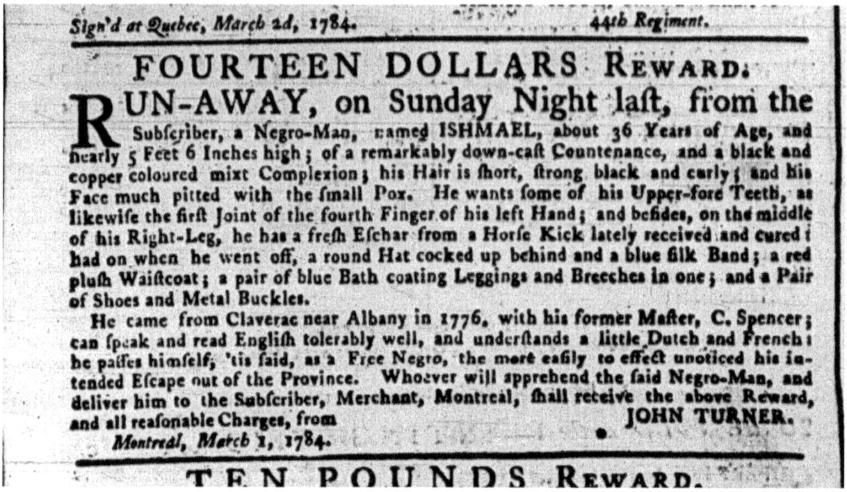

Sign'd at Quebec, March 2d, 1784. 44th Regiment.

FOURTEEN DOLLARS REWARD.

RUN-AWAY, on Sunday Night laſt, from the Subſcriber, a Negro-Man, named ISHMAEL, about 36 Years of Age, and nearly 5 Feet 6 Inches high; of a remarkably down-caſt Countenance, and a black and copper coloured mixt Complexion; his Hair is ſhort, ſtrong black and curly; and his Face much pitted with the ſmall Pox. He wants ſome of his Upper-fore Teeth, as likewiſe the firſt Joint of the fourth Finger of his left Hand; and beſides, on the middle of his Right-Leg, he has a freſh Eſchar from a Horſe Kick lately received and cured: had on when he went off, a round Hat cocked up behind and a blue ſilk Band; a red pluſh Waiſtcoat; a pair of blue Bath coating Leggings and Breeches in one; and a Pair of Shoes and Metal Buckles.

He came from Claverac near Albany in 1776, with his former Maſter, C. Spencer; can ſpeak and read Engliſh tolerably well, and underſtands a little Dutch and French: he paſſes himſelf, 'tis ſaid, as a Free Negro, the more eaſily to effect unoticed his intended Eſcape out of the Province. Whoever will apprehend the ſaid Negro-Man, and deliver him to the Subſcriber, Merchant, Montreal, ſhall receive the above Reward, and all reaſonable Charges, from JOHN TURNER.

Montreal, March 1, 1784.

TEN POUNDS REWARD.

Figure 5.6 John Turner, "FOURTEEN DOLLARS Reward. RUN-AWAY, on Sunday Night last." *Quebec Gazette*, March 11, 1784, vol. 968, p. 3; Bibliothèque et Archives nationales du Québec, Montreal

"lost some of his fore-teeth, and has the ends of his great toes frozen off" (337), and "a mulatto" named Thomas Etherington who broke out of the jail with three white male accomplices was described as walking "somewhat lame" (Gaoler and Gray 337–338).[24]

But it was perhaps Ishmael who possessed the most evidence of abuse and physical hardship. The 36-year-old "Negro-Man" was described as "wants some of his Upper-fore Teeth, as likewise the first Joint of the fourth Finger of his left Hand; and besides, on the middle of his Right-Leg, he has a fresh Eschar from a Horse Kick lately received and cured" ([sic] Turner 326).

The enslaved also bore marks of untreated illnesses. In one such case, an unnamed Negro man was described as having "a small Scar on the left Side of his Neck joining the Jaw-bone, occasioned by a Gland not yet cur'd" ([sic] "RUN AWAY from Mr *Orillat's* Farm" 318).

As Trevor Burnard has argued for the enslaved in Jamaica, the enslaved in Nova Scotia and Quebec also lived in a world of *radical uncertainty* (165). We must therefore contemplate the too easily overlooked or underestimated scars, both emotional and psychological, which were not necessarily visible to observers. For instance, the stammer of the "Negro Man" named Brouce, which was documented in his fugitive notice of October 6, 1766 in the *Quebec Gazette*, may not have been a "normal" speech impediment, but rather a manifestation of a nervous disorder ("RUN-AWAY, the 25th Instant" 315). Brouce's psychological suffering may have been exacerbated by what appears to have been his rental to a Montreal merchant named John Grant by his owner, Lieutenant-Colonel Gabriel Christie (Mackey 531 note 13).[25]

Conclusion

Fugitive slave advertisements not only documented how the enslaved dressed, but also how their bodies appeared. As such, owners took great pains to describe the runaway's mannerisms, expressions, and physical habits, things over which they had once exerted extreme even sadistic control. As Charles Joyner has argued:

> Slaveholders' intervention in the bodily appearance of their slaves could even extend to expectations about gesture, movement, and general demeanor—how slaves reacted when spoken to, how they walked, where they directed their gaze, whether they appeared content. Though he liked being kind to "his people," Robert F. W. Allston, a South Carolinian with a great many slaves, declared that he "imperatively require[d] of them ... cheerfulness in their work, wherever and whatever it is."
>
> (Quoted in White and White 49)

That whites sought to control not just the labor of the enslaved, but also their attitudes toward that labor is evidence of the extreme surveillance and control under which they lived.

Returning to the naming of scars, branding or whip marks brings up yet other issues. The grueling and barbaric nature of slavery, and the ubiquity of corporal punishment and arduous and dangerous labor practices meant that the bodies of the enslaved were transformed over time. Newly arrived Africans in the Americas would have undergone a radical physical transformation that began with the material deprivation central to the harrowing shipboard experience of the Middle Passage (Rediker). The lack of a proper and differentiated diet (mainly one which included more than carbohydrates) meant that enslaved Africans routinely arrived in the Americas both infirm and malnourished, afflictions that were necessarily evident in their bodies—hence the practices of washing and oiling the enslaved prior to auction in various locations in the Americas (Smithers).

But furthermore, the bodies of enslaved Africans quickly became marked by the signs of neglect, torture, and abuse due to the violence of slave owners and their surrogates. As White and White have ably argued:

> Throughout the centuries of their enslavement the bodies of African and African American slaves were surfaces on which were inscribed the signs of inferior status. Partly, of course, this mutilation was the inevitability of slaves' allotted role, laboring at tasks that were hard and physically dangerous in a time and place where medical care was severely limited. Badly set legs, missing fingers, and mangled feet were commonplace.[26]
>
> (White and White 48)

The archive of fugitive slave advertisements allows us to recover the condition of the bodies of the enslaved and at times to infer or even to pinpoint the occurrence of the violent inscription of marks of punishment and torture by white slave owners and others. Hence, we are able to gain a window into the lives of the enslaved.

While there exists irrefutable evidence that the bodies of the enslaved in Jamaica were commonly marked by violence, Canadian fugitive slave notices also documented scars, amputations, and illnesses, which were the product of dangerous work regimes and corporal punishment. Furthermore, the isolating nature of life in slave minority contexts like Nova Scotia and Quebec (where one or a small number of slaves lived in the same residence or on the property of their owners) provided an abundance of privacy in which to enact various forms of abuse, punishment, and torture away from prying eyes.[27] While far more research is needed to determine if specific practices like branding and scarification were respectively employed or prohibited in Nova Scotia and Quebec, in conjunction with other primary sources like slave owner journals, correspondence, and estate inventories, the Canadian fugitive slave archive will allow us to understand the nature of the punishment and abuse from which enslaved Africans were routinely fleeing.

Notes

1 The term "wench," which originally referred to a bold or forward girl of loose character and evolved through slavery into a synonym for a black or colored female servant or a Negress, is telling (Ogilvie 619).

2 The advertisement placed by Gibb and Prior confirms the pattern of the white projection of an abject sexuality onto enslaved females in its revelation of the age of an enslaved black girl, who was described as a "Young healthy Negro Wench," as a mere 12 or 13 (337). While black males faced a strategic infantilization, black females faced acceleration toward womanhood. Both were necessary to preserve white access to black female sexuality, which within the matrilineal order of slavery was exploited to "breed" new slave children, which became the property of the enslaved female's owner.

3 Waldstreicher also mentions that postmasters often functioned in a similar fashion.

4 I am grateful to Sylvia Hamilton for sharing with me her idea of fugitive slaves as freedom-runners (Sylvia Hamilton, personal communication, November 7, 2015).

5 Two places where the fugitive slave archive may pale in comparison to photographic archives of the enslaved are Cuba and Brazil, where slavery was not abolished until 1886 and 1888 respectively (Bergad xiii). For more on photography of the enslaved in Brazil, see Prussat.

6 Immediate can mean several moments like the point of commodification when enslaved Africans were often inspected in the slave castles of the West African coast or the moments of purchase once in the Americas, whether by auction or not, when slave owners or their surrogates proceeded to rename the enslaved.

7 The Virginia planter Robert "King" Carter (the richest planter in the state), who owned a plantation on the Rappahannock River, instructed his overseer to initiate a process of renaming of enslaved Africans at the point of purchase (Berlin 251–252).

8 For Césaire, colonization in its entirety was thingification.

9 The McNiells owned another enslaved "NEGRO MAN named CUFF, about 38 years of age," who ran away on May 28 or 29, 1785 (McNiell). Elizabeth McNiell placed the notice offering a six-dollar reward for his return. Archibald had died, according to Mackey, at the hands of a "Malecite Indian" in the summer of 1784 (Mackey 327–328, 538 note 45).

10 See, for instance, "RAN-AWAY, on the 11th of September last" (317); Johnston and Purss 329. The first notice was for an escaped female named Susannah (aged about 27) and the second for a pregnant female named Bett (aged about 18).

11 The discrepancy between the number of people listed (42) and the number of people incarcerated (35) is because two prisoners left the work house, only to be returned again in the same year.

12 Wilson was imprisoned from April 19 to May 10, June 7 to July 9, July 12 to August 9, August 9 to August 11, September 1 to September 5, September 5 to October 26, and on 9 December for 23 days. The ledger does not list a date of release for Wilson's last incarceration. The fact that Wilson was imprisoned from September 1 to September 5 and then re-incarcerated on September 5 can be explained by the fact that he escaped on that day and was apparently quickly apprehended. This fact is confirmed in the ledger in the column headed "by whom discharged," under which it was indicated "ran away." However, regarding Wilson's release and re-imprisonment on August 9, it would appear that he committed some new crime after his release, since no such notation is present. Of the seven times he was imprisoned, Wilson apparently escaped twice, as the ledger indicated that he ran away on August 11 and September 5. The last name of the man named William seems to have been spelled two ways in the ledger. In entries #11 and #17, the last name is spelled "Wilson" and in entries #28, #30, #36, #37, and #41 it is spelt "Willson."

13 The lack of clarity about the number of women is due to the name of prisoner # 31, Kit Nichols.

14 Love's first name was most likely George.

15 None of the prisoners' supposed crimes appear to have been very serious, since the periods of incarceration ranged from one to 52 days. Those who served one day included: Peter (a black man), #24 Esther Roberts, #25 Dina Roberts, and #26 Else McCullogh. It was William Willson (#37) who was held for 52 days. None of the prisoners was sentenced to death.

16 Notes on the ledger indicate that it was examined by Justices of the Peace John Newton, George Smith, and Daniel Wood, who ordered Hugh Kelly to be paid £25 3s. 6d. The ledger was verified by Clerk of the Peace, Thos (Thomas) Wood on January 11, 1791.

17 The microfilm reel does not include a copy of the issue prior to February 8, 1794. Although we can assume that Wallace also ran advertisements for Belfast's return on March 1 and March 8 1794 (vol. vii, nos. 405 and 406), these issues are also missing from this reel.

18 However, Cooper also documented a discussion with the carpenter who claimed that drivers commonly would strike the ground with their whip instead of the slave if the overseer or another white person were not present (58).

19 The enslaved were also often named after months of the year. For instance, one of the enslaved people that the governor, John Wenthworth, dispatched to Surinam (Dutch Guiana) in the 1780s from Halifax was named January (Riddell, "Slavery in the Maritimes" 366 note 11).

20 The estate inventory is 17 pages in length. On page 7 on the third and fourth lines under the title, it reads "by the sale of Thursday (Black Girl) to John Bishop—20.0.0".

21 According to William Renwick Riddell, Louison was listed as "a negro woman" in the advertisement ("Notes on the Slave" 319, 323–324).

22 I have discussed elsewhere how the presence of enslaved adult males at Vineyard Pen in Jamaica worked to somewhat circumscribe the violent sexual acts of Thomas Thistlewood, the eighteenth-century English overseer who systematically raped or sexually coerced the majority of enslaved females under his care. See Nelson, "Imagining Slavery in Antigua and Jamaica"; Morgan; and Burnard.

23 Porter escaped with Silas Ruen, who Richardson estimated as 18 years old. The notice specified that Richardson was willing to pay two guineas for the return of each man.

24 Thomas Etherington's accomplices were Noah Drew, Moses Little Bailey, and Recompence Tiffany. Etherington was accused of "stealing in a dwelling house" (Mackey 338).

25 Mackey believes that Brouce (Bruce/Brous) may have been the same person who was banished from the province in 1773.

26 It is also important to note that such medical care was often strategically denied to a population who slave owners saw as mere animals.

27 In Montreal, the enslaved resided with their owners, either in the same home or on the same property. For instance, the June 1780 inventory of the Quebec home of the tailor Hugh Ritchie listed "a Negro boy" amongst his other possessions—"a black Stallion, a Cow, Two Calashes mounted, a Cart mounted, a Cart Harness, a Harness for the Calash"—which were held in the stable (Mackey 536 note 34). This was not the case in Jamaica. Jamaican plantations were customarily composed of hundreds if not thousands of acres of land, with the Great House, houses for the managers, works (mill, distillery, etc.), and separate Negro villages where the enslaved lived on property, which was customarily chosen for ease of surveillance from the vantage point of the often elevated Great House.

References

"Account of Persons Committed to the Work House (Or House of Correction) of Halifax and etc. from the 1st day of January to the 31st day of December 1790, both days inclusive," *Prisoners in Bridewell 1790–1831 and County Gaol 1751–1849. NSARM:* RG 34–312, Series J, vol. 4.

"ADVERTISEMENT. *To be* SOLD *by* AUCTION." *Quebec Herald*, April 14, 1791. Rpt. in "Appendix I: Newspaper Notices." In *Done with Slavery: The Black Fact in Montreal 1760–1840*. By Frank Mackey. McGill-Queen's University Press, 2010, p. 334.

Bergad, Laird W. *The Comparative Histories of Slavery in Brazil, Cuba, and the United States.* Cambridge University Press, 2007.

Berlin, Ira. "From Creole to African: Atlantic Creoles and the Origins of African-American Society in Mainland North America." *William and Mary Quarterly*, vol. 53, no. 2, 1996, pp. 251–288.

Bickell, R. *The West Indies as they are: or a Real Picture of Slavery: but more particularly as it exists in the Island of Jamaica. in three parts with notes.* London, 1825.

"BROKE out of His Majesty's Gaol in Quebec." *Quebec Gazette*, May 4, 1786. Rpt. in "Appendix I: Newspaper Notices." In *Done with Slavery: The Black Fact in*

Montreal 1760–1840. By Frank Mackey. McGill-Queen's University Press, 2010, pp. 328–329.
Brown, William. "BROKE out of his Majesty's Gaol." *Quebec Gazette*, May 4, 1786. Rpt. in "Appendix I: Newspaper Notices." In *Done with Slavery: The Black Fact in Montreal 1760–1840*. By Frank Mackey. McGill-Queen's University Press, 2010, pp. 327–328.
——. "RAN AWAY from the Printing-Office in Quebec." *Quebec Gazette*, December 24, 1778. Rpt. in "Appendix I: Newspaper Notices." In *Done with Slavery: The Black Fact in Montreal 1760–1840*. By Frank Mackey. McGill-Queen's University Press, 2010, p. 321.
——. "RANAWAY from the Printing-Office in Quebec." *Quebec Gazette*, January 29, 1778. Rpt. in "Appendix I: Newspaper Notices." In *Done with Slavery: The Black Fact in Montreal 1760–1840*. By Frank Mackey. McGill-Queen's University Press, 2010, p. 320.
——. "RANAWAY from the Printing-office in Quebec." *Quebec Gazette*, November 27, 1777. Rpt. in "Appendix I: Newspaper Notices." In *Done with Slavery: The Black Fact in Montreal 1760–1840*. By Frank Mackey. McGill-Queen's University Press, 2010, p. 319.
——. "RUN-AWAY FROM the Printing-Office in *Quebec*." *Quebec Gazette*, September 23, 1779. Rpt. in "Appendix I: Newspaper Notices." In *Done with Slavery: The Black Fact in Montreal 1760–1840*. By Frank Mackey. McGill-Queen's University Press, 2010, p. 322.
Burnard, Trevor. "The Sexual Life of an Eighteenth-Century Jamaican Slave Overseer." In *Sex and Sexuality in Early America*. Edited by Merril D. Smith, New York University Press, 1998, pp. 163–189.
Césaire, Aimé. *Discourse on Colonialism*. 1972. Translated by Joan Pinkham, Monthly Review Press, 2000.
Cooper, Thomas. *Facts Illustrative of the Condition of the Negro Slaves in Jamaica: with Notes and Appendix*. London, 1824.
Freeman, Constant. "RUN AWAY from the Schooner Lucy." *Quebec Gazette*, June 5, 1788. Rpt. in "Appendix I: Newspaper Notices." In *Done with Slavery: The Black Fact in Montreal 1760–1840*. By Frank Mackey. McGill-Queen's University Press, 2010, p. 331.
Gaoler, Jacob Kuhn and EDWD. WM. Gray, Sheriff. "BROKE out of and escaped from the Common Gaol." *Montreal Gazette*, November 21, 1796. Rpt. in "Appendix I: Newspaper Notices." In *Done with Slavery: The Black Fact in Montreal 1760–1840*. By Frank Mackey. McGill-Queen's University Press, 2010, pp. 337–338.
Garner, Steve. "Whiteness as Terror and Supremacy." In *Whiteness: An Introduction*. Routledge, 2007, pp. 13–33.
Geurout, Pre. "RAN AWAY FROM the Subscriber." *Quebec Gazette*, August 14, 1783. Rpt. in "Appendix I: Newspaper Notices." In *Done with Slavery: The Black Fact in Montreal 1760–1840*. By Frank Mackey. McGill-Queen's University Press, 2010, p. 325.
Gibb and Prior. "FOR SALE A Young healthy Negro Wench." *Montreal Gazette*, December 28, 1795. Rpt. in "Appendix I: Newspaper Notices." In *Done with Slavery: The Black Fact in Montreal 1760–1840*. By Frank Mackey. McGill-Queen's University Press, 2010, p. 337.

Gilliland, William. "SIX DOLLARS REWARD." *Quebec Gazette*, September 19, 1771. Rpt. in "Appendix I: Newspaper Notices." In *Done with Slavery: The Black Fact in Montreal 1760–1840*. By Frank Mackey. McGill-Queen's University Press, 2010, p. 318.

Gray, EDWd. Wm, Sheriff. "WHEREAS the Night between the 4th and 5th instant." *Quebec Gazette*, September 18, 1777. Rpt. in "Appendix I: Newspaper Notices." In *Done with Slavery: The Black Fact in Montreal 1760–1840*. By Frank Mackey. McGill-Queen's University Press, 2010, p. 319.

Hipps, George. "RUN away from Mr George Hipps." *Quebec Gazette*, November 5, 1778. Rpt. in "Appendix I: Newspaper Notices." In *Done with Slavery: The Black Fact in Montreal 1760–1840*. By Frank Mackey. McGill-Queen's University Press, 2010, p. 321.

——. "RAN AWAY from my service." *Quebec Gazette*, August 20, 1778. Rpt. in "Appendix I: Newspaper Notices." In *Done with Slavery: The Black Fact in Montreal 1760–1840*. By Frank Mackey. McGill-Queen's University Press, 2010, p. 321.

Johnston and Purss. "RAN-AWAY from the subscribers." *Quebec Gazette*, March 8, 1787. Rpt. in "Appendix I: Newspaper Notices." In *Done with Slavery: The Black Fact in Montreal 1760–1840*. By Frank Mackey. McGill-Queen's University Press, 2010, p. 329.

Joseph, J. "RUN AWAY From the Subscriber in the Night of the 13th Instant." *Quebec Gazette*, July 28, 1791. Rpt. in "Appendix I: Newspaper Notices." In *Done with Slavery: The Black Fact in Montreal 1760–1840*. By Frank Mackey. McGill-Queen's University Press, 2010, pp. 334, 540 note 58.

Klepp, Susan E. and Roderick A. McDonald. "Inscribing Experience: An American Working Woman and an English Gentle Woman Encounter Jamaica's Slave Society, 1801–1805." *William and Mary Quarterly*, vol. 58, no. 3, 2001, pp. 637–660.

Martinot, Steve. "Introduction." In *The Machinery of Whiteness: Studies in the Structure of Racialization*. Temple University Press, 2010, pp. 1–34.

McNiell, Elizabeth. "RANAWAY *the 28th or 29th of last Month*." *Quebec Gazette*, June 9, 1785. Rpt. in "Appendix I: Newspaper Notices." In *Done with Slavery: The Black Fact in Montreal 1760–1840*. By Frank Mackey. McGill-Queen's University Press, 2010, pp. 327–328.

Melvin and Burns. "BY PUBLIC AUCTION." *Quebec Gazette*, August 21, 1788. Rpt. in "Appendix I: Newspaper Notices." In *Done with Slavery: The Black Fact in Montreal 1760–1840*. By Frank Mackey. McGill-Queen's University Press, 2010, p. 331.

Michener, Abel. "RAN away." *Nova Scotia Gazette and the Weekly Chronicle*, 1 August 1786, vol. XVI, no. 1060. *NSARM:* PANS MFM #8160, reel #8160.

Morgan, Philip D. "Slaves and Livestock in Eighteenth- Century Jamaica: Vineyard Pen, 1750–1751." *William and Mary Quarterly*, vol. 52, no.1, 1995, pp. 47–76.

Nelson, Charmaine L. "Imagining Slavery in Antigua and Jamaica." In *Slavery, Geography, and Empire in Nineteenth-Century Marine Landscapes of Montreal and Jamaica*. Routledge, 2016, pp. 217–275.

——. *Slavery, Geography, and Empire in Nineteenth-Century Marine Landscapes of Montreal and Jamaica*. Routledge, 2016.

Ogilvie, J. *The Imperial Dictionary of the English Language: A Complete Encyclopedic Lexicon, Literary, Scientific, and Technological*. Edited by Charles Annandale, vol. 4, Blackie and Son, 1884.

Ohri, Aditi. "'Just Imported and to Be Sold': Creolization and the Slave-Master Relationship in Eighteenth-Century Nova Scotia." In *Towards an African Canadian Art History: Art, Memory, and Resistance.* Edited by Charmaine A. Nelson, Captus Press, forthcoming 2017.

Pritchard, Azariah. "RUN away from Subscriber." *Quebec Gazette*, May 22, 1794, supplement. Rpt. in "Appendix I: Newspaper Notices." In *Done with Slavery: The Black Fact in Montreal 1760–1840.* By Frank Mackey. McGill-Queen's University Press, 2010, p. 337.

Prussat, Margrit. "Icons of Slavery: Black Brazil in Nineteenth-Century Photography and Image Art." In *Living History: Encountering the Memory of the Heirs of Slavery.* Edited by Ana Lucia Araujo, Cambridge Scholars Publishing, 2009, pp. 203–230.

"RANAWAY from Carleton-Island." *Quebec Gazette*, August 10, 1780. Rpt. in "Appendix I: Newspaper Notices." In *Done with Slavery: The Black Fact in Montreal 1760–1840.* By Frank Mackey. McGill-Queen's University Press, 2010, p. 323.

"RAN-AWAY, on the 11th of September last." *Quebec Gazette*, October 19, 1769. Rpt. in "Appendix I: Newspaper Notices." In *Done with Slavery: The Black Fact in Montreal 1760–1840.* By Frank Mackey. McGill-Queen's University Press, 2010, p. 317.

Rediker, Marcus. *The Slave Ship: A Human History.* Penguin, 2007.

Reynolds, Andrew. "Forty Shillings Reward." *Royal Gazette and Nova-Scotia Advertiser*, September 7, 1790, vol. iii, no. 77. *NSARM* (January 5, 1790–December 25, 1792): PANS MFM #8164, reel 8164.

Richardson. "Four Guineas Reward." *Nova Scotia Gazette and Weekly Chronicle*, September 5, 1780, vol. 10, no. 744. *NSARM* (September 6, 1774–December 26, 1780): PANS MFM #8158, reel 8158.

Riddell, William R. "Notes on the Slave in Nouvelle-France." *Journal of Negro History*, vol. 8, no. 3, 1923, pp. 318–323.

——. "Slavery in the Maritime Provinces." *Journal of Negro History*, vol. 5, no. 3, 1920, pp. 359–375.

Ritchie, H. "RAN-AWAY, From the Subscriber." *Quebec Gazette*, November 4, 1779. Rpt. in "Appendix I: Newspaper Notices." In *Done with Slavery: The Black Fact in Montreal 1760–1840.* By Frank Mackey. McGill-Queen's University Press, 2010, pp. 323, 536 note 34.

Rock, John. —. Estate Inventory, September 25, 1776. *NSARM*: PANS MFM #(19)420, RG48, reel 420, #61.

——. "Ran away from her Master John Rock." *Nova Scotia Gazette and Weekly Chronicle*, September 1, 1772, vol. 3, no. 105. *NSARM* (1772–1774): PANS MFM #8155, reel 8155.

——. "Ran away from her Master John Rock." *Nova Scotia Gazette and Weekly Chronicle*, September 8, 1772, vol. 3, no. 105. *NSARM* (1772–1774): PANS MFM #8155, reel 8155.

——. "Ran away from her Master John Rock." *Nova Scotia Gazette and Weekly Chronicle*, September 22, 1772, vol. 3, no. 105. *NSARM* (1772–1774): PANS MFM #8155, reel 8155.

"RUN AWAY from Mr *Orillat's* Farm on the Island of Montreal." *Quebec Gazette*, September 7, 1775. Rpt. in "Appendix I: Newspaper Notices." In *Done with Slavery: The Black Fact in Montreal 1760–1840.* By Frank Mackey. McGill-Queen's University Press, 2010, p. 318.

"RUN-AWAY, from *James Crofton*." *Quebec Gazette*, May 14, 1767. Rpt. in "Appendix I: Newspaper Notices." In *Done with Slavery: The Black Fact in Montreal 1760–1840*. By Frank Mackey. McGill-Queen's University Press, 2010, p. 315.

"RUN-AWAY, the 25th Instant, from Mr Grant." *Quebec Gazette*, October 6, 1766. Rpt. in "Appendix I: Newspaper Notices." In *Done with Slavery: The Black Fact in Montreal 1760–1840*. By Frank Mackey. McGill-Queen's University Press, 2010, p. 315.

Saul, J. "RAN AWAY FROM the Subscriber on Thursday." *Quebec Gazette*, 9 September 1784. Rpt. in "Appendix I: Newspaper Notices." In *Done with Slavery: The Black Fact in Montreal 1760–1840*. By Frank Mackey. McGill-Queen's University Press, 2010, pp. 326–327, 332, 537 note 41.

Shepherd, Jas. Esq. "BROKE out of his Majesty's Goal." *Quebec Gazette*, February 23, 1786. Rpt. in "Appendix I: Newspaper Notices." In *Done with Slavery: The Black Fact in Montreal 1760–1840*. By Frank Mackey. McGill-Queen's University Press, 2010, pp. 328–329.

Smithers, Gregory. "Missionaries, Settlers, Cherokees, and African-Americans, 1780s to 1850s." In *Science, Sexuality, and Race in the United States and Australia, 1780s to 1890s*. Routledge, 2009, pp. 99–121.

Stoler, Ann L. *Along the Archival Grain: Epistemic Anxieties and Colonial Common Sense*. Princeton University Press, 2009.

Terry, Judith. "Introduction." In *Journal of a West India Proprietor: Kept during a residence in the Island of Jamaica*. By Matthew Gregory Lewis. Oxford University Press, 1999, pp. xiv–xv.

"To be SOLD, By PUBLIC AUCTION." *Nova Scotia Gazette and Weekly Chronicle*, March 23, 1773, vol. 3, no. 134. *NSARM* (1772–1774): PANS MFM #8155, reel 8155.

Tucker, Reuben. "Twenty Dollars Reward." *Royal Gazette and Nova-Scotia Advertiser*, June 18, 1799, vol. 11, no. 597. *NSARM*: PANS MFM #8168, reel 8168.

Turner, John. "FOURTEEN DOLLARS Reward. RUN-AWAY, on Sunday Night last." *Quebec Gazette*, March 11, 1784, vol. 968, p. 3. Rpt. in "Appendix I: Newspaper Notices." In *Done with Slavery: The Black Fact in Montreal 1760–1840*. By Frank Mackey. McGill-Queen's University Press, 2010, p. 326.

Waldstreicher, D. "Reading the Runaways: Self-Fashioning, Print Culture, and Confidence in Slavery in the Eighteenth-Century Mid-Atlantic." *William and Mary Quarterly*, April 1999, pp. 243–272.

Wallace, Michael. "Twenty Dollars Reward." *Weekly Chronicle*, February 8, 1794, vol. vii, no. 402. *NSARM*: MFM 8165.

—. "Twenty Dollars Reward." *Weekly Chronicle*, February 15, 1794, vol. vii, no. 403. *NSARM*: MFM 8165.

—. "Twenty Dollars Reward." *Weekly Chronicle*, February 22, 1794, vol. vii, no. 404. *NSARM*: MFM 8165.

——. "Twenty Dollars Reward." *Weekly Chronicle*, March 15, 1794, vol. vii, no. 407. *NSARM*: MFM 8165.

White, Graham and Shane White. "Slave Hair and African American Culture in the Eighteenth and Nineteenth Centuries." *Journal of Southern History*, vol. 61, no. 1, 1995, pp. 45–76.

Wood, Marcus. "John Gabriel Stedman, William Blake, Francesco Bartolozzi and Empathetic Pornography in the *Narrative of a Five Years Expedition against the Revolted Negroes of Surinam*." In *An Economy of Colour: Visual Culture and the Atlantic World, 1660–1830*. Edited by Geoff Quilley and Kay Dian Kriz. Manchester University Press, 2003, pp. 129–152.

——. "Rhetoric and the Runaway: The Iconography of Slave Escape in England and America." *Blind Memory: Visual Representations of Slavery in England and America, 1780–1865*. Manchester University Press, 2000, pp. 77–142.

Chapter 6

The work of death

Massacre and retribution in Southampton County, Virginia, August 1831

Christopher Tomlins

Clarify the value of the exception, of the event, of rupture.
Alain Badiou (*Polemics* 8)

Hegel's dialectic of lord and bondsman is famous, and justly so. It has a place in Marxism, in psychoanalysis, in postcolonial studies, indeed "in any critical discourse that wrestles with an idea of the 'other' as that against which the self is defined" (Cole 578).

How does it go? Hegel argues that recognition of oneself *as* a self comes only through struggle with another, in which each risks its life in attempting the other's "destruction and death." Struggle breeds awareness that "*life* is as essential to [the self] as pure self-consciousness," and that the other is a distinct and opposed mode of consciousness. The one is independent, "its essential nature ... to be for itself"; the other is dependent, "its essence ... life or existence for another." The one is lord, the other bondsman. "A form of recognition has arisen that is one sided and unequal" (Hegel 232, 234, emphasis in original, 236).

Consciousness of lordship "on its own account" obtains recognition by the negation of the other. But in obtaining recognition through the other, each is set on a dialectical course that will "pass into the opposite of what it immediately is" (Hegel 234, 237). Instead of the bondsman existing only as a relation to lordship, we come to consider the bondsman in and for itself.

How does the bondsman overcome its initial cancellation of self-existent awareness? Through work and labor. By labor, the bondsman's consciousness attains "direct apprehension" of its self as independent (Hegel 238).

This is of course highly abstract. The historian's urge is to historicize the abstract, to discover its originating specificities (Cole; Buck-Morss). Here, however, I wish to continue to recognize the salience of the abstraction, for Hegel is locating his dialectic quite precisely outside the interpretive constraints of any particular materiality. I do not mean to deny that the vocabulary of lord and bondsman has originating specificities, but I want also to join Slavoj Žižek in recognizing its immanent universality: "The commonplace according to which we are all thoroughly grounded in a particular contingent lifeworld," Žižek writes, "so that all universality is irreducibly coloured by and embedded in that lifeworld, needs to be turned round. The authentic moment of discovery, the breakthrough, occurs when a properly universal dimension *explodes from within a particular context and becomes "for-itself," and is directly experienced as universal*" (152, emphasis in original).

Here I turn to the dialectic of lord and bondsman to help explain the massacre of 55 members of white slaveholding families that took place over a span of approximately 12 hours on Monday August 22, 1831 in St. Luke's Parish, Southampton County, Virginia, and also the retributive juridical killing of 18 slaves, accused of felonious conspiracy and rebellion and murder of those free white persons that followed. I contend that the massacre was an explosion beyond a particular lifeworld, and that the centrality of work to the bondsman's "direct apprehension" of its self as independent was a key component in that explosion. I will also argue that the dialectic helps explain the specifically juridical form of killing that followed the massacre.

If we are to believe Thomas Ruffin Gray's famous *Confessions*, Nat Turner used the pungent phrase "the work of death" to describe the killings that were the focal point of his rebellion (Gray 12). The phrase was not uncommon. It meant killing, and its associated experiences (Faust xiv). But what kind of killing? The killings that lie at the center of the Southampton rebellion were not a "spree." Nor were they some shambolic nightmare conjured by "a hate-driven madman" who, according to Eugene Genovese, "had no idea of where he was leading his men or what they would do when they got there" (210–211). The killings were not indiscriminate, but purposeful. They followed a logic. But what was their logic? Was it revenge? Was killing incidental to some other purpose, such as flight or revolution? Or was it central and essential to what Turner desired to achieve? And what did it mean, particularly to a slave, to describe dealing death as "work?"

Three days in August

> Us neber shot a hog … us always used an axe.
>
> Joseph Holmes (in Rawick VI 193)

The killing began in the early hours of Monday August 22, 1831 at the house of Joseph Travis, approximately five miles west of the hamlet of Cross Keys, 13 miles west of the little town of Jerusalem, Southampton County's only urban center and the county seat. In the words quoted in the *Confessions*, "we determined to enter the house secretly, and murder them whilst sleeping" (Gray 12). Nat Turner scaled a ladder, opened a second-floor window, descended the stairs and unbarred the door. Prevailed upon by his companions to strike first, Turner attempted to kill Travis with a hatchet as he lay asleep, but managed only a glancing blow. "[H]e sprang from the bed and called his wife." Turner's associate, Will

[Francis], "laid him dead with a blow of his axe." Travis' wife, Sarah, was killed the same way as she lay in bed. So too were Sarah's son, Putnam Moore, and Travis' apprentice, Joel Westbrook; their heads were hacked off. Recalling after their departure an infant child left alive in the house, "Henry and Will returned and killed it" (Gray 12).

The killing had been decided at a meeting held less than a mile away and only a few hours before the invasion of the Travis house. The meeting had been called to agree upon a plan "to rise and kill all the white people" (Southampton County Court 90). What would transpire accounted for far fewer than "all" but still enough to render Turner's August rebellion remarkable throughout the country.

Without dwelling on every blow, we can acknowledge certain salient characteristics of what took place. First, this was an extremely violent event. Second, the people who took part were perfectly ordinary people, some of whom became involved reluctantly. There is no evidence that any of them had previously been perpetrators of violence, although doubtless many of them had been subjected to violence. Third, there are signs throughout the event that the perpetrators experienced considerable stress, but also that as they proceeded, the group became more purposeful. In other words, once they had nerved themselves to begin killing, it became easier as they went on. They became familiar with killing, their actions became more considered, and both the course they followed and their practices had a logic (histories).

Fourth, there are also signs of extreme excitement. One example occurs about nine hours after the first killings at Travis', after 11 households had been destroyed, 30 whites had been killed, and the initial group of seven conspirators has grown to more than 30. Turner describes how as they gathered at a ransacked farmhouse belonging to Newit Harris, "the men shouted and hurraed ... some were in the yard, loading their guns, others drinking" (Gray 14). At this point, they knew the rebellion had been discovered and there was no longer any point in stealth. What followed was the single most devastating act of destruction, the attack on Levi Waller's farm, where there were 17 whites—two adult males, two adolescent males, and the remainder mostly women and small children. The men possessed loaded guns, but fled. Ten were killed at Waller's—the women and children, mostly hacked or beaten to death, brains "knocked out," bodies "piled in one bleeding heap" (Pleasants 51).

Finally, the reaction of Southampton's white population in the days that followed, before convention began concealing actuality beneath layers of Victorian discretion, was raw shock at the rebellion's deadliness and its sheer violence: commentators spoke of families destroyed in an infection of madness; of horrible massacres; of horrible ferocity; of bloodthirsty wolves preying on helpless women and children; of knives and axes, knocking out brains, and cutting throats; of corpses horribly mangled; of blind purposeless fury and inhuman butcheries (Tragle 36–56).

Massacre

> Harrowing was the squealing of the victims;
> quick was the stroke that slew them.
>
> John Sergeant Wise (1899)

To call what took place on August 22 in Southampton County a "massacre" is to invoke a particular way of understanding the event. Begin with the word itself. Etymologically, the meaning of the English word "massacre" is derived from the identical Middle and Old French words *massacre*, meaning butchery. They in turn are derived from post-classical Latin *macella*, which means a shambles or butcher's shop. The common first syllable (mas) tracks post-classical Latin *macia*, meaning a bludgeon, or *mace* in Anglo-Norman, which is also a variation on vulgar Latin *matteuca*, or cudgel, derived from classical Latin *mateola*, meaning an agricultural implement, from which the English words "mattock" and "maul" descend (*Oxford English Dictionary*; Semelin, "In Consideration" 378; Levene 7–9).

"Massacre" thus unites several otherwise distinct concepts: killing in the manner of animal slaughter, in which those killed lack means of self-defense; killing in the manner of a vocation that requires bodily effort, as in the work of slaughtering animals and butchering meat, or agricultural work such as felling trees, hammering posts, or chopping firewood; close proximity between killer and killed, as within the confines of a slaughterhouse or a butcher's shop; and the use of physical force to overwhelm those killed, as in stabbing, slitting, chopping, or bludgeoning. Originally associated with the slaughter of animals for food, massacre came in the late sixteenth century to be associated with the killing of people in the manner of animals—in other words, repetitious slaughter—with ritual, purgative connotations. Massacre is taken to imply multiple or repeated killings, but the etymological emphasis on the *manner* of killing means that it can also describe single killings, such as exemplary and ritual executions, or extravagantly theatrical murders (Corbin 69, 88–97).

Applied to the killing of people, massacre is thus associated with physical excess. As the principal modern student of massacre, the French sociologist Jacques Semelin, puts it, "blood spewing everywhere, unthinkable atrocities, bodies torn asunder" (Semelin, *Purify* 70). This suggests massacre has an arbitrary, insane quality. But to Semelin, this is not so. Massacre, he writes, is "a way of seeing some 'Other' being, of stigmatizing him, debasing him, and obliterating him before actually killing him" (Semelin, *Purify* 70). Semelin describes this as a discursive process composed from three elements—identity, purity, and security. Identity means the creation of a collective self as "one" against the "other" from a "common past of suffering"; purity defends the integrity of the newly created collective self, whether in religious or secular terms, against the corruption that the other represents; security is the undertaking to rid the collective self of the threat posed by the other, to destroy the other in order to forestall the inevitability of its violence. To Semelin, the inflammatory process of identity formation creates a mythic *imaginaire* of omnipotence and destruction focused on the other, "a sacrificial violence that aims to 'regenerate' the group at the expense of an 'other.'" Citing René Girard's well-known study *Violence and the Sacred*, he calls this a crystallization of identity through purification, a "logic of the sacred through murder" (Semelin, *Purify* 77, 90–92; Semelin, "Vocabulary" 196–198; Girard).

Semelin stresses that massacre is less a *murderous* process than a physically *destructive* process, directed at persons and their property. As such, massacre is extremely demanding on the perpetrator, both psychologically and physically. Psychologically, massacre demands that some ordinary people learn how to kill others—others whom they know, amongst whom they live, and with whom they may have perfectly normal relations until the process of destruction is initiated. "It is not easy for a man to resolve to kill a fellow human, even if he gives himself good reason for doing so" (Semelin, *Purify* 246, 325). Perpetrators must become inured, they must learn how to routinize their capacity to destroy so that it can be repeated as often as required. Some learn quickly, deriving pleasure from bloodshed. Others experience profound unease or traumatic stress. Some mitigate their stress with alcohol. Others obfuscate their participation or quietly abscond (Semelin, *Purify* 267; Mohamed; Browning 61–69, 80–85, 100).

Most simply persist, assimilating the process of killing and destroying to "work" (Semelin, *Purify* 254, 269). There are at least three reasons why "killing" becomes "work" in this way. First, killing (particularly repeated killing) is extremely laborious: "To slaughter human beings requires a high degree of physical and above all mental exertion" (*Purify* 254–55). Second, killing on the scale of massacre borrows its methods from work: it borrows the means (that is the tools), it borrows the tendency to develop habitual practices (repetition and routine), and it borrows the mode of organization—a division of labor amongst leaders who direct but rarely kill, executioners who kill frequently, and ancillary personnel, who kill on occasion but mainly assist those who kill frequently. Third, the most populous segment of perpetrators of massacre corresponds sociologically to a "workforce"—overwhelmingly male, single, and young, even adolescent, in the age range of 13–25 years old (*Purify* 186–189, 195, 210, 268, 269–270, 279–280; Browning 161).

Massacre is analogous to work for a fourth reason: it is a transformative process. On one side, victims become something other than merely corpses. It is common and not at all inappropriate to argue that massacre involves a transformation of the body into something *less* than it was. Perpetrators feel a need to disfigure this fellow human as quickly as possible to forestall the possibility that recognition of a common humanity will stand in the way of killing the victim. But the acts of killing—chopping, hacking, mangling, and mutilating—also represent much *more* than killing. These are somatic transformations that expose, penetrate, and occupy the material form of the victim. They are what Arjun Appadurai calls a "vivisectionist" exhibition that puts new personal realities on display. Extreme bodily violence fashions new intimacies between former social intimates, it is a "counterperformance" of their former relationship that destroys a prior order of life and re-creates the victim as something drastically different than before—helpless, weak, vulnerable, *opened* up to inspection (Appadurai 917–920). Witness reports repeatedly use the adjective "mangled" to describe the bodies of the victims of the Turner rebellion.[1] Victims' bodies become the site upon which prior relational uncertainties or conflicts are resolved "through brutal forms of violation, investigation, destruction, and disposal" (Appadurai 920).

Just as it transforms victims' bodies, massacre transforms its agents. One can certainly argue that massacre renders its agents *less* than human—and, indeed, in the case of the Turner Rebellion, this was, unsurprisingly, the consensus of white opinion. Though many descriptions were applied to them—monsters, savages, brigands—most commonly the rebels were referred to as "wretches" and "bandits," that is, as exiles and outcasts from human society.[2] But, however briefly, massacre can also mean the formation amongst perpetrators of a new collective identity, a new consciousness, endowed with a new integrity and new capacities. Here, then, is "death" as "work" in its Hegelian mode, in which "self-existence comes to be felt explicitly" for the first time as the agent's "own proper being" through the action of fashioning; in which labor creates a new self-awareness, a discovery of "having and being a 'mind of his own'" (Hegel 239). White commentary attempted to deny the massacre any meaning other than madness and degeneracy "more marked by its ferocity than its force" (Tragle 48). But meaning is to be found precisely in ferocity. Turner's work of death was work he required of his companions in the service of their self-transformation, through a cancellation and destruction of the other, from bondsmen subordinated by fear, "consciousness repressed within itself," into autonomous actors possessed of "real and true independence" (Hegel 239).

Insurrection

> He knocked some honky down and beat him to death
> … he killed white men, white babies, white women,
> white cats, white dogs, everything that was in the
> neighborhood.
>
> Anonymous (in Ellison et al. 82)

If the logic of the Southampton massacre lay in Turner's attempt to transform its perpetrators from subservience to self-awareness through "the destruction and death of the other" (Hegel 232), it remains to ask whether the event itself had any distinct instrumental purpose.

Examining individual instances of massacre, Semelin discerns three fundamental political dynamics or rationalities on display: subjugation, eradication, and insurrection. Killing in the service of subjugation means that a population is subjected to the terror of destructive example to produce an effect in the remainder, such as surrender and subservience, as in wars of colonial conquest (Semelin, *Purify* 327–330). Killing in the service of eradication means killing not to subjugate a population, but to destroy it in order to remove it physically from a position in command of resources desired by another or from a position in which it is perceived as a threat. Eradication may be exemplary, designed to induce an existing population to move elsewhere, as in settler colonialism's wars on indigenous populations (Tomlins 133–183; Madley), or it may be totalized, intended to eliminate the entirety of a population, as in the Holocaust.

Killing in the service of insurrection differs from these in two respects. First, subjugation and eradication are usually the work of state actors or state sympathizers; killing in the service of insurrection almost by definition is not. Second, subjugation and eradication both exhibit a capacity to escalate into elimination; state actors usually possess the resources to make escalation a viable possibility if less intense forms of coercion prove ineffective. Insurgents usually do not possess the capacity to escalate. At most, they can multiply—do what they are already doing, but with greater frequency.

To terrify the target population is an objective in all three of Semelin's rationalities of massacre. In the third case, however, terror is not simply a means but an end. Insurgents are fully aware that they have no presence in the relevant public sphere, either because they are an excluded minority or because the armature of the target group is too formidable to penetrate: spectacular violence enables them to gain sufficient purchase on the target group's attention to shock the system it dominates (Merari 213, 229, 230; Semelin, *Purify* 347, 348–351).

In appearance, the Southampton massacre was killing in the service of insurrection. As Turner explained himself, the first objective was to gather resources—weapons and participants—sufficient to secure freedom of movement while killing to preserve secrecy. Once secrecy had been lost, killing became more explicitly part of the design; freedom of movement was subordinated to killing: "my object to carry terror and devastation wherever we went" (Gray 14). Corpses became expressive propaganda: "mangled bodies" to intimidate pursuers. Finally, with resources maximized and opponents terrorized, the moment came to spread the traumatic shock. "I determined on starting for Jerusalem" (Gray 15). Turner sought new resources—arms and ammunition—to multiply both frequency and freedom of action. Jerusalem was the logical source.

What followed was failure. Turner never reached Jerusalem. But Turner's failure had little to do with any fault in his plans, which he pursued boldly with everything he had at his disposal. Eugene Genovese, to the contrary, he knew what he was doing, and why. Failure lay instead in the relationship between the insurgents' "struggle for life" and the circumstances—the grid of constraints—that bound them. They could not overcome the crucial distinction that Michel de Certeau draws between "tactics" and "strategy."

To invoke Certeau is to leave the sociology of massacre for social anthropology, in particular for "the models of action characteristic of … the dominated element in society," those fated to use only what is left over by the dominant rather than to produce for themselves (Certeau xi–xii). This is less of a leap than it might seem, for a moment's reflection will show that we remain within the terms of Hegel's dialectic. Certeau's "users" are analogous to Hegel's unawakened bondsmen, confronted by lordship, their own existence for themselves deferred or canceled. Just as the bondsman begins to attain self-consciousness through work, Certeau's users "make innumerable and infinitesimal transformations within their cultural economy in order to adapt it to their own interests and their own rules" (xiii–xiv). They use whatever is available, their own "toolkit[s] of personal and cultural knowledge" (Hinton 30). Turner and his comrades engage in work of their own construction built from their own ways of using what comes to hand, from local, practical knowledge—"clever tricks, knowing how to get away with things, 'hunter's cunning,' maneuvers" (Certeau xix); what James Scott (309–341) calls *mētis*, the ways of the weak. Here is an example from the *Confessions*:

> Sam and Will went to the door and knocked. *Mr. Francis asked who was there, Sam replied, it was him, and he had a letter for him*, on which he got up and came to the door, they immediately seized him, and dragging him out a little from the door, he was dispatched by repeated blows on the head.
>
> (Gray 12–13, emphasis added)

Still, they are unable to overcome the positionality of the weak. Theirs is not the realm of "strategy," but of "tactics."

For Certeau, strategy is "the calculus of force-relationships which becomes possible when a subject of will and power can be isolated from an 'environment' "; that is, when the subject becomes for-itself and thereby attains an autonomous spatiality. Tactics, by contrast, is "a calculus which cannot count on [an autonomous spatiality] ... A tactic insinuates itself into the other's place, fragmentarily, without taking it over in its entirety, without being able to keep it at a distance." In the calculus of tactics, the actor is a creature of circumstance. It "must play on and with a terrain imposed on it and organized by the law of a foreign power" (Certeau xix, 37).

Turner's rebellion is, from the very beginning, a calculus of tactics, undertaken " 'within the enemy's field of vision' ... within enemy territory" (Certeau 37). Turner and his confidantes do not have the option of strategy. They acknowledge this quite explicitly. "Many were the plans formed and rejected by us," says Turner. "The time passed without our coming to any determination how to commence ... forming new schemes and rejecting them" (Gray 11). When they decide to begin, it is not a strategic (autonomous) decision, but one taken in answer to a demand imposed from elsewhere—a sign from God (11). And even then, they must still decide *how* to begin, "to concert a plan as we had not yet determined on any" (11). Once under way, the rebellion "operates in isolated actions, blow by blow" (Certeau 37). It has no place of its own, no base from which to operate, to which to return. It has to rely on mobility and to seize on possibilities as they present themselves. It must surprise its adversaries and poach on their territory.

The fate of the rebellion is a manifestation of the limits inherent in the calculus of tactics. Its defeat is a victory of space over time, of strategy over tactics, of *techné* over *mētis*, of power over trickery and local knowledge. At first, the terror of the rebellion empties the terrain of white families. But gradually and inexorably, the whites fill it again. By re-establishing their command of place, they block the rebellion's trajectory. They fill the channels that connect point to point, neighborhood to neighborhood. One group follows the rebels' tracks; another group rides into their faces. When the rebels try to go around "through a private way," they find their target destination guarded. They spend the night in fear of white patrols converging upon them. When they attempt to recruit the next morning, they are "immediately fired upon" and retreat headlong. In their retreat, they run into yet another "party of white men" and disintegrate. The whites take back the roads; they force the rebels back onto footpaths; they patrol everywhere. Their control of space becomes absolute (Certeau 38).

"That place"

> O Jerusalem, Jerusalem, which killest the prophets,
> and stonest them that are sent unto thee.
>
> Luke 13:34

Nat Turner's "work of death" describes a particular kind of human labor—the violent destruction of others—in the service of a transformative struggle for life: what one might call a process of destructive creation. The logic of the attempt was dialectical, the explosive realization of life through its release from the constraints of the lifeworld of slavery, such that enslaved life could become "for-itself" and directly experienced as universal, transforming the perpetrators and abettors and circumspect beneficiaries of massacre from slaves into free agents.

But the attempt failed. Some of the insurgents were killed, some were captured, and some ran off (Gray 16–17). Rather than produce the desired universal, the dialectic collapsed back into circumstance. The crowning Hegelian sublation did not occur. Instead, the course of the dialectic proved disjunctive (Benjamin, "Program" 106), lurching back from Bondsman to Lord, Slave to Master. Hegel had argued that the consciousness of lordship obtained its recognition through negation of the other, the bondsman, and that in doing so, what lordship in fact demonstrated was its dependence, giving rise to the beginnings of the bondsman's wisdom, the seed of antithesis and eventual sublation. Orlando Patterson argues differently. The master was not so dependent upon the slave. True, "the degradation of the slave nurtured the master's sense of honor," but "as a ready object for the exercise of his sense of power." And beyond the relationship of master and slave lay the free white population who shared in the collective honor of the master class (99). An ambivalent black minority and a timocratic white majority were tough nuts for rebellious slaves to crack.

Still, Southampton slaveholders could not rest easy. Turner said he had only given up hope "for the present" (Gray 17). The dialectic was disjunctive rather than non-existent. It might lurch back again. To secure their lifeworld, slaveholders had their own work of death to do.

Here too we see strategy ascendant over tactics. Retribution was not immediate—there was no continuation of *massacre* in the form of an answering mass *atrocity*. Revenge killings certainly took place, but as David Allmendinger has recently shown, they were not legion (289–299). Rather, the slaveholders' work of death was in Certeau's terms a further "triumph of place" (Certeau 36). They invested in what was their established advantage, namely the *techné* of legal process, situated in a specific place, the town of Jerusalem. For Turner, the town had been an objective only because he thought arms and ammunition might be found there—resources that could buy him more time. For those he sought to destroy, the town was a different kind of resource, not temporal but spatial, a strategic knot in a net of authority that extended across all the counties of the state, and stretched above and beyond to Richmond, the state capital. As Southampton's county seat, Jerusalem was an empowered place, home to the County Court and its special trial jurisdiction of Oyer and Terminer, reserved for the capital crimes of slaves.

Jurisdiction—literally the speaking of law—is of course a spatial concept. Law is spoken from a place of authority outward to its surrounds (Dorsett and McVeigh, 14–15; McVeigh 12–13). Jurisdiction is thus of a piece with strategy. It also answered massacre in kind. The tactics of insurrectionary massacre had wrought somatic transformations on its victims; correspondingly, the court opened up the bodies of slaves to inspection. At least temporarily, massacre had stunned and invaded the lifeworld of slavery. The task of the court was to restore that lifeworld. Its process was panoptic, a resumption of mastery through sight, specifically the sight of those who had witnessed. Witnesses transformed what was alien to the lifeworld of slavery, rebellious slaves, into objects "observed and measured, and thus control[led] and 'include[d]'" within the court's "scope of vision" (Certeau 36).

Fifty-four slaves and two free men of color were either killed in the course of the Turner Rebellion or sentenced to death in its aftermath. Of the 54, 15 died in circumstances deemed atrocities by contemporary white authority. Six were bystanders, some of whom may have been implicated in the rebellion. Two were insurgents killed before capture whose bodies were mutilated. Seven were suspected insurgents killed upon capture (Allmendinger 90–95).

Fifty-five blacks appeared before the Southampton County Court on charges of participating in the rebellion. Five were free people of color, of whom one was eventually hanged. Of the 50 slaves, 43 were committed for trial, 30 were convicted and 18 were hanged. The remainder had their sentences commuted to transportation (Tragle 229–245).

All the defendants had counsel and all pleaded not guilty. The court proceeded expeditiously, not because time was of the essence to its processes, but because delay would invite the mob to substitute atrocity for the court and so undo the net of juridical authority. Trials began a week after the rebellion had collapsed. Over the next nine days, 27 defendants were tried, or 60% of the total. Most trials lasted only an hour or two. During this initial phase, 21 were condemned to death, nine with recommendations of commutation. Thereafter, the court met less frequently, and its proceedings were marked by more frequent discharges. The highlight, of course, did not arrive for ten weeks, when a bench of ten magistrates, double the required quorum, met to try Nat Turner and, inevitably, sentenced him to hang (Tragle 221–245).

In all essentials, the court did exactly what courts do in situations of social disorder. It established its authority expeditiously, administered a just measure of pain mingled with mercy, and finally answered the social demand for "closure" with righteous condemnation of the elusive ringleader. David Allmendinger holds that throughout: "In trial procedure the magistrates observed the letter of the law" (231). In other words, defendants had counsel appointed to represent them, a record of proceedings was kept, and the required quorum of five justices was always present. Some disagree. Daniel Fabricant's examination of Turner's trial alleges improprieties in criminal procedure in that case that impugned the integrity of the court (343–352). However, by his own admission, the improprieties he alleges did not amount to illegalities (350). And here we approach the heart of the matter of the legal response to massacre. The point is not that, as Fabricant puts it, "Nat's trial" or any of the other trials "must stand as a whitewash of justice." It is not that "the requirements of the law were commonly set aside ... when they came into ... conflict with the need to control blacks" (352, 353), for they were not—rather, the reverse. It was precisely "the need to control blacks" that law expressed. The court's job was to ensure that law, and not the mob, would perform control and retribution. Law was the oil in the hinge upon which the dialectic swung back from *Knecht* to *Herr*. Just as in the rebellion, here was no *indiscriminate* work of death. Indeed, the two were at one in the end—punishment—to which their work was dedicated, albeit that those punished by the rebels and by the courts were of different sorts and conditions, and were punished for different reasons.

The point is that as Southampton's answering agent of retribution, law was just like the rebels, a *perpetrator* of violence. To return to Žižek, what we have here is another "authentic moment of discovery," another "breakthrough," another moment when "a properly universal dimension *explodes from within a particular context and becomes "for-itself," and is directly experienced as universal*" (152, emphasis in original). In his own assessment of the trials, Alfred Brophy has described the magistracy as "negotiating between competing considerations of the desire for vengeance, the need for punishment to terrify future rebels, and the need for some restraint in the violence" (1862). But law here is not negotiating, it is not an arena of struggle. Moments such as this reveal law for-itself, and law for-itself does not negotiate. Rather, as Walter Benjamin puts it, "in the exercise of violence over life and death, more than in any other legal act, *the law reaffirms itself*" ("Critique" 242, emphasis added).

The usual place

> Meat is the common zone of man and the beast,
> their zone of indiscernibility.
>
> Gilles Deleuze (17)

The 18 condemned were hanged "at the usual place of execution"[3] on eight different dates in September, November, and December, 1831. Most were dead before September was half over.

Few accounts of the hangings exist. Turner's execution, the likeliest to attract attention, was marked by two abbreviated reports that squabbled over the details. In one "He exhibited the utmost composure throughout the whole ceremony ... and told the sheriff in a firm voice, that he was ready. Not a limb nor a muscle was observed to move." In the other he seemed "utterly reckless in the awful fate that awaited him, and even hurried the executioner in the performance of his duty!" (Tragle 140; *Richmond Enquirer*).

The two accounts of Turner's end offer radically different assessments of the conduct of the condemned, but both underscore the importance of witnessing to execution. This too is part of the work of death. In nineteenth-century hangings, witnessing—seeing and hearing—is a crucial element. The occasion is intended to be a public spectacle, witnessed. Still, neither report helps us understand what was actually seen. What was the actuality of hanging by the neck at the end of a rope until one died? What did it look like?

The mechanics are simple. Hanging is death by strangulation, a halter around the neck of the condemned, cinched tight by the weight of the suspended body and its struggles against suffocation. Death usually resulted from asphyxia or apoplexy rather than a ruptured spinal cord, for that required careful judgment of the length of the rope, the weight of the condemned, and the length of the drop, all rare before the second half of the century (Gatrell 45–54).

Like all the rebels, Turner was hanged from a tree branch, not a scaffold; no careful calculation of bodyweight, rope length, and drop here. This was death by slow suffocation. Compression of the neck forces blood into the brain, discoloring and swelling the face, and causing grotesque distortion of the facial features. Sometimes the eyes of the condemned would be forced part way out of their cavities, the tongue would protrude, the lower jaw would "retract," and "a bloody froth of mucous" would be forced from mouth and nostrils (Taylor 654–655). Hanging causes muscular contractions and convulsions, involuntary urination, and defecation. Men might become erect and ejaculate; women bled from the uterus. Like any other violent, mutilating death, death by hanging was physical destruction of the body. Hanging re-created the condemned as something drastically different from the human body it had been moments before: something helpless, weak, and vulnerable, "choking, pissing, and screaming" (Gatrell 30, 46).

And in Turner's case, like many before him, hanging was not the end of it. His body was to be dissected, its insides turned out, opened up for inspection. The intent was to destroy the corpse of the condemned so completely that nothing was left for burial. William Sidney Drewry, who took oral histories about the Turner Rebellion from old people in Southampton County at the turn of the twentieth century, writes that Turner's body was flayed, its flesh rendered into grease, its skin used to make mementos, and its skeleton claimed for anatomical use (102). Whether all this is actually so cannot be proven—Drewry was relying on 70-year-old memories—but it seems entirely likely, for Drewry's account conforms to the normal outcome of criminal dissection practices. In England, for example, the meat of the dissected murderer John Holloway, hanged in 1831, was separated from the bones and the skeleton was preserved for anatomical use in the Sussex County Hospital (Gatrell 69). Three years before, Suffolk General Hospital had become home for the skeleton of William Corder, hanged in Bury St. Edmunds for the murder of Maria Marten (Gatrell 257).

Corder is of particular interest, because the well-documented treatment of his body, postmortem, is as good a guide as one might obtain to the undocumented treatment of Turner's body. Cut down from the scaffold, Corder's body was taken to the Bury Shire Hall, where it was first "exposed to public view" and then opened up by the county surgeon. At length, after the body's secrets had been exposed as best they could be, attention turned to Corder's other parts. His bones were "cleared of the flesh" in preparation for rewiring as an anatomical skeleton. "A great portion of the skin has been tanned," it was reported, "and a gentlemen connected to the hospital intends to have the Trial and Memoirs of Corder bound in it" (Gatrell 256–257). The gentleman made good on his intentions. As Drewry had discovered, public hangings created a demand for souvenirs. The volume in question remains on public display to this day in a Bury St. Edmunds museum (258). Law, says Certeau, "engraves itself on parchments made from the skin of its subjects ... It makes its book out of them" (140).

The radiance of justice

> It's a Peculiar Apparatus.
>
> Franz Kafka (3)

At law's core lies the body scourged with words. Law's penalties incise the bodies of the condemned. Kafka's punishment machine wrote with a harrow. At about the sixth hour of the harrow's work, too exhausted to scream anymore, the condemned would begin slowly to comprehend his sentence. "You've seen," the Officer says to the Traveler in the story, "that it's not easy to figure out the inscription with your eyes, but our man deciphers it with his wounds." And as death approaches and realization dawns, the face of the condemned begins to glow with the radiance of justice (Kafka 11, 14; see also Minkkinen 358–359).

Massacre also scourges bodies to create text. In Southampton County, what Appadurai calls "bodily brutality perpetrated by ordinary persons against other persons with whom they may have ... previously lived in relative amity" (907) created a text that followed Semelin's "logic of the sacred through murder" to its own radiance of justice. This justice owed nothing to law; its text was one of "brutal intrusions of justice beyond law" (Žižek 178). Turner's work of death was what Walter Benjamin would later call divine violence ("Critique of Violence" 252).

Law answered massacre with its own work of death. For Hegel, punishment followed the same dialectical logic as consciousness: "crime logically implies its punishment ... the dialectic naturally moves from crime to punishment as punishment follows crime." For Hegel, in fact, crime was self-contradictory; it was "a negation of right" that "carrie[d] within itself its own negation—the reaffirmation of right through punishment" (Dubber 1583 note 33).

But law's retribution could not cancel what brutal intrusion had created. The Southampton dialectic, we have seen, was disjunctive. And this was as true of its lurch from bondsman back to lord as in its initial lurch from lord to bondsman. Punishment could not negate the crime of massacre, because massacre had not been a negation of right. Rather, massacre was a rupture of the reality endured by wretches and bandits, the reality of their enslavement; it had torn into that reality and its attendant logic of right. It had put in its place not negation, but what Alain Badiou describes as an *event*. "An event" says Badiou, "is the creation of a new possibility. An event changes not only the real, but also the possible. An event is at the level not of simple possibility, but at the level of possibility of possibility" ("Is the Word 'Communism' Forever Doomed?"; see also *Hypothesis* 182). At the level of "possibility of possibility," the dialectic's disjunctions could persist. They did.

Notes

1 To mangle is "to hack, cut, lacerate, or mutilate (a person or animal) by repeated blows; to reduce (a body, limb, etc.) by violence to a more or less unrecognizable condition." Mangle is derived from Anglo-Norman *mangler* or *mahangler*, which means to mutilate, and is likely related to *mahaignier*, to maim and perhaps the Middle Dutch *mangelen*, which means to mingle, exchange, fight, or come to grips with. *Oxford English Dictionary*, entry for "mangle," *v.*[1], etymology.

2 On the centrality of the outcast as "enemy" to Anglo-American colonization, see Tomlins 176–177. The meanings of "wretch" include both one who is an "exile," and one who is "sunk in deep distress, sorrow, misfortune, or poverty," both quite fitting in application to African slaves in Virginia. *Oxford English Dictionary*, entry for "wretch."

3 This is taken from the Southampton County Court's generic death sentence.

References

Allmendinger, David F. Jr. *Nat Turner and the Rising in Southampton County*. Johns Hopkins University Press, 2014.

Appadurai, Arjun. "Dead Certainty: Ethnic Violence in the Era of Globalization." *Development and Change*, vol. 29, 1998, pp. 905–925.

Badiou, Alain. *The Communist Hypothesis*. Verso, 2010.

——. "Is the Word 'Communism' Forever Doomed?" November 2008, www.lacan.com/essays/?page_id=323.

——. *Polemics*. Verso, 2006.

Benjamin, Walter. "Critique of Violence." In *Walter Benjamin: Selected Writings*. Edited by Bullock and Jennings, Harvard University Press, 2004, pp. 236–252.

——. "On the Program of the Coming Philosophy." In *Walter Benjamin Selected Writings*. Edited by Bullock and Jennings. Harvard University Press, 2004, pp. 100–110.

Brophy, Alfred L. "The Nat Turner Trials." *North Carolina Law Review*, vol. 91, no. 5, 2013, pp. 1817–1880.

Browning, Christopher R. *Ordinary Men: Reserve Police Battalion 101 and the Final Solution in Poland*. Harper, 1993.

Buck-Morss, Susan. *Hegel, Haiti, and Universal History*. University of Pittsburgh Press, 2009.

Bullock, Marcus and Michael W. Jennings, eds. *Walter Benjamin: Selected Writings, Volume 1, 1913–1926*. Harvard University Press, 2004.

Certeau, Michel de. *The Practice of Everyday Life*. Translated by Steven Rendall. University of California Press, 1984.

Cole, Andrew. "What Hegel's Master/Slave Dialectic Really Means." *Journal of Medieval and Early Modern Studies*, vol. 34, no. 3, 2004, pp. 577–610.

Corbin, Alain, *The Village of Cannibals: Rage and Murder in France, 1870*. Harvard University Press, 1992.

DeLeuze, Gilles. *Francis Bacon*. Continuum, 2005.

Dorsett, Shaunnagh, and Sean McVeigh. *Jurisdiction*. Routledge, 2012.

Drewry, William Sidney. *The Southampton Insurrection*. The Neale Company, 1900.

Dubber, Markus Dirk. "Rediscovering Hegel's Theory of Crime and Punishment." *Michigan Law Review*, vol. 92, no. 6, 1994, pp. 1577–1621.

Ellison, Ralph et al. "The Uses of History in Fiction." *Southern Literary Journal*, vol. 1, no. 2, 1969, pp. 57–90.

Fabricant, Daniel S. "Thomas R. Gray and William Styron: Finally, A Critical Look at the 1831 *Confessions of Nat Turner*." *American Journal of Legal History*, vol. 37, no. 3, 1993, pp. 332–361.

Faust, Drew Gilpin. *This Republic of Suffering: Death and the American Civil War*. Vintage, 2009.

Gatrell, V.A.C. *The Hanging Tree: Execution and the English People, 1770–1868*. Oxford University Press, 1994.

Genovese, Eugene D. "William Styron's *The Confessions of Nat Turner*: A Meditation on Evil, Redemption, and History." In *Novel History: Historians and Novelists Confront America's Past (and Each Other)*. Edited by Mark C. Carnes. Simon & Schuster, 2001, pp. 209–219.

Girard, René. *Violence and the Sacred*. Johns Hopkins University Press, 1977.

Gray, Thomas Ruffin. *The Confessions of Nat Turner, the Leader of the Late Insurrection in Southampton, Va. As fully and voluntarily made to Thomas R. Gray, in the prison where he was confined, and acknowledged by him to be such when read before the Court of Southampton … &c.* Lucas & Deaver, 1831.

Hegel, Georg Wilhelm Friedrich. *The Phenomenology of Mind.* Translated by J.B. Baillie. Harper & Row, 1967.

Hinton, Alexander Laban. *Why Did They Kill? Cambodia in the Shadow of Genocide.* University of California Press, 2005.

Kafka, Franz. *In the Penal Colony.* Translated by Ian Johnston. Kartindo Books, 2013.

Levene, Mark. "Introduction." In *The Massacre in History.* Edited by Mark Levene and Penny Roberts, Berghahn Books, 1999, pp. 1–38.

Madley, Benjamin. "Reexamining the American Genocide Debate: Meaning, Historiography, and New Methods." *American Historical Review*, vol. 120, no. 1, 2015, pp. 98–139.

"Mangle." *Oxford English Dictionary*, www.oed.com.

McVeigh, Sean. ed. *Jurisprudence of Jurisdiction.* Routledge-Cavendish, 2007.

Merari, Ariel. "Terrorism as a Strategy of Insurgency." *Terrorism and Political Violence*, vol. 5, no. 4, 1993, pp. 213–251.

Minkkinen, Panu. "The Radiance of Justice: On the Minor Jurisprudence of Franz Kafka." *Social & Legal Studies*, vol. 3, no. 3, 1994, pp. 349–363.

Mohamed, Saira. "Of Monsters and Men: Perpetrator Trauma and Mass Atrocity." *Columbia Law Review*, vol. 115, no. 5, 2015, pp. 1157–1216.

Patterson, Orlando. *Slavery and Social Death: A Comparative Study.* Harvard University Press, 1982.

Pleasants, John Hampden. "Dispatch to the *Constitutional Whig*." August 25, 1831. In Tragle, *Southampton Slave Revolt*, pp. 50–52.

Rawick, George P. ed. *The American Slave: A Composite Autobiography.* Greenwood Press, 1972–1979.

Richmond Enquirer, November 18, 1831.

Scott, James C. *Seeing Like a State: How Certain Schemes to Improve the Human Condition Have Failed.* Yale University Press, 1998.

Semelin, Jacques. "In Consideration of Massacres." *Journal of Genocide Research*, vol. 3, no. 3, 2001, pp. 377–389.

——. *Purify and Destroy: The Political Uses of Massacre and Genocide.* Columbia University Press, 2007.

——. "Toward a Vocabulary of Massacre and Genocide." *Journal of Genocide Research*, vol. 5, no. 2, 2003, pp. 193–210.

Southampton County Court, *Minute Book.* 1830–1835. www.brantleyassociation.com/southampton_project/southampton_project_list.htm#Court_Minute_Books.

Taylor, Alfred Swaine. *The Principles and Practice of Medical Jurisprudence.* John Churchill & Sons, 1865.

Tomlins, Christopher. *Freedom Bound: Law, Labor, and Civic Identity in Colonizing English America, 1580–1865.* Cambridge University Press, 2010.

Tragle, Henry Irving. ed. *The Southampton Slave Revolt of 1831: A Compilation of Source Material.* University of Massachusetts Press, 1971.

Wise, John Sergeant, *The End of an Era.* Boston: Houghton, Mifflin Company, 1899.

"Wretch." *Oxford English Dictionary*, www.oed.com.

Žižek, Slavoj. *Violence: Six Sideways Reflections.* Picador, 2008.

Chapter 7

Civilizing missions and humanitarian interventions

Into the laws and territories of First Nations

Irene Watson

Introduction

For First Nations Peoples, the matrix of colonial power remains a fixture on our territories and colonial violence has never ended. This is the cruel and inhuman, the ongoing colonial project. In this chapter I write about the impact of the colonial project on the continent now known as Australia. After their "discovery," the First Nations Peoples' lands later dubbed "Australia" were landmarked by Cook for a military takeover;[1] the doctrine of *terra nullius*—the lands belonged to nobody—ensured that they became sites where acts of violence were sanctioned. Violence was deemed a necessary part of civilizing missions by the conquerors, intent upon "saving" the "natives" from our "native selves." In Australia, it was widespread and essentially it was acts of violence which founded the Australian colonial states. The following is one example of attitudes which propelled colonial foundation violence; it is an excerpt from an 1840 speech given by Governor Gawler with respect to the introduction of the *Bill to Deal with Aboriginal Evidence in Court*:

> The British constitution is the growth of a thousand years; it cannot be imposed on a nation in a day. It is adapted for Britain—the country which stands highest in the world in the scale of religion, civilization, and improvement; it cannot be fully received or properly appreciated even by civilized nations of an inferior class, much less by the savages of Australia, who stand in the lowest degree in all the earth in religion, government, arts, and civilization. In all these respects they are morally, as in material things they are physically, the antipodes of Britain—and it is not an easy thing to make antipodes meet.
>
> ("Legislation" 2–3)[2]

There was no intention to make a meeting of the First Nations Peoples and the invader, but rather to eradicate the savage by force of arms and then to gather the survivors into missions to be "civilized" and ultimately assimilated into a slave-like identity. Our ancestors were intended to become a future workforce for the new colonies.

Our ancestors experienced a violent colonial frontier, and this body of violence conducted since the invasion of 1836 (and even earlier) has been translated into colonial law; violence was the foundation of the colonial legal system and is now integral to Australian law. Thinking and talking about our ancestors as native savages is of the past, but it was the fabric and the foundation of the colonial legal system then. Now that same preoccupation with the native—still deemed dysfunctional—continues and still resonates a colonial violence. It remains the foundation of the contemporary Australian legal system, and acts of colonial violence are ongoing. And "civilizing missions" continue, but they go under new names—one such being "humanitarian state intervention." But by whatever name they go, they still translate as acts of violence intended to maintain control over the lives and territories of First Nations.

The foundation of the Australian colonial project embodies an "originary violence" in which the state retains a vested interest in maintaining the founding order of things. Inequalities and iniquities are maintained for the purpose of sustaining the life and continuity of the state, and this I have argued[3] occurred again when the Australian Commonwealth enacted the Northern Territory Emergency Response Act 2007 (known as the NT Intervention). The history of the power and force of Australian colonialism fits well with the argument that the origins of law are in violence.[4] However, it is apparent that the same theory does not concern the origins of First Nations laws.[5] Our laws are known to us as being of the land and the natural world which we exist within. Relationality is at the core of our being and we know of ourselves in relation to all things in our natural world. So the law constitutes our relationship to all that we live with.

The capacity to hold our relationship with law has been affected by the colonial project, but many of us nevertheless retain it and hold our law ways despite this. Colonialism's military power became legitimized as law, and that law became deemed to be universal—as though no other way of being law-full is known to the world. The laws of the colonizing states have been taken up as being of universal application, and thus laws founded in violence were legitimized in both the colonially constructed domestic state law and international law. Derrida wrote on "law" as though its acknowledged origins were a universal phenomenon. But they were not, for First Nations had and still have a way not violence-founded, but law-full. However, while the power of the colonizers has framed and constructed itself as being "law," the laws of the afflicted First Nations have been portrayed as non-existent. Nonetheless, they are still here, but the ways of the colonized and the colonizer are different. First Nations know law differently. The laws of First Nations originate in Kaldowinyeri.[6] Kaldowinyeri is a place of creation or as our songs record, the time of the first sunrise, and a place of law-fullness.

In "Australia," "civilizing missions" have occurred since the 1788 British invasion of New South Wales, and the colonizers are still at it, but the civilizing missions are now known as "human rights interventions of the state." Armed with the idea that they are enacted in the "best interests" of Indigenous Peoples, they continue to this day to enable the processes of colonialism. In 2007, the

Australian federal government used a trumped-up mainstream media campaign which focused on the "dysfunctional" conditions in which First Nations live in the Northern Territory to move in on the existing Aboriginal Land Rights (Northern Territory) 1976 structures, which enabled collective recognition of the land rights of traditional owners.[7] In the "best interests" of Aboriginal women and children, international and domestic laws originally enacted to prevent racial discrimination were suspended.[8] Further to this, Aboriginal Land Rights legislation was overridden by the Commonwealth package of Northern Territory Emergency Response laws.[9] In 2016, nine years later, the Australian emergency response laws in respect of the Northern Territory remain in force while the United Nations' criticism of their limits and legitimacy continues to be ignored by the Australian state. In this instance, the state went in under the cover of "humanitarian intervention," but in my view the actual intention was an extension of the colonial project, revealing similarities with Cook's military mission in the 1770s. I argue that there was always and continues to this day to be a vested interest in keeping the colonial project alive, and that is why the events, such as so called "human-rights interventions," will continue to be enacted, so as to retain the colonial hierarchies.[10] This chapter will critique current positions and attempts to limit the colonial project, and the violence which always attends it.

Kaldowinyeri is law

Many First Nations Peoples have different knowledges of the origins of law. We know that law is everywhere in the land and the natural world. We are belonging to and surrounded by law. We are in relationships with law, and all of those relationships are by humans as beings of law and all living things are beings of law.[11]

The laws of the colonial states are hierarchical and understand life forms as being of property and not of themselves. Breaches of First Nations' law occur on a daily basis within colonial states—in the form of environmental degradation, acts of ecocide, and acts of genocide, the removal of our children, assimilation policies and cruel and inhuman punishments as a result of the over-imprisonment of Indigenous Peoples.[12] But if we listen, we can hear law-full voices speaking back against violations of First Nations' laws. First Peoples are well able to comment on the nature of colonial laws; colonialism was imposed upon us by force, our old people felt that force, and today we continue to feel it. We feel the effects of colonial power, but it is not operating within our law—it is a force which intends our annihilation and it cannot be law as First Nations Peoples' epistemologies would have it framed. Even if we can call colonial power "law," its constructed regulations are sourced in the violence of the colonial project itself, and it is a thing which has been legitimized and maintained by its own inherent violence. How is this law? We know law differently and there is no universal way of knowing law.

Why is colonial power called law? The military deployments of colonial powers enabled the baggage of their imported "laws" to be passed off as legitimate, but in truth they emerged from that military power. The invaders ignored the law of First Peoples as if it was nothing, and stated repeatedly that there were no laws before their arrival. The empty "terra nullius" space was construed in the places where our ancient laws existed—and still exist.

Walter Benjamin's way of knowing was from a European center and his pronouncement of laws' violent origins derives from a Euro-centered space.[13] What did he know or not know of First Peoples and how relevant is Euro-centered thinking to the dilemma of colonization and First Peoples? As a First Nations scholar, I have experienced and know the violent origins of colonial power, and also know and see that another way of being exists and has done since time immemorial. The laws set up by the colonial powers became universalized by the debates between those powers and grew into contemporary international law. And they ignore those other ways, pre-colonial ways of being. The fact that they have been ignored notwithstanding, these ways still survive today; still under duress, but they nevertheless survive.[14]

The people of many First Nations have been with and part of our lands from the time of the first sunrise.[15] We have had our own names for the land, but after the invasions and dispossessions, our natural world has become known by other names: Australia, Canada, the US, New Zealand, etc. Yet, in spite of colonial violence, many of our ancient names have survived these annihilating and renaming processes. My people, the Milmenrura of the Tanganekald, have held on to our name, even though following the colonial application of martial law in the 1840s, my ancestors were hunted down in what became known as the Coorong massacres and our population was decimated. The intent of colonialism was the death of our peoples, our identities, and our ancient names.[16] Many have gone, but many have also survived. The imperialists mapped the world and translated north as being at the top and south at the bottom, creating a geographical hierarchy. We also know that a Euro-centered view of the world once took it to be flat; interestingly, our old people always knew that planet earth was a sphere, a cyclical body of law and motion.

Some see their world as the normative and other ways of knowing as strange. Our old people observed hawks carrying fire sticks to ignite bush to flush out prey; they observed that the lighting of fire was for survival, for food, and that bird and human equally shared ways of being alive. We learnt fire-stick farming[17] from our relation—the Kirrakee, or Brown Hawk, for she and we are at one in our sharing of life and knowledges. Evidence of our ways is found in our languages. How many words are there in any number of First Nations languages which are used to describe a natural phenomenon, such as clouds? Some nations use as many as 52 words. And this is while the English language has many more words for killing, slaughter, torture, and many others that are related to violence (Means and Johnson 6). Ontological and epistemological differences are evident and can be located in language. Similar deep knowledges of the relationships between people and the earth were once held in the places now known as Europe, but were lost and are now translated as myth—not real, not law, and having no real connection and relationships to other beings.

From violence to recognition

In other works, I have considered the effect of state and international law for contemplating the possibilities for "indigenous recognition";[18] I have argued that what are represented as laws of recognition[19] have the potential to derail and disempower First Nations' struggles for both our freedom from colonialism and increase the risk of genocide. Genocide manifests in the body of state assimilationist laws and policies. Discussed arrangements, which would affect an illusion of recognition, would not mean any real possibility of a freedom to decolonize on First Nations' terms and from within our laws, cultures, languages, and frameworks. Conjuring illusions of recognition enables states to appear as though they are protecting the interests of First Peoples, in keeping with the civilizing mission. But the fallout from this position carries its own colonial violence and madness. How could "rights recognition" be a bad thing? Or, alternatively, what is so wrong with the opportunity being offered to Indigenous Peoples to assimilate? What is wrong is that assimilation—becoming like them—is genocide and it works against the survival of distinct First Nations Peoples.

First Nations Peoples have not sought recognition of who we are; we know who we are. First Nations' dialogues with colonial states, the United Nations, and other international institutions has been a process of seeking avenues for peace, survival, and relief from the genocidal effects of the colonial project[20] that is still grinding on. We continue to seek mechanisms which will provide relief from the assimilatory-genocidal processes of the colonial states, but the talk of recognition remains just that—talk—because recognition by the colonial powers seems to provide no avenue to anywhere other than back into the corridors of assimilation into the colonial state. The idea of First Nations seeking "recognition" from the colonial states negates the truth: we have always been on our territories and we were here first. First Nations have our own names, our own languages, and our own territories, laws, peoples, and ways of being in the world. However, the alternative narrative, this "truth" of the colonizer continues to be constructed: the "natives" need to be seeking recognition. Recognition of what? Of our humanity? We know we are human, but we also know that the human is only one part of life; the simple "rights of the human" cannot exist in isolation. Our ways of thinking are different from those who have led and still maintain the colonial project. Why would we appeal for recognition: just to enable a better fit into the assimilatory project of the state? We are already, we have been here forever. Why would one seek recognition from the colonial state which has no real concept of who we are? What does it mean to be recognized by the very culture which intends our demise? Would recognition enable us to become more like the colonial society, to fit into the web of the genocidists? Would it better enable us to be no longer native and related to the land, but instead separated, fragmented, and civilized, aliens too? And what is it which could be recognized? What is the will of the state,—could it recognize our being beyond that of a people who can only ever be absorbed and assimilated? Many First Nations resist the politics of recognition and resist the idea that we are in need of civilization, that we are unsettled peoples in need of settlement and assimilation. In this space of resistance we continue to say: "we have always been and we will always be, in relation to our lands and laws."

We are ancient peoples who have shared relations with hundreds of other First Nations and we are by our names and connections to our country evidence of those relations with country and with each other. We are the First Peoples of places which originated inter-nation relationships. We are the first internationals—but we are different from those whom we know now as international states. And again, the history of our inter-national cooperation with each other is unacknowledged, "unrecognized," buried by the myths of *terra nullius*, and another part of that ignoring of the fact of our existence in any form at all.

So we resist, and this resistance takes many forms. An obvious one is to challenge the idea that the center of our world is Europe and European epistemologies. Since the time of colonization, the idea that Europe is the center of all worthwhile thought has dominated, and a significant resistance to hierarchical ways of knowing the world has taken the form of centering First Nations' epistemologies instead. This move challenges the idea that there is no horizon other than the European and the European colonial matrix which currently dominates the human rights recognition agenda. It is also a challenge to the idea of a Eurocentric universal and that that is all there is.

Much of the literature and discussion concerning the recognition of indigenous rights is anthropocentrically centered on a colonially constructed identity. Our First Nations which were enclosed by that now called Australia were bound by song lines. The songs held the peace and the boundaries between the nations, and were respected and upheld; that was the law. But as we know at the invasion, our laws were translated differently and were deemed "terra nullius" and non-sovereign. And the native was deemed not-human, and thus fell outside colonial frameworks of recognition. Anghie noted that "the history of the non-European states is told principally in terms of the civilizing mission" (21) and colonial states are still in the business of initiating and controlling discourses on the subject of Indigenous recognition. More recently within Australia, the discussion about possible constitutional recognition of First Nations is out there for public consumption.[21] What it means beyond the *terra nullius* narrative is as yet unknown, but there is little to suggest that it means much more than the continuation of that same narrative: the *terra nullius* body dressed as "recognition." Nothing will have changed. The *terra nullius* fabrication continues to cover the raw law of our ancestors and will continue to do so until a process of decolonization occurs and we begin again.

Current debates on "recognition" within the colonists' circles have no interest in acknowledging that the lands stolen—the vast continents stolen—did not belong to people in a proprietorial enslaved way, but that we belonged in our ancient relationships with the land. And there is no interest in acknowledging that discredited doctrines of discovery and *terra nullius* underpin the foundations of these contemporary settler states. The subject of First Nations' laws falls outside colonial-state discourses of recognition, because it has the potential to unsettle and fracture their unlawful foundations; as such, it is avoided (*Mabo v. Queensland* 30).

Violence by other names

The violent acts of old were intentional acts of genocide; the acts which continue today still intend genocide, but take other forms. Much has been made of the "stolen generations" of the past, but the forcible removal of First Nations' children continues. Now it takes place under the guise of state welfare policies deemed to be in the best interests of the children. Past acts of genocide were not named as such then and the contemporary acts are not now. Now being characterized as in "their" best interests, they are still part of a program of forced assimilation, and that is an act of genocide. In Australia, however, it is passed off as legitimate and in the name of the progress of the underdeveloped.

What is deemed genocide in other places is here translated as a "civilizing mission" for the native. In truth, it is not about "the best interest of the native," but more about enabling the ongoing colonial project to profit from First Nations' resources and cultures. The laws of the colonialists are not about rights or recognition, but more about maintaining a "rights and recognition" project which will keep the world open to further exploitation and harvesting. From the beginning of the colonial project, punishment of First Nations Peoples was essential and necessary to its success. The public face was the mission of civilization, purported to bring "light" to native lives, but the cover of civility was used to justify discovery, *terra nullius* determinations, invasions, and war. These methods were deployed to steal, plunder, and dispossess us of our land. More than punishment, the "civilizing mission" was the attempted annihilation of Indigenous Peoples. In Australia, the imposing ideology of "terra nullius" was translated to mean that our peoples did not exist, but was also realized to mean that our lawfulness as First Nations was denied and erased.

Similarly, the wholesale colonial state annexations of First Nations' territories and resources were promoted as being necessary to save the natives from "their own inherent savagery." It was (and is) a curious leap of logic—that the price of our "civilization" was the total forfeiture of our living spaces and culture, and that by that we would become better. But still, that was (and is) the demand: all ways of the native were to change; the need for change was legitimized by the invader settler society's perception of heathen, backward peoples. Those who survived the frontier violence were to be assimilated and absorbed. And although this was the plan—by the nineteenth century, the British had almost decided that slavery was against popular opinion, so colonial utterances (on paper) had to be "reformist"—the reality for us was often slavery. After all, what better way to occupy landless indigents? The policies of the past and those of the contemporary contexts are not dissimilar; a cruel and potent violence lies within them all.[22] In Australia, the colonial frontier killing fields are history, but they have been replaced by new ways of killing the natives. In this context, there is no limit to the progress of the colonial project, only an insatiable appetite for the others' territories and resources. And now that most of earth's territories have been colonized and are being mined, we now observe, incredulous, the intentions behind the promotions of space travel.

When we look around for powers committed to supporting and upholding the position of First Nations, there are very few. When we consulted the United Nations (given as it was to lofty, embracing sentiments) and its recent development of the United Nations Declaration on the Rights of Indigenous Peoples (UNDRIP), we soon realized that this document is able to do very little beyond smoothing the pillow of a perceived dying set of problems and ushering in the inevitable assimilation of the global population of First Nations. The reference to self-determination in the UNDRIP is hollow, as the opportunities for member states to relinquish power and to enable self-determination are limited by Article 46, which ensures that the interpretation of the UNDRIP remains limited by and within the domestic paradigm of the state.[23]

Many appeals for recognition under international law have been made by First Nations and all have thus far failed, mainly because international law—from a statist perspective—has been created by and in the interests of colonialism itself. International law grew out of the distinctions made between civilized and non-civilized states, and those distinctions enabled and confirmed that international law applied only within a civilized "family of nations." The UNDRIP does little to shift the confinement of First Nations from the "domestic paradigm" of an occupying settler state. Charmaine White Face provides a critique of the UNDRIP and of how it performs as a domestic instrument in the hands of state power. Currently, there is no possibility of international mechanisms providing relief from the pressures of colonialism, due to colonialism's constituting in and being foundational to international law. In colonialism's shaping of international law, its refusal to recognize the laws of First Nations, and the concomitant disasters which entail, we are left to consider the following question: is it possible that we might reconstruct international law so that it is liberated from its colonial origins? Recentering Indigenous law would be a good basis on which to start, but the limitations of the current framework of international law and the further problems around accounting for the impact of colonialism on First Nations Peoples makes any shift difficult to achieve.

Different laws—different origins

There is no universal approach to law's origins; our Peoples grew from the first sunrise when the magpies raised the sky and light fell on the earth; our laws were not founded in violence. There is no universal principle of law's foundations, but many have claimed that a universal fusion has made them, and us, one. First laws are still alive and stand apart, separate from coloniality.

The impact of colonial violence on the lives of First Nations is long in our history, but we had a life and cultures before the invasion of our territories and the colonial projects set up shop. To reiterate, First Nations' legal systems do not originate on violent foundations. Our law songs and stories teach about a different way of being in the world, a way not stranded in the past, but living in the continuing present. The law is the law is the law, it just is. Kaldowinyeri—the "dreaming"—means law, and its meaning involves the story of how law unfolds. First Nations' laws are not imposed; peoples live with law. Law is known; there is no "mystical foundation of authority" in law. We are all related and live in relationship to law; law is intimately known and founded in the environment which surrounds us. However, the frame which the colonial states use to deny Indigenous Peoples as beings of law is that Kaldowinyeri is perceived as being other-worldly, not exactly real, inhabiting the realm of myth and story, but many First Nations Peoples know a way in which song is the foundation of law. It survives under the duress of becoming further obscured, reconstructed, and contained by colonialism.

Colonial law's origins are sourced in the violence of the colonial project, a history which cannot be erased. The politics of recognition, the reconstruction of a property law right (as in Mabo), or even the signing of treaties (none of which has yet happened in Australia) cannot erase the history of the horrors of colonialism. Violent foundations have enabled, legitimized, and constructed the current framework of "recognition" and its limits. But power upheld by violence to construct and name law is not lawful. International law is known as law, but it is sourced in colonialism; colonialism made that which is now "international law."

I am advocating rethinking law. Western law systems are violent in their origins: why translate the lawlessness of coloniality into the world's authority? First Nations' laws are not violent in their origins; I have argued, from a First Nations position, that law is not power and violence. To acquiesce to the idea of law's authority being mandated by violence is to ignore other ways of being; it is to confirm that the only way of being is sourced in violence, and doing so raises the following question: is that all there was and will be?

Contemporary examples of the ongoing life of the colonial project are evident in state interventions within First Nations' territories and as in the past; these interventions enable an unlawful foundation to continue wielding its power. Contemporary human rights interventions serve as re-enactments of the original invasion of our territories. In the past, colonial powers attempted to explain that their interventions were legitimized as being in the best interests of the native and they still do.

First Nations' ongoing experience of cruel and unusual violence

The colonial project's use of violence has changed little across the centuries of the colonial project; in the past, frontier violence was a process of war, massacre, and incarceration, all used to reduce numbers and the capacity to resist. Today incarceration, which carries its own species of violence, is the main method used to control First Nations. Outright massacres have slowed, but "humanitarian interventions" are still in full usage to control the lives of First Nations Peoples—where and how we live—and the threat of death, by "accident" or "in custody," is still ever-present. Contemporary mechanisms of control are not so different from those which were applied in the past; they still work their violent effect. Up until the 1960s, across the Australian states, the Aborigines Acts determined every aspect of our lives and how those lives were lived. We woke to the sound of the bell, children were separated from kin, and our lives were either contained within Aboriginal reserves or we were thrust out, banished. Contemporary interventionist laws, reminiscent of the past, still control how people are going to live, and all this is done and declared in our "best interests" and is seen as taking action to protect "human rights." Cruelty, violence, punishment: is it unusual? Within the scope of the colonial project, it is quite methodical, quite typical. And very little distinction exists between the various methods used across the centuries; they were all aimed at the same objective. Violence was and continues to be used to legitimize and normalize the settler states' unlawful foundations, and to control and contain the First Nations in order to enable the colonizers' occupations and harvesting of our stolen territories.

The formal declaration of decolonization has not ended the colonial project, it has merely provided the illusion of a decolonized globe which is more than ever ravaged by colonialism (Anghie 32). Yet in spite of this, First Nations ways survive and still run. It is the classic knot of colonial "impossibility" and First Nations' resistance and survival of what is "known" to be impossible.

Concluding remarks

Some may consider this work to be entirely bleak. I disagree. It is instead, in my view, an optimistic approach to a future which project "progress" lays at the feet of humanity. First Nations' thinking is different to that which posits laws being founded in violence and as a result positions another way of thinking about the world. This difference offers an opportunity to think about how we might create a system of non-imperialist, non-hierarchical laws, of the international, and laws which redress global suffering and genocide. I am confident and optimistic because many First Nations already have a way of being and a model for nations living together in peace and non-violence. Before Cook, there were hundreds of distinct First Nations living on the continent now known as Australia who held ancient systems of law and had lived side by side for thousands of years; this ancient international legal system secured the life of hundreds of distinct nations. We know our history from our ancient songs which record our laws and their origins in the natural world without the necessity for conquest of each other.

In thinking on what is to be done, simply, we need only to continue to be who we already are—First Nations Peoples—and to become more of who we are as we gain the space and places to simply be ourselves. To enable that space, there is a need for colonialism to take its boot off our necks, so that we are able, with all other life forms, to breathe, to breathe life back into the spaces and places of our old ones, and to breathe life back into the center, as the earth has done, as the law has done, forever. To simply continue to be who we are. This may appear impossible, but it is from where we began and still remain. It is a way which has worked for thousands of years in our past and it will continue to work—for that is the law. Perhaps the colonialists may learn to "be realistic, demand what they see as the impossible" so that we may live (Nancy 100).[24]

The experiences of cruel and inhuman punishments remain for First Nations People, and these will continue as long as the colonial project continues to be empowered. At present, there is no end in sight. Advice as to what might bring about its ending is as old as the colonial project itself: our old people have always spoken back, speaking up the peace and offering ways for the colonizer to come back into the territories of First Nations in peace. In Australia, more than 200 years after they shot their way in, we are still here offering them the same advice. That advice hasn't been properly heard, so we continue to demand: we must begin again, not with "recognition," but with a smoking,[25] a cleansing, and a teaching of the laws of the lands, and then perhaps when the colonizers understand our ways and our laws, they will find a way of freedom from their own violent foundations.

Notes

1 See Cook's secret instructions to take possession of Native lands: www.foundingdocs.gov.au/resources/transcripts/nsw1_doc_1768.pdf.
2 A quote taken from the proceedings of the South Australian Council, September 25, 1840. South Australia was invaded by colonizers in 1836 following the passing of the British South Australia Act of 1836, and the Parliamentary system of the colony of South Australia was established in 1856.
3 See Watson, "In the Northern Territory Intervention" 45.
4 See Derrida 927, 931, 943, and 971–977.
5 While I write from my history, that of the Tanganekald, Meintangk, and Boandik Peoples of the south-east of South Australia (and without speaking for) other First Nations of "Australia" and elsewhere, similar positions exist regarding the laws of First Nations of other regions, that is, they are also founded in relationality.
6 A word of the Tanganekald language, meaning law-full way. It is more commonly translated by the colonizer as the "dreaming"; this provides a limited understanding of Kaldowinyeri, one contained by myth and story, which also negates its core meaning as being about law.
7 The campaign drew upon a report on violence in Aboriginal communities in the Northern Territory, prepared by Wild and Anderson.
8 A Request for Urgent Action was made by a group of First Nations Peoples living under the effects of the Northern Territory Intervention to the UN Committee on the Elimination of Racial Discrimination in February 2009. The Request for Urgent Action argued that the suspension by the Commonwealth of Australia of the Racial Discrimination Act 1975 and the Australian government's failure to consult adequately with affected Aboriginal communities violated arts 2, 5, 6 and 7 of the Convention on the Elimination of All Forms of Racial

Discrimination (opened for signature 21 December 1965, UNTS 660, entered into force 4 January 1969). The Request for Urgent Action resulted in a request by the Chairperson of the Committee for the Elimination of All Forms of Racial Discrimination that the Australian government lift its suspension of the Racial Discrimination Act. The government was also requested to redesign the measures of the "emergency response" in consultation with the Aboriginal communities affected by the legislation.

9 Amendments made to the Aboriginal Land Rights (Northern Territory) Act 2006 created 99-year individual leases over lands which were previously held under the Land Rights Act as communal ownership, while decision making regarding traditional lands has shifted from traditional owners back to administrative control held by the Commonwealth government.

10 For a further discussion of the intervention, see Watson, "In the Northern Territory Intervention."

11 For a discussion of Aboriginal Law, see Watson, *Aboriginal Peoples*.

12 In recent years, the Australian state has held inquiries into state child removal policies of the nineteenth and twentieth centuries; these were reported in the Australian Human Rights and Equal Opportunities Commission (HREOC) report (Wilson), which raised the question of genocide, in the form of forced removal of Aboriginal children from their nations. See also Reynolds for an historical approach to genocide in Australia; and for a more recent account, see Watson, "Genocide, the State, and Original First Nations." The contemporary picture is in fact no better; Aboriginal children are still removed, by way of the criminal justice system. Juvenile detention statistics within Australia reveal the highly disproportionate levels, compared to non Indigenous juveniles, of First Nations children incarcerated. Australian Bureau of Statistics data shows that in 2012–2013, the daily average detention rate for Aboriginal and Torres Strait Islander young people was 364.8 per 100,000 10–17 year olds. This was around 24 times the rate for non-Indigenous young people (15.4 per 100,000 10–17 year olds) (quoted in Steering Committee for the Review of Government Service Provision 4.100); see also Richards; and Weatherburn. Nationally, 14 267 Aboriginal and Torres Strait Islander children were on care and protection orders at June 30, 2013. The rate for Aboriginal and Torres Strait Islander children increased from 11.3 per 1,000 children at June 30, 2004 to 49.3 per 1,000 children at June 30, 2013 (quoted in Steering Committee for the Review of Government Service Provision 4.81). The removal of Aboriginal children from their families by welfare agencies is also increasing dramatically, with rates comparable to the worst times in history.

13 Benjamin, writing during the rise of Nazism in Europe, was a German Jewish philosopher who argued that the first function of violence is its law-making function. Violence's second function, he theorizes, is its "law preserving function" (*Reflections* 284).

14 An idea Benjamin might have discounted as being the "dogma of sacredness" ("On the Critique of Violence" 26).

15 One of our songs of the first sunrise is sung by the magpies, their song is sung again and again, and will always be sung while the magpie still sings.

16 For an early legal account of the issues which arose regarding the illegality of invoking martial law against the Milmenrura, see Lendrum.

17 Fire-stick farming was a land management practice which was applied across the continent of Aboriginal Australia (for an introductory discussion, see Gammage). This way of living with the land was demonized just days after 9/11, in an article by journalist Paul Toohey.

18 See Watson, *Aboriginal Peoples*.

19 For example, the laws of native title and heritage protection do not provide First Nations with the power to care for country in the ways in which we are obliged to do so, but are rather laws intended to assimilate First Nations into the Australian property law system.
20 An example of these processes is found in the early negotiations concerning the drafting of the United Nations Declaration on the Rights of Indigenous Peoples, (UNDRIP); however, these processes have had a limited impact on offsetting assimilation. For further discussion on these limitations, see Venne.
21 A Commonwealth of Australia, Joint Select Committee on Constitutional Recognition of Aboriginal and Torres Strait Islander Peoples held an inquiry into constitutional recognition: see www.aph.gov.au/Parliamentary_Business/Committees/Joint/Constitutional_Recognition_of_Aboriginal_and_Torres_Strait_Islander_Peoples.
22 The persistence of colonialism has been masked by postcolonial theory; "postcolonial" is a loaded term, used loosely, and as Spivak notes, the term "postcolonialism" itself "is like throwing words around and is as meaningless as the idea of decolonization—that is, the idea is thrown around without being based in any truth of decolonization or moving beyond the event of colonialism" (quoted in Watson, *Aboriginal Peoples* 25).
23 The idea of the domestic paradigm has been deployed in the work of Isabelle Schulte-Tenckhoff.
24 The phrase was coined in 1967 by "Che" Guevara.
25 Aboriginal smoking ceremonies are an ancient law-full process, which continues to this day. Ceremonies are continued for the purpose of cleansing the space, so as to enable life to go on in a law-full way.

References

Aboriginal Land Rights (Northern Territory) Act. Commonwealth of Australia, 2006.

Anghie, Antony. *Imperialism, Sovereignty and the Making of International Law*. Cambridge University Press, 2008.

Benjamin, Walter. "On the Critique of Violence." In *One-Way Street and Other Writings*. By Benjamin. Translated by J.A. Underwood. Penguin, 2009.

——. *Reflections*. Schocken Books, 1986.

Derrida, Jacques. "Force of Law: The Mystical Foundation of Authority." *Cardozo Law Review*, vol. 11, 1990, pp. 920–1046.

Gammage, Bill. *The Biggest Estate on Earth: How Aborigines Made Australia*. Allen & Unwin, 2011.

"Legislation for the Natives," *Southern Australian*, October 2, 1840, pp. 2–3.

Lendrum, S.D. "The Coorong Massacre: Martial Law and the Aborigines at First Settlement." *Adelaide Law Review*, vol. 6, 1977, pp. 26–43.

Mabo v. Queensland (No. 2), 1992, 175 CLR 1.

Means, Russell and Bayard Johnson. *If You've Forgotten the Names of the Clouds, You've Lost Your Way*. Treaty Publications, 2012.

Nancy, Jean Luc. "What is to Be Done." Translated by Irving Goh. *Diacritics*, vol. 42, no. 2, 2014, pp. 100–119.

Racial Discrimination Act. Commonwealth of Australia, 1975.

Reynolds, Henry. *An Indelible Stain? The Question of Genocide in Australia's History*. Viking, 2001.

Richards, Kelly. "Trends in Juvenile Detention in Australia." *Trends & Issues in Crime and Criminal Justice*, no. 412, Australian Institute of Criminology, 2011.
Schulte-Tenckhoff, Isabelle. "Re-assessing the Paradigm of Domestication: The Problematic of Indigenous Treaties." *A Review of Constitutional Studies*, vol. 4, 1997, pp. 239–289.
Steering Committee for the Review of Government Service Provision. *Overcoming Indigenous Disadvantage: Key Indicators 2014*. Productivity Commission, 2014.
Toohey, Paul. "Scheming Blacks behind Fires: Farmers." *The Australian/Weekend Australian Magazine*, September 22, 2001, 18.
Venne, Sharon. "NGOs, Indigenous Peoples and the United Nations." In *NGOization Complicity, Contradictions and Prospects*. Edited by Aziz Choudry and Dip Kapoor. Zed Books, 2013, pp. 75–101.
Watson, Irene. *Aboriginal Peoples, Colonialism and International Law: Raw Law*. Routledge, 2015.
——. "Genocide, the State, and Original First Nations." In *Towards International Normativity, Between Mimetism and Dissemination*. Edited by Vincent Negri and Isabelle Schulte-Tenckoff. A. Pedone, 2016, pp. 171–186.
——. "In the Northern Territory Intervention, What is Saved or Rescued and at What Cost?" *Cultural Studies Review*, vol. 15, no. 2, 2009, pp. 45–60.
Weatherburn, Don. *Arresting Incarceration: Pathways out of Indigenous Imprisonment*. Aboriginal Studies Press, 2014.
White Face, C. *Indigenous Nations' Rights in the Balance: An Analysis of the Declaration on the Rights of Indigenous Peoples*. Living Justice Press, 2013.
Wild, Rex and Pat Anderson. *Ampe Akelyernemane Meke Mekarle "Little Children are Sacred": Report of the Northern Territory Board of Inquiry into the Protection of Aboriginal Children from Sexual Abuse*. Northern Territory Government, 2007.
Wilson, Ronald. *Bringing Them Home: Report of the National Inquiry into the Separation of Aboriginal and Torres Strait Islander Children from their Families*. Australian Human Rights and Equal Opportunities Commission, 1997.

Chapter 8

The rhetoric of abolition

Continuity and change in the struggle against America's death penalty, 1900–2010

Austin Sarat, Robert Kermes, Adelyn Curran, Margaret Kiley, and Keshav Pant

Introduction

Today the US seems to be on the road to abolishing the death penalty. Support for capital punishment, which for the last quarter of the twentieth century appeared firmly entrenched, is weakening. Moreover, across the US, the number of death sentences dropped from a high of 311 in 1994 to 49 in 2015 (Death Penalty Information Center (DPIC), "Fact Sheet"). Mirroring this trend, the number of executions peaked in 1999 and has been steadily declining over the past 15 years, reaching a 24-year low in 2015 (DPIC, "Fact Sheet"). While 31 states still retain the death penalty, 27 of those states and the federal government did not execute anyone in the past year (DPIC, "States with and without").

There are, of course, many possible explanations for the changing situation of capital punishment. Relatively low rates of violent crime and the growth of life in prison without parole are two such explanations. However, if the American death penalty is eventually ended, it will be in no small part because abolitionists altered their political and legal arguments and, in so doing, successfully reframed the death penalty debate.

Communications scholar Robert Entman broadly defines the term "framing" as "any effort to influence public opinion through the formulation of messages" (Schaffner and Sellers xi). Issues of political import in a democracy are almost always being framed "as various political entrepreneurs [attempt] as best they can to affect the debate given changes in the stream of information coming in from forces beyond their control" (Baumgartner et al. 14). The framing of complex issues involves social, cultural, and political elements. In this way, debates surrounding the death penalty resemble other hot button issues in the US.

The importance of framing in political contexts is illustrated by the struggle for gay and lesbian rights. Teresa Godwin Phelps notes that an "unprecedented shift in the rhetoric used about gays and lesbians—the names they are called, the kinds of images and metaphors that describe them, the stories about them" paved the way for the Supreme Court's recognition of gay marriage in *Obergefell* (Phelps

57). A large reason for the change, Phelps argues, was "the strategic rhetorical choices made by gay activists and advocates" (65).

In the past half-century, the framing of the death penalty debate has shifted and evolved dramatically. Perhaps the most important factor in this evolution has been the fact of wrongful convictions in death penalty cases. Since 1976, more than 150 people have been exonerated from death row (Unnever and Cullen 26). Abolitionists have used the phenomenon of wrongful conviction to change the story about capital punishment and the public's understanding of what is at stake when the state kills.

Frank Baumgartner and his colleagues examined this change in anti-death penalty rhetoric. Focusing exclusively on the last part of the twentieth century, they traced the emergence of what they called "the innocence frame," which "diverts attention away from theoretical and philosophical issues of morality to focus simply on the possibility of errors in the criminal justice system" (Baumgartner et al. 9). Furthermore, Baumgartner et al. noted the way in which "the process of 'framing,' defining an issue along a particular dimension (e.g., fairness and innocence) to the exclusion of alternate dimensions (e.g., morality, constitutionality, or cost)" completely shifted the grounds of debate (4). They argued that the innocence frame came to dominate public discussion of the death penalty beginning in the early 1990s.

Building on Baumgartner et al.'s work, Austin Sarat argues that abolitionist rhetoric has so radically shifted that we are living in an era of what he calls "the new abolitionism," an era in which moral, philosophical and pragmatic opposition to the death penalty has been, he claims, displaced in importance by rhetoric that highlights problems in the processes of guilt determination and sentencing. "The campaign to abolish capital punishment," Sarat observes:

> no longer takes the form of a frontal assault on the morality or constitutionality of state killing. Instead, arguments against the death penalty occur in the name of constitutional rights other than the Eighth Amendment, in particular due process and equal protection. Abolitionists today argue against the death penalty claiming that it has not been, and cannot be, administered in a manner that is compatible with our legal system's fundamental commitments to fair and equal treatment.
>
> (Sarat, "Recapturing the Spirit" 9)

Sarat's argument underscores dramatic changes in the framing of abolitionist arguments against the death penalty.

A change of the kind that Sarat describes can also be seen in jurisprudential opposition to capital punishment over the past 40 years. The opinions of Supreme Court Justices William Brennan, Bryon White, Harry Blackmun, and Stephen Breyer in high-profile death penalty cases dating back to *Furman v. Georgia* in 1972 capture the evolution of anti-death penalty rhetoric.

While Justice William Douglas' opinion in *Furman* gave voice to elements of what emerged later as the new abolitionism, Brennan's *Furman* opinion drew heavily on a moral or philosophical interpretation of the 8th Amendment. Brennan noted that the argument about the death penalty is, at its core, a battle that has "been waged on moral grounds" (*Furman v. Georgia* 17). "The country," he suggested, "has debated whether a society for which the dignity of the individual is the supreme value can, without a fundamental inconsistency, follow the practice of deliberately putting some of its members to death" (*Furman v. Georgia* 17). In Brennan's view, capital punishment is cruel and unusual, and thus unconstitutional, because "the deliberate extinguishment of human life by the State is uniquely degrading to human dignity" (*Furman v. Georgia* 19).

Justice White joined Brennan in voting to strike down the death penalty, but he did so more on pragmatic than moral grounds. For White, the problem with capital punishment was that it was "so seldom imposed" that it ceased to be "a credible deterrent or to contribute to any other end of punishment in the criminal justice system" (*Furman v. Georgia* 28). The death penalty amounted to the purposeless infliction of pain. As White put it:

> I accept the effectiveness of punishment generally, and need not reject the death penalty as a more effective deterrent than a lesser punishment. But common sense and experience tell us that seldom-enforced laws become ineffective measures for controlling human conduct, and that the death penalty, unless imposed with sufficient frequency, will make little contribution to deterring those crimes for which it may be exacted.
>
> (*Furman v. Georgia* 28)

More than two decades after *Furman*, Justice Blackmun turned his attention from the philosophical, moral, and pragmatic problems with capital punishment to procedural problems with what he labeled "the machinery of death." In his 1994 dissent in *Callins v. Collins*, Blackmun argued that:

> no combination of procedural rules or substantive regulations ever can save the death penalty from its inherent constitutional deficiencies ... The problem is that the inevitability of factual, legal, and moral error gives us a system that we know must wrongly kill some defendants, a system that fails to deliver the fair, consistent, and reliable sentences of death required by the Constitution.
>
> (*Callins v. Collins* 1142)

Although Blackmun mentioned the "moral error" of the death penalty, he focused, to a much greater degree than either Justice Brennan or White, on defects in its administration and gave voice to a new abolitionist perspective.

That perspective informed Justice Breyer's dissenting opinion in *Glossip v. Gross*, a 2015 case in which the Supreme Court approved the use of midazolam as a lethal injection drug. Justice Breyer offered a wide-ranging account of possible constitutional problems with America's death penalty. Breyer cited three main defects: "(1) serious unreliability, (2) arbitrariness in application, and (3) unconscionably long delays that undermine the death penalty's penological purpose" (*Glossip v. Gross* 2). All three of Breyer's reasons for opposing capital punishment highlighted faults in the administration of the death penalty.

The salience of new abolitionist rhetoric was also seen in the American Bar Association's (ABA) resolution in 1997, which called for a moratorium on capital punishment. The ABA resolution said that "the death penalty as currently administered is not compatible with central values in our Constitution" (Sarat, "When the State Kills" 254). Like Blackmun and Breyer, the ABA "embraced the new abolitionism, eschewing a direct address to state violence and relying instead on an indirect, though nonetheless devastating critique. This effort, while speaking to some of the most pressing issues facing today's capital punishment system, recaptures the spirit of *Furman*" (Sarat, "Recapturing the Spirit" 27). The ABA example suggests the relevance and usefulness of new abolitionist rationales in fora other than the Supreme Court.

Our research seeks to understand when, how, and where the framing of arguments against capital punishment has changed. We focus on politics and popular culture rather than jurisprudence and law. While others have focused exclusively on the national level, we studied the framing of abolitionist arguments in three American states: Connecticut, Kansas, and Texas.[1] Each is located in a different region of the country and each has its own distinctive death penalty history.

Moreover, we extended the time period for the analysis of the rhetoric of abolition beyond the period previously studied by Baumartner et al. and Sarat. We studied the framing of arguments against the death penalty from 1900 to 2010. In this analysis, we ask whether the development of the "new abolitionism" at the state level tracked national developments and whether it evolved in similar or different ways in three different death penalty jurisdictions.[2]

We begin with Texas, the long-time capital of America's death-belt.

Texas

Texas has a long and storied death penalty history dating back to the period before it became a state. Throughout most of that history, executions were carried out in the locality in which the crime was committed or the criminal was captured. Records dating back to before the founding of the Republic of Texas reveal that from 1819 to 1923, there were 394 legal executions in Texas, 390 by hanging and four by firing squad (Marquart et al. 12). Of course, like all southern states during this period, there were also frequent extra-judicial lynchings, forms of private revenge for which records were not kept.

In May 1922, an outbreak of lynchings in central Texas led state officials to consider policy changes to curb the unsanctioned violence (Marquart et al. 13). The state decided to centralize all executions in the Huntsville prison and to adopt the electric chair in 1924 (Marquart et al. 17). Officials hoped that by removing the responsibility for executions from local authorities and using a more advanced mode of execution, they could professionalize and further legitimize state killing (Marquart et al. ix).

Texas' use of capital punishment continued unabated until 1964, when the state halted executions. Texas also joined the national moratorium after the Supreme Court's *Furman* decision in 1972 briefly ended capital punishment. In 1982, six years after the Court's reinstatement of capital punishment in *Gregg v. Georgia*, the first person was put to death under Texas' updated sentencing statute. Despite its slow post-*Gregg* start, the state quickly accelerated its use of the death penalty. By 1992, Texas was leading the nation in death sentences and executions (Marquart et al. 130). Nevertheless, throughout this period, abolitionists in Texas mounted a continuing effort against the death penalty.

Looking back over the course of the last century reveals that the framing of anti-death penalty arguments in Texas has exhibited elements of both continuity and change. At the start of the twentieth century, almost 67% of abolitionist arguments were made in philosophical, moral, and religious terms. By the century's end, only about 40% of abolitionist arguments were framed in that way.

Arguments about the high cost and/or lack of deterrence associated with capital punishment have remained a relatively constant feature of capital punishment criticism in Texas. At the start of the twentieth century, about 25% of abolitionist arguments raised issues involving cost and/or deterrence. A similar proportion did so at the start of this century.

In contrast, arguments focused on the arbitrariness of the death penalty system, arguments consistent with the new abolitionism, have markedly increased in prominence since the 1960s. Those focused specifically on the death penalty's unreliability (the innocence frame) have shown a similar increase from the 1980s to the present day. In the early decades of the twentieth century, slightly more than 10% of abolitionist arguments in Texas criticized the death penalty's administration. By the end of the century, arguments about defects in the death penalty's administration in our sample more than tripled in frequency from what was seen at the start of the last century.

In Texas, the new abolitionism seems to have emerged much earlier than one would surmise from Baumgartner et al.'s analysis. In addition, although by the end of the twentieth century, it provided an important new tool in the struggle against the death penalty in that state, in terms of sheer frequency, abolitionists continued to rely more on moral, religious, and pragmatic arguments than on arguments about innocence and arbitrariness.

Typical of the kind of moral and religious arguments found in Texas during the period of our study is one that appeared in February 1924 in the *Canton Herald*. When "life is taken," this early twentieth-century opponent of the death penalty said, "it is in direct refutation of one emphatic command which says 'thou shalt not kill' " ("Capital Punishment," *Canton Herald* 6). Here the language of command is deployed to criticize state killing. Here citizens of Texas were called to attend to four words, the Divine enunciation "thou shalt not kill."

The vast majority of these moral and religious arguments against state killing, not surprisingly, are Christian. Yet, these arguments are polarizing. They create a clear dichotomy between right and wrong, and call on the death penalty's supporters to admit the error of their ways, suggesting that they are sinners or are on the wrong side of a stark moral divide.

Thus, in 1956, columnist Harry McCormick published an article in the *Dallas Morning News* in which he said: "As one who has witnessed 27 executions, most of them in Texas, this writer could never see it as other than a form of legalized murder on the part of the state. Of course, in a democratic society the state is you and I. An execution is a deliberate act in which every Texan participates."

Equating the death penalty with murder and its supporters with murderers, long a mainstay of traditional moral arguments against capital punishment, hardly seems a way to change hearts and minds. These arguments suggest that the death penalty is an insidious and corrupting force, a cancer that must be removed.

In contrast to the relative decline in the frequency of moral and religious arguments against the Texas death penalty, pragmatic arguments constituted between 20% and 25% of all death penalty arguments in each decade of the twentieth century. During this period, arguments focused on the death penalty's failure as a deterrent were the most popular of these pragmatic arguments.

Over the course of the twentieth century, those making deterrence arguments invariably cited statistics purporting to show that the death penalty did not, in fact, deter. For instance, in 1924, Texas State Representative T.K. Irwin remarked that he knew "from a study of the statistics in eight states in the union which have done away with capital punishment that major crimes have decreased in every one of them, and not one has returned to it" ("Author of Electrocution Bill" 1). Another deterrence argument, from 60 years later, uses a similar line of reasoning:

> A recent Associated Press poll found an overwhelming majority—84 percent—of Americans approve of the death penalty. Many view it as a deterrent to violent crime. Most available statistics don't bear out their view. Murder rates in death penalty states, such as Illinois and New Hampshire, differ little from non-death penalty states of similar populations and characteristics, such as Michigan and Vermont. In some states, a decrease in homicides has followed abolition of the death penalty. And it is possible that the actual effect of a death sentence may be to incite rather than deter violence. (Graff 4-A)

As we noted above, from the 1960s to the early 1980s, Texas did not use the death penalty (Marquart et al. 147–148). Coinciding with this de facto moratorium, abolitionist rhetoric underwent a perceptible change with an increase in new abolitionist framing of anti-death penalty arguments. In fact, 80% of all the new abolitionist arguments made from 1900 to 2010 were made after 1964. The most common of them highlighted the death penalty system's bias and arbitrariness, and/or the dangers of executing an innocent person.

Our research identified arguments about five different dimensions of arbitrariness in death sentences: race, geographical location, socioeconomic condition, gender, and educational level. Although each form of bias has its own characteristics, new abolitionists incorporate them into larger arguments about disproportionality. One example of such an argument is found in an op-ed from the late 1960s:

> Penologists agree that discrimination is a justifiable argument against capital punishment since it is well known that some states have tailored capital punishment to fit the black offender ... The United States executed 449 men for rape between 1930 and 1963 and 90 per cent of those condemned were Negro ... [Moreover] according to numbers kept between 1930 and 1965, 17 Southern States registered 1659 black executions to 636 white; Considering these figures, then, it is little wonder that civil rights activists are among the staunchest anti-execution workers in the nation.
>
> (Tiede 4)

As important as arguments about arbitrariness have been among recent efforts to end Texas' death penalty, even more important have been arguments about the unreliability of capital punishment and the risk of executing the innocent. From the late 1980s to the present day, increasing attention to these problems has animated abolitionist rhetoric. The following claim is typical in this respect: "an alarming number [of prisoners] are innocent of the crimes for which they were convicted. For even one man to be killed in the name of justice for crimes that he had nothing to do with is unacceptable. And for this to happen on a regular basis is a preposterous travesty of justice" (Dimitri 4A). In discussing the 81 men and one woman who had been freed from death rows between 1973 and 1999, one commentator remarked that "you can call [their release] luck. You can call it the hand of God. You can call it fortuity, serendipity. What it's not is the system working" (Dimitri 4A).

Today, in Texas as in the nation as a whole, the death penalty is in decline. New death sentences in Texas have dropped nearly 80% since 1999, when they reached their peak of 48. In 2015, juries condemned only three new individuals to death. This marked the lowest number of new death sentences since the US Supreme Court upheld Texas' revised death penalty statute in 1976. Furthermore, after hitting a high of 40 executions in 2000, Texas has slowed its pace markedly, sending only 13 people to death in 2015. Finally, there are 249 individuals on death row in Texas, the lowest that this population has been since the late 1980s.

It is, of course, not possible to say how much of the changed situation in Texas is attributable to abolitionist arguments. What we can say is that those arguments both resemble and depart from the framing of anti-death penalty arguments at the national level. In Texas, as elsewhere, during the last part of the twentieth century, the new abolitionism assumed greater prominence. Yet moral, religious, and pragmatic arguments continued to play a major role in the movement to end the death penalty in that state.

Connecticut

Connecticut has, not surprisingly, a very different death penalty history from Texas. Indeed, in 2012, the Connecticut Legislature enacted Public Act No. 12–5, prospectively abolishing the death penalty. With the passage of Public Act No. 12–5, Connecticut became the seventeenth state, and the fifth state in the preceding five years, to end capital punishment (Applebome). Furthermore, Connecticut is one of only six states—the others being Illinois, Maryland, New Jersey, New Mexico, and, most recently, Nebraska—to have recently abolished the death penalty through legislative action (Sarat, "The 'New Abolitionism'" 4).

Before 2012, Connecticut was one of only two states in New England (the other being New Hampshire) that retained the death penalty (DPIC, "States with and without"). Moreover, it is the only New England state to have executed anyone during the last half-century, putting to death Joseph Taborsky in 1960 and Michael Ross in 2005 (Goodheart 2). At the time of abolition, it had 11 inmates on death row, far more than New Hampshire, which sentenced only one person to death between 1994 and 2012 (DPIC, "States with and without").

Three years after the legislature's prospective abolition, the Connecticut Supreme Court, in *State v. Santiago*, held that the death penalty in all its forms violated the state's constitution, thus preventing its retroactive application to inmates then on death row. These legislative and judicial acts were motivated by contemporaneous societal and legal developments and, more fundamentally, reflected the shift in abolitionist rhetoric that took place during the twentieth century in America (*State v. Santiago* 17).

Over the past century, individuals from across the political spectrum in Connecticut have voiced grave concerns about the death penalty, alleging that capital punishment is a relic of a more barbaric age, that the penalty is driven by revenge, that the risk of executing innocent people is too great, that the delays that plague the system are too long, and that the money spent on the death penalty could be used more effectively elsewhere (DPIC, "New Voices"). These critics have included judges, prosecutors, legislators, social justice advocates, and the families of murder victims (DPIC, "New Voices").

From 1900 to 2010, the framing of abolitionist arguments in Connecticut followed a pattern somewhat similar to what we observed in Texas. While traditional philosophical, moral, and religious arguments against the death penalty were more prominent at the start of the twentieth century in Texas than in Connecticut, in the latter state—as in the former—they declined, but were not entirely displaced by new abolitionist rhetoric. Thus, at the start of the twentieth century, approximately half of abolitionist arguments found in our Connecticut sample focused on questions of morality and/or religion. By the end of the century, this number dropped slightly to about 45%.

The seeming persistence of such moral and religious arguments derives from a spike in old abolitionist arguments in 2005, the year of Michael Ross' execution. Ross' execution interrupted a half-century-long moratorium on state killing in Connecticut and invited what Lawrence Goodheart, the pre-eminent scholar on Connecticut's death penalty, termed "a wave of emotionalism" (201). Indeed, 2005 is the only year in the last decade in which old abolitionist arguments outpaced the new abolitionism.

In the early decades of the twentieth century, about 20% of abolitionist arguments criticized the death penalty's administration. By the end of the century, arguments about defects in the death penalty's administration increased to 32% of Connecticut's anti-death penalty arguments. This shift in the framing of the case for abolition in Connecticut is not as dramatic as the change in Texas, where new abolitionist arguments tripled in frequency. However, it is significant enough to support Baumgartner et al. and Sarat's claims concerning the increased importance of new abolitionist rhetoric during the second half of the twentieth century.

The use of pragmatic arguments against capital punishment in Connecticut was relatively consistent with what we found in Texas. At the start of the last century, about 30% of the abolitionist arguments in our sample raised issues involving cost, Life Without Parole (LWOP), and/or deterrence. These pragmatic arguments declined in frequency to about 23% by the end of the century. Furthermore, the deterrence argument again figured most prominently throughout the twentieth century, accounting for 16% of the total number of arguments made against the death penalty in Connecticut.

For example, in a 1925 editorial published in the *Bridgeport Telegram*, Lewis Lawes, a warden at Sing Sing Prison in New York, utilized one such deterrence argument and advocated the replacement of capital punishment with life imprisonment without parole, writing: "It has been so frequently said that capital punishment might deter if it were enforced. The fact remains that until the characteristics of mankind change, it can never be enforced" (Lawes 12). He continued to question the deterrent value of capital punishment by noting that the homicide rate in the US offered a "shameful contrast" to the rest of the civilized world.

Forty-six years later, in 1971, Representative Irving J. Stolberg of New Haven used similar pragmatic language to reject the argument put forth by long-time death penalty supporter Governor Thomas J. Meskill that capital punishment serves as a deterrent to murder. "Capital punishment is not and has not been a deterrent to crime," Stolberg said. "If anything, with well-publicized executions, the murder rate increases rather than decreases" (Gudauskas 3).

Typical of the kind of moral, philosophical, or religious rhetoric that was used in Connecticut to oppose the death penalty during the period of our study was the fiery commentary offered by Connecticut journalist George Ross Wells in October 1935. In that year, the Connecticut General Assembly passed legislation replacing hanging with electrocution as the method of execution for capital crimes (Goodheart 131). In addition, the state hired a professional executor to run its electric chair. Electrocution was defended as a swifter, more humane form of execution (Goodheart 166).

However, some, like Wells, rejected this view and argued that the legislation simply perpetuated what they called a barbaric system. In his *Hartford Courant* editorial, Wells wrote: "Replacing hanging with electrocution is squirting perfume on a manure heap instead of clearing it away. We have simply substituted one brutal savagery for another" (Wells 11). "It is," he continued, "as savage as war, and with one as with the other, using scientific methods makes it not in the least less savage" (Wells 11).

Twenty years after Wells, an article in the *Hartford Courant* entitled "Clergy of Three Faiths Criticize Defenders of Capital Punishment" cataloged opposition by major state religious leaders. Rabbi Abraham J. Feldman pointed to "increasing humanitarianism" in expressing opposition to Connecticut's system of capital punishment. He argued that: "We do not have the right to take a life ... Capital punishment is one of the vestiges of primitive savagery remaining with us" (Dove 8).

While this type of moralistic rhetoric decreased somewhat after the 1960s, it did not disappear. In 2005, Reverend Stephen J. Sidorak Jr., Executive Director of the Christian Conference of Connecticut, advocating the replacement of capital punishment with life imprisonment without the possibility of parole, called for Connecticut to move beyond "archaic" practices. He wrote: "At the very least, both the governor and the General Assembly owe the people of this state a morally serious reconsideration of whether or not Connecticut should return to the archaic and barbaric practice of capital punishment" (Taylor A6).

Like Texas, the framing of arguments against the death penalty in Connecticut continued to rely on a traditional moralistic framing, though here overtly religious appeals played a much less prominent role. Yet while new abolitionist language did not fully displace old abolitionist rhetoric in Connecticut, it became more common toward the end of the twentieth century.

In 1973, Connecticut modified its death penalty laws to meet the standards articulated by the Supreme Court in *Furman*. The revised statute limited the number of capital crimes and, in various ways, raised the bar that the state would have to clear to impose the death penalty (Donohue 642). Over the succeeding decades, the Connecticut legislature further reviewed and revised the state's death penalty statute, rendering the task of executing a person on death row more and more difficult. At the same time, abolitionists focused their criticism on the administration of the death penalty with greater frequency. Arguments regarding regional disparity, racial disproportionality, innocence, delay, and infrequent executions played an enlarged role in Connecticut's death penalty debate.

In the last quarter of the twentieth century, in Connecticut as in Texas, the prospect of executing the innocent emerged as a formidable argument against the death penalty. Rhetorical appeals to the "epistemological certainty of DNA evidence" had a profound effect on abolitionist discourse (Cole and Aronson 52). The cold rationality of science was added to emotionally charged narratives about the rights and wrongs of capital punishment (Cole and Aronson 47). As Sarat puts it, "the issue of innocence, more than any other factor, has changed the climate surrounding state killing" (Sarat, "Innocence" 46).

One example of this focus on innocence and error is provided by Connecticut Senator John M. Lupton, who addressed the Senate's Judiciary Committee in 1967 and advocated the abolition of the death penalty in the state. "The taking of life," he said, "is the only irrevocable step that is permitted under our American jurisprudence. All other actions under our marvelous constitutional law are, in one way or another, subject to review and, if necessary, rectification. Human frailty in error being what it is, let us pass this legislation and leave the irrevocable to the infallible" ("Assembly Urged" 20).

Forty-five years later, in 2012, Representative Terry Backer similarly argued: "As a government, we have done things that haven't quite worked out the way we had hoped ... but we are always able to go back and fix those things. Unfortunately, when we are wrong in these cases, there is no way to put them back on track" (Altimari para. 16).

The Connecticut legislature's decision to prospectively abolish capital punishment, although outside the time period of our study, is worth noting here. In 2012, opinions in the Connecticut legislature were divided on the relevance of the innocence argument to its consideration of the death penalty. The state had only executed two men in the last 65 years and the guilt of both Ross and Taborsky was never in question (Goodheart 227). As a result, during the 2012 debate in Connecticut's House of Representatives, Representative John Hetherington reminded his fellow legislators: "We have to remember that we are looking at the death penalty as it exists in Connecticut, as it is applied here" (Connecticut General Assembly, April 11, 68). He asserted that while a number of people across the US have been exonerated based upon post-conviction evidence, no one in Connecticut, at least in modern times, has been executed and later proven innocent. Thus, he insisted, "I don't think that that argument is a very strong one when you consider it in light of Connecticut's experience and the way the capital felony law is applied here" (Connecticut General Assembly, April 11, 68).

In addition to innocence, abolitionists have increasingly noted blatant geographic inconsistencies in calling the state's administration of death penalty into question. Karen Goodrow, a lawyer who represented Michael Ross, commented that when she and her colleagues hear about a death eligible case in Connecticut, their first question is always: "Where did it happen?" (Tuohy B1). This is important, Goodrow explained, because the capital sentencing rate in places like

Waterbury (a large Connecticut city) has been strikingly higher than in the rest of the state (Donohue 650). Around 33%of all death eligible cases received death sentences in Waterbury, while only 2.6% of the cases outside Waterbury received similar sentences (Donohue 655).

State legislators and judges also took note of geographic disparities, focusing on state to state differences. In the legislative debate over Public Act 12–5 in 2012, Representative Mike Lawlor noted:

> It's worth keeping in mind that in this part of the country, New Jersey doesn't have it. New York doesn't have it. Massachusetts doesn't have it. Rhode Island doesn't have it. Vermont doesn't have it. Maine doesn't have it. New Hampshire, in theory, has it. There's nobody on death row. There's not been a death penalty prosecution in recent decades. And that leaves Connecticut.
>
> (Connecticut General Assembly, April 11, 230)

Racial discrimination has also played an important role in the recent framing of Connecticut's death penalty debate. In 1973, an editorial in the *Hartford Courant* claimed that the Connecticut death penalty was "applied randomly at best and discriminatorily at worst. It violates equal protections of the laws because it is imposed almost exclusively against racial minorities and the poor" ("An Official Act" 2).

In 2009, Connecticut Representative Demetrios Giannaros pointed to the racially discriminatory way in which capital punishment has been administered in Connecticut: "There is evidence, clear evidence," he said, "that if the person who died is a white person, like me, the individual who commits the crime is more likely to face the death penalty than if the person who died was a black person or perhaps a Hispanic. This is a system that is disgraceful when it comes to fairness" (Connecticut General Assembly, May 13 n.p.)

The deliberations and decisions of both Connecticut's legislature and its Supreme Court in 2012 and 2015 respectively reflected the rhetorical shift toward new abolitionism that altered that state's death penalty debate (DPIC, "States with and without"). As in Texas, this rhetorical strategy did not go uncontested, nor did it displace other ways of framing the argument against capital punishment. Indeed, what is striking is how much the pattern in Connecticut resembles Texas where the new abolitionism emerged as a late twentieth-century refinement in the arsenal of arguments deployed against the death penalty.

Kansas

The story of capital punishment in our third state, Kansas, reveals a reluctant and halting embrace of the death penalty. The Kansas death penalty, long a mainstay of its criminal justice system, was abolished at the start of the twentieth century in 1907 and remained off the books until 1935. Although it was reinstated in 1935, the first execution in the twentieth century took place in 1944 (DPIC, "Kansas"). And, after the *Furman* moratorium was lifted in 1976, Kansas was slow to revive its death penalty, bringing it back only in 1994. While capital punishment remains legal in Kansas, no one has been executed in the state since 1965 (DPIC, "Kansas").

The broad outline of abolitionist arguments in Kansas is similar to what we observed in Texas and Connecticut. In the first decades of the twentieth century, new abolitionist arguments represented only 13% of the arguments against capital punishment found in the newspapers we examined. In the last years of our study, new abolitionism made up 32% of the arguments in our sample. The moral and religious framing of anti-death penalty arguments, which is characteristic of what we called the old abolitionism, fell from 59% in the first four decades to 43% in the last several years. Finally, pragmatic arguments against the death penalty (deterrence and cost) remained relatively constant, declining slightly from 28% at the start of the twentieth century to 25% at its end.

As in Texas, many of the old abolitionist arguments made in Kansas have been religious. An example of this kind of argument can be found in a letter to the editor published in the *Lawrence Daily Journal-World* on November 18, 1961: "To believe that capital punishment is the will of God not only circumvents the major impact of the New Testament; it also makes us forget our responsibility to a penal system in which the increasingly obvious need is rehabilitation, not just punishment" (Davis 4).

For another religious objection to the death penalty, consider the argument of Governor E.W. Hoch published by *The Sun* on February 2, 1906:

> how a Christian, one believing in the Bible, in immortality and in the preparedness necessary in this world for bliss in the next, and of the awful conditions of the lost throughout eternity, can believe in and consent to a theory that would plunge a human soul into eternity and into that immortality unprepared is beyond my comprehension.
>
> ("Capital Punishment," *The Sun (KS)* 4)

As noted above, pragmatic arguments against the death penalty have remained relatively constant throughout the past 110 years in Kansas. One such argument is found in the February 1, 1901 edition of the *Kansas Semi-Capital*:

> There are a number of states which have abolished capital punishment and every governor of these states is on record testifying that the abolition of the death penalty has not resulted in an increase in crimes. The fact appears to be that the punishment has little or nothing to do with this prevention of capital crimes, these crimes being due to uncontrollable passion or depravity law cannot suppress.
>
> ("Capital Punishment out of Date" n.p.)

Another example of a pragmatic argument against the death penalty is found in a 1935 opinion piece published in the *Hutchinson News*:

> If every murder were immediately identified, promptly captured, speedily tried, invariably convicted and subjected to the sentence at once, the thought of hanging might be more disturbing to the criminal mind than that of serving a life in prison. Distressing statistics, however, show that not one murder in 100 in this country actually serves the maximum sentence that might be imposed for his crime. With 100 to 1 odds against experiencing it, no punishment however severe is going to seem very alarming to potential criminals. It is the inevitability of punishment and not the style of it that checks crime.
>
> ("Death Penalty" 4)

Perhaps the most famous case in Kansas' death penalty history was the 1959 Clutter killings that inspired Truman Capote's book *In Cold Blood* (Kreitner). Richard Eugene Hickock and Perry Edward Smith broke into the home of Herb Clutter searching for money, and slaughtered the entire family (Robinson Library). An important figure in this saga was Harrison Smith, the defense lawyer for Hickcok. Unable to defend his client directly, Smith attacked both the efficacy and morality of the death penalty, saying it was "a miserable failure" and that it "makes a murderer of the state" ("State Presses" 1).

In Kansas, as in Texas and Connecticut, the third frame of abolitionist argument, the new abolitionism, assumed greater prominence during the last part of the twentieth century. The style of new abolitionist arguments evolved as well. In the early decades of the twentieth century, new abolitionist arguments were generally linked to moral and/or religious sentiments and arguments about deterrence. An example of this hybrid rhetoric can be found in an excerpt from a letter to the editor in the *Kansas City Star*, printed on August 7, 1915: "Many a man sentenced to life imprisonment has later been found innocent and freed. But what of your innocent man convicted and hanged? Hell will have no better offering for the murderer than for the executioner, and, in my opinion, the latter should have the worse punishment" ("Speaking the Public Mind" n.p.).

Another example of this hybrid argument is found in an article from the *Hutchinson News* on April 26, 1921:

> I think capital punishment is wrong. I do not think it ever keeps a man from committing a crime. There is too great a chance for human judgment to err, and also too many mistakes made in administration, to let me think that it is ever absolutely right for the state to take the life of a citizen. I can understand why an individual kills, or why a mob executes, because they are frenzied with excitement, but for the people of the State, calmly and deliberately and without immediate provocation, to take the life of a man or woman seems to me to be more than a mistake.
>
> ("Capital Punishment," *Hutchinson News* 4)

As new abolitionism became more prominent in the second half of the century, arguments about systemic failure began to stand on their own. Consider an excerpt from an April 4, 1960 comment in the *Lawrence Daily Journal-World*:

> Those actually put to death are most frequently the poor and the friendless. Of the 49 persons executed in the United States last year, 33 were Negroes. Some years ago a congressional committee reported that "as it is now applied the death penalty is nothing but an arbitrary discrimination against an occasional victim. It cannot even be said that it is reserved as a weapon of retributive justice for the most atrocious criminals. For it is not necessarily the most guilty who suffer it." This pattern has not changed.
>
> ("State Should Not Kill" 4)

As in Texas and Connecticut, some new abolitionist arguments in Kansas focus on innocence, others on discrimination. In 1990, the murder of a college student once again reignited the death penalty debate in Kansas (Smith). In this context, abolitionists held firmly to a framing of their arguments that focused on defects in the administration of that state's death penalty. An example can be found in an opinion piece in the *Salina Journal* dated May 22, 1990:

> For these reasons, the idea that only especially evil criminals are selected for execution is a joke. The ones who lose are poor, mentally impaired, black—and had lawyers who did not take the case seriously. The results are so unfair that half of all state death sentences have been set aside in recent years during the long process of federal habeas corpus.
>
> ("America's Rage" 4)

In 1994, soon after Kansas reinstated capital punishment (DPIC, "Kansas"), abolitionists continued to criticize the death penalty's arbitrary administration. For example:

> How many states have executed wealthy whites? There are notorious cases, you see them on "Hard Copy" and "A Current Affair." Premeditated murder for hire. They are convicted, but they are never executed. "Justice" of the rope and the tree against poor minorities continues today, and as finite human beings we have not, despite our good intentions, found a way to keep it from happening. And if this state passes capital punishment, it will continue as it has in the other 36. We will not, we will not, execute wealthy whites.
>
> (Wright 1A)

Like Texas and Connecticut, the story of efforts to abolish the death penalty in Kansas has elements of continuity and change. As in those two states, new abolitionist framing of the case against capital punishment became more prominent in the late twentieth century. However, again it did not fully displace other forms of argument. Here, as elsewhere, abolitionist efforts drew on multiple sources in a shifting, but layered array.

Conclusion

Our study suggests that the rhetorical reframing of the campaign against capital punishment that has occurred at the national level has had deep resonance at the state level. Over the course of the twentieth century in Texas, Connecticut, and Kansas, the focus on error and arbitrariness has assumed greater prominence among abolitionists. In each state, this change began to take hold in the late 1960s and 1970s, and accelerated as the twentieth century drew to its close. But our findings complicate the pictures presented by Baumgartner et.al. and Sarat since, in each state, older frames persisted and indeed continued to occur with greater frequency than the new abolitionism.

Across the country, change is afoot as the death penalty slowly but steadily retreats. Precisely how much of this change can be attributed to innovations in the rhetorical strategies of abolitionists we cannot say. However, we can say that since the new abolitionism has come to prominence in places like Texas, Connecticut, and Kansas, the debate has changed. Now, one can be opposed to the death penalty and also be a defender of the values of due process and equal protection. Such opposition can even be cast as a form of legal and political conservatism rather than as a defense of those condemned to death.

Abolitionists now argue against capital punishment because of the risk of executing the innocent, the discriminatory way in which it is applied, or the fact of its geographic arbitrariness. They can even concede that the death penalty may in some cases be morally justified or that, if it were used enough, it might deter. Instead of creating a stark moral divide or suggesting that support for the death penalty is irrational, abolitionists create common ground with those who support the death penalty, even as they invite them to see that, in its day-to-day practices, capital punishment is incompatible with widely shared constitutional commitments.

Of course, only time will tell if this rhetorical reframing will help lead the way to capital punishment's permanent demise.

Notes

* We are grateful for the indispensable help provided by Amherst College's Missy Roser and for the collaboration of Haley Cambra.

1 In each state, we examined newspaper coverage of capital punishment, drawing on newspapers that have been digitized, with minimal gaps, back to 1900. Furthermore, each state had additional digitized records available on NewspaperArchives allowing articles found in the more prominent newspapers in each state to be supplemented by articles from regional newspapers. Every newspaper article was searched using a consistent system designed to capture any article that contained, in the body or in the title, the words "capital punishment" or "death penalty" in addition to, when possible, the words "abolition," "abolish," or "abolitionism." Lastly, in

the course of our analysis, we drew upon legislative debates to contextualize and better understand the rhetoric found in the press.

2 Our research initially identified 24 unique arguments against the death penalty, which we eventually collapsed into three categories: new abolitionism, old abolitionism, and pragmatic. New abolitionist arguments criticize capital punishment for failing in terms of equal protection and due process. In contrast, old abolitionist arguments focus on the alleged immorality of the death penalty, draw on philosophical or religious sources, and invite one to sympathize with the perpetrator of a crime rather than simply opposing state killing on procedural grounds. Pragmatic arguments include arguments relating the costs associated with capital punishment, potential alternatives to capital punishment, and the ability of capital punishment to deter crime.

References

Altimari, Daniela. "House Votes to Repeal Death Penalty." *Hartford Courant*, April 12, 2012, www.courant.com/politics/hc-death-penalty-house-vote-0412-20120411-story.html.

"An Official Act of Violence." *Hartford Courant*, April 18, 1973, p. 2.

"America's Rage to Kill Puzzles Our Foreign Friends." *Salina Journal*, May 22, 1990, p. 4.

Applebome, Peter. "Connecticut House Votes to Repeal Death Penalty." *New York Times*, April 11, 2012, www.nyti.ms/1ynKmgU.

"Assembly Urged to Eliminate Death Penalty." *Hartford Courant*, February 22, 1967, p. 20.

Baumgartner, Frank R., Suzanna De Boef, and Amber E. Boydstun. *The Decline of the Death Penalty and the Discovery of Innocence*. Cambridge University Press, 2008.

Callins v. Collins, 510 U.S. 1141 (1994).

"Capital Punishment." *Canton Herald*, February 15, 1924, p. 6.

"Capital Punishment." *Hutchinson News*, April 26, 1921, p. 4.

"Capital Punishment." *The Sun (KS)*, February 2, 1906, p. 4.

"Capital Punishment out of Date." *Kansas Semi-Weekly Capital*, January 22, 1901, n.p.

Connecticut General Assembly. House Session Document, May 13, 2009, www.cga.ct.gov/2011/trn/S/2011STR00105-R00-TRN.htm. Accessed 21 February 2016.

——. House Session Document, April 11, 2012.

Cole, Simon A. and Jay D. Aronson. "Blinded by Science on the Road to Abolition?" In *The Road to Abolition? The Future of Capital Punishment in the United States*. Edited by Charles J. Ogletree, Jr. and Austin Sarat. New York University Press, 2009, pp. 46–71.

Davis, Paul. "The Odom Case." *Lawrence Journal-World*, November 18, 1961, p. 4.

"Death Penalty." *Hutchinson News*, March 9, 1935, p. 4.

Death Penalty Information Centre. "Fact Sheet," www.deathpenaltyinfo.org.

——. "Kansas." www.deathpenaltyinfo.org/kansas-1#history.

——. "New Voices," www.deathpenaltyinfo.org/new-voices.

——. "States with and without the Death Penalty," www.deathpenaltyinfo.org/states-and-without-death-penalty.

Dimitri, Dale. "The Death Penalty is Fatally Flawed." *Texas City Sun*, August 15, 1999, p. 4A.

Donohue, John J. "An Empirical Evaluation of the Connecticut Death Penalty System Since 1973: Are There Unlawful Racial, Gender, and Geographic Disparities?" *Journal of Empirical Legal Studies*, vol. 11, no. 4, 2014, pp. 637–696.

Dove, Roger. "Clergy of Three Faiths Criticize Defenders of Capital Punishment." *Hartford Courant*, March 3, 1955, p. 8.

Furman v. Georgia, 408 U.S. 238 (1972).

Glossip v. Gross, 576 U.S. (2015).

Goodheart, Lawrence B. *The Solemn Sentence of Death: Capital Punishment in Connecticut*. University of Massachusetts Press, 2011.

Graff, Don. "Death Penalty Reinstatement Results in Grim Statistics." *Baytown Sun*, March 24, 1985, p. 4A.

Gudauskas, George. "Avcollie Amendment Fails of Passage." *Naugatuck Daily News*, May 26, 1971, p. 3.

Goodheart, Lawrence B. *The Solemn Sentence of Death: Capital Punishment in Connecticut*. University of Massachusetts Press, 2011.

Kreitner, Richard. "November 15, 1959: The Clutter Family is Murdered in Holcomb, Kansas, Later the Subject of Truman Capote's 'In Cold Blood.'" *The Nation*, November 15, 2015, www.thenation.com/article/november-15-1959-the-clutter-family-is-murdered-in-holcomb-texas-later-the-subject-of-truman-capotes-in-cold-blood.

Lawes, Lewis. "Capital Punishment Should Be Abolished." *Bridgeport Telegram*, August 8, 1925, p. 12.

Marquart, James W., Sheldon Ekland-Olson, and Jonathan R. Sorensen. *The Rope, the Chair, and the Needle: Capital Punishment in Texas, 1923–1990*. Austin: University of Texas Press, 1994.

Phelps, Teresa Godwin. "The Evolving Rhetoric of Gay Rights Advocacy." In *Rhetorical Processes and Legal Judgments: How Language and Arguments Shape Struggles for Rights and Power*. Edited by Austin Sarat. Cambridge University Press, 2016, pp. 54–82.

Robinson Library. "Clutter Family Murders," www.robinsonlibrary.com/social/pathology/criminology/crimes/clutter.htm. Sarat, Austin. "Innocence, Error, and the 'New Abolitionism': A Commentary." *Criminology & Public Policy*, vol. 4, no. 1, 2005, pp. 45–54.

——. "The 'New Abolitionism' and the Possibilities of Legislative Action: The New Hampshire Experience." *Ohio State Law Journal*, vol. 63, no. 343, 2002, pp. 1–16.

——. "Recapturing the Spirit of 'Furman': The American Bar Association and the New Abolitionist Politics." *Law and Contemporary Problems*, vol. 61, no. 4, 1998, pp. 5–28.

——. *When the State Kills: Capital Punishment and the American Condition*. Princeton University Press, 2001.

Schaffner, Brian F. and Patrick J. Sellers. *Winning with Words: The Origins and Impact of Political Framing*. Routledge, 2010.

Smith, Gene. "Murders Tell Stories of How System Failed." *Topeka Capital-Journal*, November 29, 1998, www. cjonline.com/stories/112998/kan_murderstories.shtml#.V2rBfJMrL-Z.

"Speaking the Public Mind." *Kansas City Star*, August 7, 1915.

"State Presses for Death Penalty for Two in Clutter Murder Case." *Hays Daily News*, March 29, 1960, p. 1.
"State Should Not Kill." *Lawrence Journal-World*, April 4, 1960, p. 4.
State v. Santiago, 318 Conn. 1, LEXIS 228 (2015).
Taylor, Francis Grandy. "A Stand against Inhumanity." *Hartford Courant*, January 13, 2005, p. A6.
Tiede, Tom. "'I Have Never Seen a Person of Means Go to Chair,' Says Former a Governor," *Victoria Advocate*, August 15, 1967, p. 4.
Tuohy, Lynne. "Trying to Halt Ultimate Torture," *Hartford Courant*, October 24, 2004, p. B1.
Unnever, James D. and Cullen, Francis T. "Executing the Innocent and Support for Capital Punishment: Implications for Public Policy," *Criminology and Public Policy*, vol. 4, no. 1, 2005, pp. 3–38.
Wells, George R. "Men and Manners." *Hartford Courant*, October 11, 1935, p. 11.
Wright, Julie. "Death Penalty Takes Big Step: Final House OK is Likely." *Witchita Daily Eagle*, February 11, 1994, p. 1A.

Chapter 9

"Too wicked to die"

The enduring legacy of humane reforms to solitary confinement

Kelly Struthers Montford, Kelly Hannah-Moffat, and Alexandra Hunter

> There are many ways to destroy a person, but one of the simplest and most devastating is through prolonged solitary confinement.
>
> (Guenther xi)

Introduction

The Correctional Service of Canada's (CSC) use of segregation to respond to and manage federally sentenced women has repeatedly been the subject of commissions, inquiries, and public scrutiny over the last two decades. Justice Arbour's inquiry, for example, following the prolonged segregation of women in the Kingston Prison for Women in 1994 and the death of Ashley Smith in 2007 while in segregation at the Grand Valley Institution for Women in Ontario evince the CSC's historical and continued reliance on segregation to deal with resistant and "difficult-to-manage" women. In this chapter, we focus on Ashley Smith's treatment as a prisoner and the circumstances in which she died to show that the use of segregation is not an exceptional practice for the CSC. Instead, we argue that is a normalized and common response to prisoners who do not meet the behavioral expectations of the institution.

By considering the historical logics of segregation, we follow Lisa Guenther's critical phenomenology of solitary confinement to show that the subject for whom solitary confinement was designed (i.e., the autonomous human of Western philosophy) does not exist *except* when produced as a result of intensive confinement. According to Guenther, we are not atomistic individuals, but relational beings who develop our self-concept as individuals *through* our intercorporeal relations with others. Following from this, we show that at its core, solitary confinement is designed to undermine our subjectivity. By denying embodied relations with others, solitary confinement turns a person's subjectivity against themselves, resulting in the fundamental undermining of their ability to experience themselves in relation to others. Despite it being variously labeled "disciplinary segregation," "administrative segregation," "the special handling unit," or characterized as a therapeutic measure, solitary confinement is punitive in its operation (Reiter and Blair).

Consequently, we show that legal attempts that rely on the discourse of humanism to limit the state's use of segregation actually legitimize the practice as necessary to the security of the institution. Such reform attempts also redraw thresholds of minimum standards of treatment, with the result that the practice becomes increasingly immune to litigation (Guenther). Given the limits of human rights legal frameworks to effect operational change or destabilize rationales for solitary confinement, we argue that solitary confinement is better understood as practices that ethically violate our ontologies, preclude possibilities for dignity, and require a relational and intersubjective account of vulnerability (Gilson; Gruen; Guenther).

The chapter is organized as follows: first we provide an overview of the contemporary use of segregation practices in federal Canadian penitentiaries. We then analyze how solitary confinement is articulated as an acceptable and appropriate mode of confinement premised on a particular understanding of "the human" and how the motivation to isolate penal subjects is endemic to the historical rationality of the penitentiary in Canada. Because solitary confinement is rooted in humane penal reforms, we demonstrate the limits of legislative and policy efforts that mobilize human rights violations to challenge solitary confinement. We conclude by outlining relational accounts of the subject, dignity, and vulnerability that reveal solitary confinement as a practice that implicitly entails ethical violations of the prisoner, which cannot be resolved via reform or legislative oversight.

The CSC's contemporary reliance on segregation

Despite decreases in the use of long-term solitary confinement (over 60 days) for the federally sentenced prison population during the 2015–2016 reporting year, data from the Office of the Correctional Investigator (OCI) shows that solitary confinement remains a common CSC management technique. In its 2014–2015 Annual Report, the OCI noted that 48% of the current inmate population had been segregated during their sentence, and that 26% of the male population and 25% of the female population had been segregated at least once during the reporting year. The average length of segregation was 27 days.

The report included a special focus on administrative segregation. The OCI stated that it had made 31 recommendations to the CSC over the last decade pertinent to the administration and accountability of segregation, including the following: a prohibition on indefinite segregation and on the use of segregation for those who have serious mental illness, are self-harming, or are suicidal; that segregation placements include increased due process procedures; that decisions to place prisoners in segregation be independently adjudicated; that alternatives be put in place to reduce the number of young offenders in segregation; and that alternatives be developed to meet the least restrictive criteria for those with complex mental health needs. In their review of suicides in prison, the OCI concluded that segregation is an independent factor that elevates suicide risk. Despite these findings and ongoing reform recommendations, the OCI stated that the

"CSC has consistently and repeatedly rejected any call to strengthen oversight and accountability deficiencies" (2014–2015 29.)

The OCI also noted the disproportionate use of segregation to manage Indigenous and Black populations, as well as mentally ill offenders: One-third of Indigenous prisoners had experienced segregation during the reporting period and were held in segregation for the longest periods. With respect to mentally ill offenders, the OCI data clearly demonstrates that segregation is commonly used to deal with offenders who have complex mental health needs. For example, 85% of prisoners who self-injure have a history of segregation, and more than 60% of current prisoners with a history of segregation had also been housed at a regional mental health treatment center (this increases to 78.9% and 72.9% for women and Indigenous prisoners, respectively; OCI, *Annual Report 2014–2015*).

The 2013–2014 Annual Report of the OCI also identified problems with using segregation to manage self-injury among the women's prison population, noting that segregation does not further women's rehabilitation, enable program participation, or improve access to health services. Instead, women prisoners' safety and mental health are often jeopardized as a result of the distress produced in segregation (see also Bottos). Furthermore, prisoners with a history of segregation are more likely to be assessed "as high risk, high needs, low motivation, low reintegration potential and low accountability," and as having behavioral, psycho-social, and emotional needs requiring interventions (OCI, *Annual Report 2014–2015*). This could indicate that segregation has prolonged psycho-social effects for prisoners (Jackson; Motiuk and Blanchette; Roberts and Gebotys) that are not discernable and/or not reversed either upon their return to general population or upon their transfer to therapeutic correctional settings such as a psychiatric hospital.

Prolonged solitary confinement can be so harmful that the UN Human Rights Committee declared it a prohibited form of torture in 1994. Other international conventions on rights ratified by Canada prohibit its use for specific populations such as disabled persons (OCI, *Annual Report 2014–2015*). Minimum standards for the treatment of prisoners include that a person being placed in solitary confinement must be deemed fit to sustain it by the medical officer and that governments should actively be taking measures to reduce and/or abolish it (OCI, *Annual Report 2014–2015*). In 2011, the UN Human Rights Council Special Rapporteur on torture and other cruel, inhuman, or degrading treatment or punishment stated that solitary confinement is incompatible with the correctional aims of contemporary penitentiary regimes (Méndez). The Rapporteur recommended that segregation exceeding 15 days should be prohibited and stated that the solitary confinement of persons with diagnosed mental disabilities amounts to degrading and cruel treatment (OCI, *Annual Report 2014–2015*). In addition to these rights-based frameworks condemning solitary confinement, significant empirical data documents the harms of solitary confinement.

Confining the individual: producing the human

Solitary confinement has remained a constant feature of penality despite shifting penal rationalities and conceptions of the penal subject. It has long been known that prolonged isolation of individuals, regardless of their mental health at the outset, can precipitate their subjective undoing: "the symptoms of solitary confinement have remained strikingly consistent: anxiety, fatigue, confusion, paranoia, depression, hallucinations, headaches, and uncontrollable trembling" (Guenther xi; see also Haney). Often referred to as "SHU syndrome," these symptoms remain constant across settings and occur regardless of the intent of the institution (i.e., therapeutic, administrative, and punitive; Bonner; Guenther; Kupers, "How to Create"; Miller and Young).

Guenther argued that solitary confinement, and all forms of intensive confinement, will be similarly experienced across jurisdictions, prisons, and other institutions that subject prisoners to isolation. This is because the ultimate effect of this form of confinement is to prevent and undermine meaningful relations, which are not only constitutive to our subjectivity as persons, but, more importantly, are fundamental to our subjectivity as relational beings.

Empirical evidence demonstrates widespread agreement that solitary confinement tends to exacerbate prior mental health problems and can lead to the development of previously undetected mental health problems (Arrigo and Bullock). Over a decade ago, psychologist Craig Haney concluded that "empirical research on solitary and supermax-like confinement has consistently and unequivocally documented the harmful consequences of living in these kinds of environments" (130). Since then, research studies and inquiries have continued to expose the numerous harmful psychological effects of segregation on general prison populations, women prisoners, and vulnerable sub-populations, including those with prior mental health issues and those with a tendency to self-harm. The psychological distress caused by isolation has been noted as comparable in experience to physical torture (Metzer and Fellner).

Drawing on data from the US, Guenther showed that despite the fact that supermax units provide the requirements for human survival and can include amenities such as television, there is a fundamental difference in prisoners' well-being depending on the form of interpersonal interaction they have. For example, there is a marked difference when prisoners "visit" with their loved ones via closed-circuit television (CCTV) (and are thus prevented from being in physical contact or proximity) versus an in-person visit. Because of our need for inter-subjective modes of relating, forced solitude can function as a weapon deployed against the prisoner:

> Solitary confinement works by turning prisoners' constitutive relationality against themselves, turning their own capacities to feel, perceive, and relate to others in a meaningful world into instruments of their own undoing. This self-betrayal is only possible for beings who are complicated, whose

> subjectivity is not merely a point but a hinge, a self-relation that cannot be sustained in absolute solitude but only in relation to others.
>
> (Guenther xiii)

If it is the case that as relational beings we develop a sense of ourselves emotionally, psychologically, and even spatially (i.e., having a sense of our bodies in space) via significant embodied interactions with others, it follows that these symptoms are related to our deprivation not only of contact, but also of embodied relations that are significant to the prisoner.

When deprived of such relations, the prisoner may become disoriented to the point of losing a sense of self and existence:

> They see things that do not exist, and they fail to see things that do. Their sense of their own bodies—even the fundamental capacity to feel pain and distinguish their own pain from that of others—erodes to the point where they are no longer sure if they are being harmed or are harming themselves.
>
> (Guenther xi)

Women experience segregation as rejection, abandonment, invisibility, and as a denial of their existence (Canadian Human Rights Commission). Isolation has been reported as a contributing factor to higher rates of self-harm and suicidal thoughts in women prisoners in Britain (Kruttschnitt and Vuolo). Given the consistency of the harms of solitary confinement across geographic settings and differing population demographics, it seems that it is not just that solitary confinement prevents meaningful relationships that can be sustained via written communication or telecommunication. As Guenther argued, there is something specific about being cut off from other beings in space that undermines our subjectivity and our ability to know where we begin and where we end. As a practice central to the logic of the penitentiary, solitary confinement emerged as a part of humane reforms that presupposed a specific subject—an atomistic independent individual—who can only be actualized in the segregation cell (Guenther).

Historical underpinnings: contemporary continuity

As noted above, the institution of the penitentiary as an appropriate means to punish was and continues to be rooted in calls for humane reform. Troubled by the spectacle of public shaming, physical torture, and execution, reformers in Europe and North America during the late eighteenth century and the first half of the nineteenth century claimed that the penitentiary would provide a humane means to reform the criminal. In contrast to the mere enactment of punishment upon the body, reformers thought penitentiaries would be an enlightened and productive means of responding to criminal offenses and criminal offenders (Foucault; Guenther; McCoy). Central to the promise of the penitentiary was the notion that solitary confinement would allow for the reformation of prisoners by providing the conditions in which they could become disciplined and productive citizens.

Solitary confinement, originally premised on the notion that solitude would provide the conditions for penance and reform, was designed around Western philosophy's dominant ontology of "the human." The human of Western philosophy is a European male who is a rational, autonomous actor. He does not depend on others, nor is he determined by his environment or his body (Derrida; Guenther). However, this version of the human ignores the multiple ways in which humans are sustained by, and participate in, constant relationships of interdependence with humans, non-humans, and the more-than-human world. Because dependence has long been associated with femininity, disability, and animality, relationships of dependence are simultaneously disavowed by this particular understanding of the human and are positioned as a condition to be overcome (Derrida; Hall).

The segregation cell is one of few locations in which this Cartesian version of the human is actualized and experienced:

> Non-incarcerated subjects are free to invest in the fictions of objectivity, autonomy, self-sufficiency, and individuality, all the while relying on their embodied experience of affective and intercorporeal depth to sustain a meaningful sense of Being-in-the world. Only incarcerated subjects are forced to actually *exist* in such fictions, or to be broken by them.
>
> (Guenther 187)

According to Guenther, by preventing the conditions for sustaining a sense of one's self in relation to others, humanist frameworks prevent the recognition that solitary confinement will almost always be detrimental to those incarcerated. The intent and design of this practice has not resulted in the effects imagined by reformers; as Canadian prison advocate Michael Jackson noted, "it is a paradox of history that a central feature of that correctional strategy—solitary confinement—has come to epitomize the most disturbing abuse of power that exists in the Canadian penitentiary today" (*Prisoners* 6). From its inception, the Canadian penitentiary system was invested in the promise of solitude as a means to reform criminals, but also relied on practices of intensive confinement to manage and punish recalcitrant prisoners.

By the 1830s, politicians in Upper Canada had accepted the penitentiary as an effective and humane means of addressing crime and criminality by reforming the morality and habits of the poor. Within this political climate of "progressive" punishment, Kingston Penitentiary opened in 1835. Kingston was based on the "silent system" of imprisonment, with section VIII of the administrative regulations describing the duty of prisoners to "labour diligently and preserve unbroken silence ... not exchange a word with one another under any pretext whatever, nor communicate with one another ... must not exchange looks, wink, laugh, nod or gesticulate to each other" (quoted in Jackson, *Prisoners* 28). Although prisoners were not permitted to communicate with one another (although they did), nor were they separated physically from one another; they worked and ate together. Isolation was used by the administration of Kingston Penitentiary to deal with "incorrigible" criminals, and was still seen as a more humane and less violent option to that of corporeal punishment, which it supposedly replaced (McCoy 226).

Solitary confinement in the US can be characterized by three waves, each deployed as a means to achieve the shifting goals of the penitentiary system (Guenther). The first wave was characterized by the notion that prolonged solitude would cause the prisoner's introspection and redemption. Led by religious and moral reformers in the mid-nineteenth century, solitary confinement was positioned as being able to "transform the criminal into an upright citizen or, in Benjamin Rush's words, 'a republican machine'" (Guenther xvi). The prison became indexed as a location where the isolation of the prisoner was tethered to their moral reformation.

The second wave of solitary confinement was characterized by a will to rehabilitate, not redeem, the prisoner. This was framed by a belief in the rehabilitative potential of the behavioral sciences, made possible in a context of post-Korean War in the 1960s and 1970s. Scientists had developed behavior modification regimes that they claimed would treat and cure prisoners' anti-social behavior, with the goal of producing productive members of society (Guenther).

The third wave of solitary confinement shifted to the needs of the control prison, and is the form of solitary confinement that shapes current practices. Beginning in the 1980s, the function of solitary confinement shifted; it was no longer to redeem or rehabilitate the prisoner, but to manage populations according to the administrative and security requirements of the institution. In this case, administrators use solitary confinement to teach prisoners:

> To adapt to the rules and structures of the prison itself. We are living in the era of the control prison, where the immobilization of inmates has become an end in itself rather than a way of breaking through to the inwardness of criminals' souls or even the outwardness of their abnormal behaviour. Prisoners have become risks to be managed, resistances to be eliminated, and organisms to be fed, maintained, and even prevented from taking their own lives.
>
> (Guenther xvi)

In other words, prisoners are not viewed as individuals, but rather as "units of behavior" that can be arranged according to the (security) needs of the prison. Within this frame, solitary confinement is used to incapacitate prisoners so that the prison can be more efficiently governed. It is not for the achievement of a future-oriented project, such as adapting to life outside upon the termination of a sentence, though correctional policies might state otherwise

(Guenther); rather, it is part of a broader machinery of penal managerialism that continuously calculates criminal risk vis-à-vis institutional security concerns (Garland).

Guenther's examination of the logics of solitary confinement and their shifting investments in the context of particular moments of carcerality in the US has applicability to Canada, where the practice, since its inception, has also been used to punish and have offenders conform to norms of institutional behavior. Shortly after the opening of Kingston Penitentiary, rumors of the use of violence against prisoners, the sexual assault of women prisoners by guards, starving prisoners, and general mismanagement surrounded the institution (Jackson, *Prisoners*; McCoy). The Brown Commission was convened in 1848 by the reform government to examine Warden Henry Smith's management of Kingston Penitentiary.

The Commission focused on finding evidence of cruelty and corruption. In attempting to enforce the silent system, Smith had relied on corporeal punishment for those who violated their duties as prisoners. For instance, boys aged 10 and 11 were lashed and flogged using rawhide or a cat-o'-nine-tails (a multi-tailed whip) for behavior typical of children, such as talking, laughing, and idleness (Jackson, *Prisoners*; McCoy). Testimony delivered to the Brown Commission shows that "the box" or "dark cell" (i.e., solitary confinement) was explicitly used to punish a difficult-to-manage female prisoner, Charlotte Reveille.

As part of its investigation, the Brown Commission charged Warden Smith "in goading Charlotte Reveille, a Convict, by way of excessive punishment, into a state of insanity, or aggravating the malady under which she laboured" (Brown Commission 203). Reveille was imprisoned at Kingston Penitentiary from 1846 to 1849. As per the testimony of prison staff, a surgeon, and a psychologist interviewed in this commission, some constructed Reveille as violent, crude in her manner of speech (she used expletives), and destructive to prison property. Staff also claimed that Reveille's requests for medical attention were often frivolous and attention-seeking. The institutional infractions for which Reveille was punished included: "refusing to walk," "bad language," "outrageous behaviour," "refusing to wear shoes," "tearing blankets," "cursing the Matron," and "grossly insulting the Surgeon" (Brown Commission 203). According to the Warden's Punishment Ledger examined by the Brown Commission, Reveille's conduct was responded to by the "dark cell," "rawhide," "box, and bread and water" (204). Prison staff reported to the commission that the Surgeon requested that she be "put in some place where she could neither see nor hear" (quoted in Brown Commission 205).

After more than a year of Reveille being placed intermittently in solitary confinement, and a suicide attempt made by her, the Surgeon for Kingston Penitentiary was asked by the Board of Inspectors to provide a diagnosis as to her mental condition. In 1848, Dr Sampson declared her to be suffering from "moral insanity," yet the Warden and Inspectors disagreed with this assessment and did not transfer her to "a Lunatic Asylum" (Brown Commission 324). Further testimony by staff and Dr Sampson showed disagreement as to whether the dark cell or box could "injure a Convict's health" (205). She was characterized as very ill as a result of the punishment inflicted upon her, but was diagnosed as "too strong and too wicked to die" (205). What is clear is that staff defended their use of isolation on the grounds that they provided her with the necessities to keep her alive (such as adequate food and stimulation such as knitting).

The Commission determined that while Reveille arrived at Kingston Penitentiary in bad health and was predisposed to mental illness, it had "no doubt that the severe punishment she received, has greatly aggravated her maladies, physical and mental" (Brown Commission 208). Despite Kingston Penitentiary being modeled on the silent model of the Auburn Penitentiary in New York (Hayman), where prisoners were meant to silently labour together and solitude would provide the conditions for prisoners to repent or redeem themselves, solitary confinement was explicitly used to *punish* prisoners who violated institutional norms of behavior. The punitive function of solitary confinement is therefore not a contemporary practice in Canada linked only to the control prison; rather, it has historically been relied upon to control difficult-to-manage women, despite concerns that it was detrimental to physical, emotional, and mental health.

Political, academic, and institutional support of isolation practices did not decrease following the Brown Commission. Instead, proposals for its reform were put forward. The main recommendation of the Brown Commission was to implement a separate system wherein prisoners would be separated for a standard period at the outset of their custodial sentence. The separate system had become "penal orthodoxy" in England during the second half of the nineteenth century, with all prisons in England administered under this system as per the English Penal Act of 1865 (Jackson, *Prisoners* 31).

This regime of imprisonment entailed the solitary confinement of prisoners in cells that included an attached workshop. During this time, it was explicitly recognized by government officials that this mode of imprisonment was not therapeutic but an enduring form of punishment. Following the Brown Commission, the Penitentiary Act of 1851 permitted the construction of a maximum of 50 solitary cells consistent with the "solitary" or "separate" system, though this was not acted upon because these larger cells were more expensive to build and the labour performed individually by prisoners was less profitable for the prison by way of external contracts than was communal labour.

Yet, the will to isolate did not dissipate amongst prison officials. J.G. Moylan, the inspector of penitentiaries from 1875 to 1895, was steadfast in his belief that solitary confinement was a superior means to the congregate system in terms of achieving discipline among the prison population. Drawing on evidence from Europe and the US (e.g., a German prison director who attested that 99% of prisoners could endure solitary confinement for their entire life without harm, and Belgian officials who lauded the low recidivism rates of prisoners held in isolation), Moylan suggested that all prisoners be held in solitary confinement at the outset of their sentence. He wrote:

> The isolation of newly received convicts, for eight to nine months, for the object mentioned by Sir Walter Crofton (the proponent of the Crofton regime of isolation) [for reflection, repentance and religious instruction] and of incorrigibles for at least 18 months, to reform and prevent them from corrupting those who are well inclined, can be tried with all safety.
>
> (Quoted in Jackson, *Prisoners* 36)

While his vision for the isolation of all prisoners was not implemented to the degree of Moylan's recommendation, the practice of isolating prisoners became a common strategy to manage the recalcitrant prisoners whom the penitentiary had failed to rehabilitate (Jackson, *Prisoners*).

The isolation of incorrigible prisoners was solidified with the quick construction of the "Prison of Isolation" at Kingston Penitentiary in 1890, which opened in 1892 with 108 cells. This occurred within an academic and legal climate where the rehabilitation of prisoners was to include a supervised transition and reintegration into the community (McCoy). Incorrigibles, on the other hand, were positioned as a threat to the security of the institution, whose idleness and immorality could contaminate the general population; administrators posited that they required individualized approaches (Jackson, *Prisoners*).

Jackson described the Prison of Isolation as "Canada's first super-maximum institution" (*Prisoners* 37). Cells at the Prison of Isolation were larger than those at Kingston Penitentiary, as prisoners were to work and live in their cells for 23 hours a day. A regime of solitude and silence was expected: they were to exercise alone (under the supervision of a guard) for one hour a day, were given a restricted diet for the first three months, and were not permitted visitors or letters during this same time period. After the first three months, if prisoners exhibited good behavior, they could receive an ordinary prison diet. Three months after this, subject to their good conduct, they would be permitted to return to the general cells at Kingston Penitentiary. Prison authorities praised the Prison of Isolation as a successful tool of discipline, as it afforded individual attention and treatment that "rarely fails to have the desired effect" (quoted in Jackson, *Prisoners* 39).

The harms of this form of imprisonment were dismissed by the institution's surgeon, Dr Phelan, who emphasized the difference between solitary imprisonment of the past (placing prisoners in dungeon-like cells without light and physical and mental stimulation) versus the separate or isolation system structuring the Prison of Isolation. Dr Phelan praised the isolation system as "the best place as a safeguard to mental equipoise" and that claims as to its psychological harms were "fictitious stories" (cited in Jackson, *Prisoners* 39). Medical experts supported the prolonged isolation of prisoners who did not follow prison rules.

Isolation of this sort was deployed to make prisoners disciplined, productive, and laboring citizens.

From its inception, the logic of the Prison of Isolation functioned to manage security threats via the incapacitation of prisoners:

> Although the Prison of Isolation was steeped in reform ideas, its true purpose was to give keepers and officials at Kingston greater control over what they considered to be the worst elements in the prison population. Thus, it gained both political and administrative support where countless other reform initiatives had failed.
>
> (McCoy 251)

As such, the use of isolation as a punitive measure to manage resistant and recalcitrant prisoners is endemic to its logic, regardless of the reformist intentions of its proponents.

The Prison of Isolation—Canada's only penal institution where solitary confinement was the focal point of a regime of punishment—closed in 1908 due to a decline in prisoner admissions. It was reopened in 1911 and was used intermittently until in 1921, when it was converted into general population cells for Kingston Penitentiary. While these cells continued to be used to segregate incorrigibles, the system of separate confinement ended as prisoners resumed working together during the day.

This brief overview of the rationale and political will to isolate demonstrates that solitary confinement is historically embedded in humane reforms. As such, attempts to resist or curtail its use that rely on a legal discourse of "humane treatment" remain consistent with the logic that have continually rendered solitary confinement an articulable mode of captivity. This understanding provides insight as to why these practices have remained immune to abolition and instead are recalibrated (and renamed) according to changing notions of crime, offenders' criminality, penal rationalities, and shifting political climates. In the next section, we discuss legal challenges to practices of solitary confinement to show that instead of undermining this practice, they can actually affirm the ongoing use of solitary confinement. Specifically, we show that certain consequences of legal challenges and policy reforms can further codify and lower the minimum *legal* standards of treatment of prisoners, while making solitary confinement increasingly litigation-proof (Guenther; Reiter).

Cruel and unusual: the limits of rights-based litigation and policy reforms

In 1975, seven plaintiffs held in segregation in the "Penthouse" of the British Columbia Penitentiary sued the Government of Canada (*McCann v. The Queen*) on the grounds that their treatment constituted cruel and usual punishment under section 2(b) of the Canadian Bill of Rights. Further, they challenged that conditions of their confinement violated sections 1(a) and 2(e) of the Canadian Bill of Rights as their right to a fair hearing was denied. The plaintiffs had spent a combined 11-and-a-half years in solitary confinement between 1970 and 1974, with one plaintiff, Jack Emmett McCann, having spent a total of 1,471 days in solitary confinement (which included uninterrupted periods of segregation lasting 754 days and 342 days). The plaintiffs testified that they were subjected to isolation for 23-and-a-half hours per day, constant illumination, beatings by guards, tear-gassings, and forced medication; they further testified that they did not have hot water in their cell and were goaded into self-harming by guards who would give them razor blades when others in segregation engaged in such behavior. Two additional prisoners, Tommy McCaulley and Jacques Bellemaire, were also held in these conditions, but were not included as plaintiffs (Jackson, *Prisoners*).

McCaulley committed suicide by hanging after having ongoing hallucinations of a machine he believed to be in his cell (and which he set a fire to destroy). Bellemaire was not in a suitable psychological state to be included as a plaintiff; other prisoners believing that his prolonged solitary confinement had driven him "mad." The presiding judge, Mr Justice Heald, ruled that their confinement constituted cruel and usual punishment. As to due process, Justice Heald ruled that because their segregation was "administrative," in the sense that prison management needed discretion to act immediately to quell institutional disturbances, to require due process prior to segregation would result in a chaotic prison environment in which the administration had little power.

The Court's ruling of cruel and unusual punishment had little effect on the institution's use of segregation, nor did the ruling call into question the practice of segregation. Lasting changes following the ruling included a name change, from the "Penthouse" to "Super-Maximum Unit," larger windows in the cell doors, dimmed lights between 12 am and 6am, and the location for exercise moved from the hallway outside of the cells to an indoor central control area (Jackson, *Justice*). As such, the charge and finding of cruel and unusual punishment did not challenge *the logic* of isolating and caging prisoners. Rather, the institution's discretion to use segregation as a security measure was reiterated, clarified, and ultimately strengthened.

Segregation: the CSC's approach to difficult-to-manage-women

The CSC's use of segregation to manage federally sentenced women has come under legal scrutiny and challenge over the past 30 years. In each case, the CSC remains invested in the practice of segregation and resistant to operational change. In April 1994, shortly after CSC committed to its landmark women-centered reform initiative based on *Creating Choices: The Report of the Task on Federally Sentenced Women* (1990), an incident occurred at the Prison for Women that threatened its reputation and shook public confidence in the national correctional system. A popular investigative documentary program, "The Fifth Estate," broadcast a video of a cell extraction at the prison performed by a male Institutional Emergency Response Team (IERT) from the Kingston Penitentiary for Men. The video showed images of the mistreatment of women in segregation including the unarmed, partially clothed women prisoners being removed from segregation cells by the IERT who were dressed in full riot gear.

Prisoners were left in cold and damp segregation cells wearing paper gowns, and guards also placed them in restraints and leg irons. They were subjected to body cavity searches on dirty cell floors and were denied basic necessities like toilet paper and sanitary products. These prisoners also had minimal access to legal counsel and advocates. These events led to a Commission of Inquiry headed by Justice Louise Arbour, who conducted a lengthy investigation and extensive policy hearings. Two years later, in 1996, she released her report, "Commission of Inquiry into Certain Events at the Prison for Women in Kingston," which led to the resignation of the Commissioner of Corrections (Hayman 140).

This report was one of the most candid and pointed critiques of the CSC's management of prisoners. Arbour reported that despite the numerous rules, policies, and laws that governed the conduct of frontline prison staff, institutional administrations, and prisoners, "one sees little evidence of the will to yield pragmatic concerns to the dictates of a legal order … the Rule of Law is absent, although rules are everywhere" (Arbour 180). Arbour's report made multiple recommendations for change directed at ensuring that the CSC would strengthen its administrative accountability to the rule of law—changes that would also institutionalize protections to uphold prisoners' rights.[1]

The Commission made very specific recommendations about the use and oversight of administrative segregation (Arbour, Recommendation 9, 255–256). The report also called for the development of alternatives to segregation and best practices for diffusing difficult situations and managing prisoners in crisis (Arbour 187–188). The CSC took several steps to formally respond to Arbour's concerns and made significant efforts to strengthen policies and procedure to ensure compliance with the law. However, the past 20 years of annual reports of the Correctional Investigator, the recent Corner's Inquest into the death of Ashley Smith, and research conducted by independent scholars and experts confirm that most of the same issues identified in Arbour's report persist. For example, transparency and accountability in operations, and a lack of willingness to be scrutinized by others are still issues of great concern (see Arbour 192).

In 2003, as part of changes to managing high-risk women and the implementation of the Intensive Intervention Strategy (IIS), the CSC introduced a management protocol for managing higher-risk women in maximum security (and those already housed in administrative segregation). The CSC referred to this as "a detailed framework, based on legislation and CSC's segregation and transfer policies, to keep staff, other inmates, the public and the inmate herself safe" (CSC, *Ten-Year Status Report*, n.p.). However, the 2008/2009 Annual Report of the Office of the Correctional Investigator called for this protocol to be immediately rescinded because it was not having the intended improved safety effects and women were not being reintegrated back into the Secure Units in a timely manner. As of 2010, the protocol had been used for a total of seven women (CSC, *Management*).

That same year, the CSC report *Management of Higher-Risk Women: Results of Consultation on an Alternative to Management Protocol* concluded that the protocol was not having its intended effect and committed to finding alternative ways to manage higher-risk women (see Kerr for a discussion of the history of the protocol). Although the protocol has been terminated (date uncertain), its replacement is not clearly articulated in any publicly available CSC material. Because of this lack of transparency, it is difficult to discern how women being housed in administrative segregation are being managed, especially those with long-term placements. The continued lack of transparency and accountability in the management of administrative segregation is an ongoing concern.

Segregation and homicide: Ashley Smith's death and the CSC's commitment to isolation

Ashley Smith, a 19-year-old prisoner in the care of the CSC at the Grand Valley Institution for Women in Kitchener, Ontario, died on 19 October 2007 from a self-affixed ligature around her neck as guards watched. At the age of 14, Ashley was originally sentenced for to 30 days in youth custody for throwing crab apples at a postal worker. In the youth system, Ashley did not behave according to institutional norms and accrued behavioral infractions and additional criminal charges. As a result, she was sentenced to serve a federal sentence. She did not fare better in adult institutions, being the subject of 150 security infractions in close to a year, most of which were about her engaging in self-harm. Because she was perceived as "difficult-to-manage," she was mainly housed in solitary confinement for the duration of her incarceration.

In the context of Ashley's use of ligatures to self-harm, staff often wore full riot gear to enter her cell to remove them and used force as required in an attempt to ensure her safety. Force included physical handling, various restraints, and Oleoresin Capsicum (also referred to as inflammatory, OC, or pepper) spray or mace. Ashley's self-harming was so frequent that staff removed ligatures from her neck as often as six or seven times a day. Although she was mostly compliant with the removal of ligatures, she sometimes used the opportunity to wrestle with, spit on, and/or bite the guards. As a result of her repeated self-asphyxiation, her face was permanently discolored; she had broken facial blood vessels, experienced frequent nosebleeds, and lost vision in one eye.

During the course of less than a year, the CSC moved Ashley 17 times between various institutions within four of the CSC's five regions (three federal penitentiaries, two treatment facilities, two external hospitals, and one provincial correctional facility; Hannah-Moffat and Klassen). Each transfer "reset" her segregation clock, meaning that the CSC was able to circumvent the legally required segregation review at day 7 and day 30, wherein the review must justify the prisoner's continued segregation. During flights between regions, Ashley was sometimes duct-taped to her airplane seat. Upon arrival at each new institution, she would be immediately placed in segregation and at times physically or chemically restrained.

Ashley's cell effects were restricted to the degree that she was prohibited from having a food tray and was only given two sheets of toilet paper at a time. Her living conditions were barren: her cell was without tiles or light fixtures, and the sprinkler was covered as she used these to self-injure. The segregation shower was adapted so that she could not access metal to self-injure. A guard explained that Ashley "would lie down on the floor in front of the food slot on the dried tar left from the tile adhesive, right against the door where we couldn't see her well" (Union of Canadian Correctional Officers 8). It is clear that Ashley's environment in segregation provided little stimulation and extreme isolation. The interaction with others that she experienced was often negative. Ashley and advocates on her behalf officially grieved the conditions of her confinement, but these grievances were dismissed by officials as baseless.

Frontline staff sought advice on how to better manage Ashley, strategies to prevent her self-injuring, and ways to access help for her. Senior prison administrators, on the other hand, were apprehensive about the increasing reports documenting the use of force when guards entered her cell. Consequently, management ordered staff not to enter Ashley's cell until they had determined that her breathing had stopped. When frontline staff violated this order—i.e., when they entered Ashley's cell when she self-harmed but was still breathing—they were disciplined by their managers. On October 19, 2007, Ashley died from self-strangulation—guards, who were watching on camera, did not access her cell in time. Three guards faced criminal charges for causing death by criminal negligence, though the Crown attorney eventually dismissed these charges. After six years of deliberation, a coroner's inquest ruled Ashley's death a homicide.

For those familiar with corrections in Canada, Ashley's death was preventable, but not unpredictable or unusual. Ashley's treatment is consistent with common institutional practices such as segregation, and physical and chemical restraints practices that violate the rights of prisoners. Though commentators had hoped that the Coroner's report into Ashley Smith's death would yield changes in correctional practices, the report and the CSC's reception of it, revealed again that prisons are institutions of punishment and cannot be tasked with treating or managing complex social problems.

As with the Brown Commission and the Arbour Commission, it is difficult to determine with certainty whether the Ashley Smith Inquest had any effects on the CSC's use of segregation and segregation-like practices, or its management of individuals with mental health issues or self-injurious behaviors. A year after the Coroner's jury made their recommendations, the CSC officially responded in December 2014. Its response largely consisted of it reiterating existing CSC policy and practices. The CSC's Response to the Coroner's Recommendations refers to a number of changes and new forms of assessment and practices (CSC, *Response* 813), but the details of these assessments, practices, and programs are not publicly available for review.

The CSC dismissed the Coroner's jury recommendations that "indefinite solitary confinement" be abolished, that long-term segregation not exceed 15 days, and that restrictions be imposed on the length and number of times that prisoners can spend in segregation, including a requirement of no more than a cumulative total of 60 days in a calendar year (CSC, *Response*). A similar recommendation made by Arbour that was not operationally implemented. The CSC's response to its critics, independent inquiries, and the Ombudsman notably reaffirmed its legal authority to use segregation and its necessity in managing the prison population. It stated that segregation it is not intended for punitive use, but rather to:

> facilitate an investigation or to protect the safety and security of individuals and/or the institution. The purpose of administrative segregation is to maintain the security of the penitentiary or of any persons by not allowing an inmate to associate with other inmates when he or she meets the legislative requirements outlined in the CCRA.
>
> (CSC, *Response* 8)

In its rejection of the jury's recommendations, the CSC admitted that although segregation is antithetical to healthy outcomes, it required discretion to engage it as a security management tool. Furthermore, because administrative segregation does not require the same levels of due process that a disciplinary segregation placement entails, administrative segregation is used as a punitive measure that circumvents legal requirements that include external oversight, sharing of information with the prisoner, and a maximum of 30 days' confinement (OCI, *Annual Report 2014–2015*). Whether or not the CSC intends to punish the prisoner in question via the use of solitary confinement does not negate the fact that the prisoner can experience it as such.

In the latest annual report of the OCI, segregation remains an issue requiring scrutiny, despite decreases in its use over the reporting year. Specific to women with complex needs, administrative segregation remains commonly used. The OCI remained skeptical that placing prisoners in segregation could accomplish therapeutic goals, especially when counseling and healthcare occurs via the food slot of a segregation cell. This concern demonstrates the fundamental isolation and deprivation of intercorporeal relationships that segregated prisoners can experience.

The most recent OCI annual report (2016), as with its previous annual report (2015), recommended legal limits surrounding the length and uses of segregation, as well as encouraging the CSC to commit to recommendations surrounding the death of Ashley Smith. Yet, legal challenges and reforms have not challenged the practice of solitary confinement as a whole; rather, they have intensified calls to limit its use for *specific* populations (e.g., those with diagnosed mental illnesses), presupposing that solitary confinement is still a suitable method of control for others. This approach negates the fact that solitary confinement can precipitate distress and mental illness among otherwise healthy persons (Guenther; Kupers, "How to Create") who would remain subject to instituted isolation despite the fact that this form of confinement can cause ailments that would prohibit its use.

It is evident that a commitment to more "humane" forms of punishment do not preclude the development and use technologies of violence. However, as Reiter and Guenther argued, legal challenges to solitary confinement have legitimized and solidified these practices while rendering them increasingly resistant to rights-based advocacy. For example, the decision in the US Eighth Amendment case, *Madrid v. Gomez*, found that solitary confinement constituted cruel and unusual punishment for specific prison sub-populations: those who were diagnosed as having a mental illness or those with an "unreasonably high risk" of developing mental illness while confined. The effect of this decision did not challenge the logic of solitary confinement or undermine its use; instead, it "ended up reinscribing the violence of prolonged solitary confinement within law" (Guenther 128).

Human rights-based challenges specific to the conditions of solitary confinement have also had the unintended effect of producing legal minimum standards of treatment the norm under which prisoners are confined:

> By failing to condemn solitary confinement outright as a form of cruel and unusual punishment and by delineating exactly what the law would permit—sometimes down to the specific dimensions of an isolation cell—many district and federal courts have ended up inscribing a "just measure of deprivation" within the law, even in cases where they have explicitly affirmed prisoners' human rights.
>
> (Guenther 132)

Within a human rights framework, law has worked to set out minimum standards of treatment for the isolation of prisoners. In so doing, these minimum standards become normalized as the standard under which prisoners can be held in isolation while institutions can claim procedural compliance.

We have highlighted the seeming immunity of solitary confinement to legal challenge and the limits of rights-based litigation to abolish this technology of violence. In the next section, we propose new interventions for understanding the harms of solitary confinement, not only as the violation of rights, but also as ethical violations of our ontologies as relational beings, our dignity, and the necessity of recognizing vulnerability as complex and multi-faceted.

Ontological violations: ethical implications

Because solitary confinement is rooted in humane prison reforms that presuppose an atomistic and rational human subject, Guenther's critical phenomenological account of solitary confinement highlights the need for an alternative account of the subject. For Guenther, the need for intercorporeal relationships to sustain us is not exclusive to humans, but to all animals who develop a "sense of self as an individuated subject with a unique perspective on a shared world" via our relations with others (155). Solitary confinement should be understood not as a violation of our human rights premised on an implicit right to freedom and dignity reduced solely to law, but as a violation of our ontologies as relational beings. The harms of being forcefully confined to oneself exceed dehumanization, and for Guenther are better understood as effecting a *deanimalization* of the subject. She described this as a process entailing:

> The reduction of a living, relational animal to a nonrelational thing to be stored, exchanged, or even destroyed without regard for its particular ways of being in the world. Perhaps human dignity is best protected when it is claimed not as the unique, exclusive property of the human but as a structure of open relationality shared with other living beings.
>
> (Guenther 157)

Guenther's call for an alternative account of the subject implies a recognition that we are interdependent beings who develop an understanding of ourselves through our relations to others in a shared world. The Commissioner's Directive for administrative segregation outlined that solitary confinement is used "to contribute to the safety of staff and inmates and to the security of the institution by providing a safe and humane administrative segregation process" (CSC, Commissioner's Directive 709). Yet a relational account of the subject undermines the conceptual premise of this justification, namely that solitary confinement can be reformed or used appropriately for certain populations (who can putatively be unharmed).

If meaningful intercorporeal relationships are vital to our subjectivities, then solitary confinement, regardless of intent or reform, remains an ethical violation of our most profound selves as "*living beings*, sensible flesh with corporeal relations to other embodied beings and to an open field of overlapping experience in a shared world" (Guenther 155). It is these aspects of our subjectivities that a human rights framework fails to account for. An interdependent and relational account of the subject also highlights how dignity will fail to be obtained through legal appeals to rights.

Whereas dignity is framed within human rights discourse as an intrinsic possession that can be taken away, Gruen argued that dignity is instead a relational property that can only be realized as matter of treatment and perception. According to Gruen, the politics of sight in the space of the prison functions to undermine possibilities for dignity. Because the prison has an interest in keeping prisoners alive and uses solitary confinement as the ultimate enactment of this interest, prisoners in solitary are kept constantly visible. This precludes possibilities for dignity because privacy is obliterated; prisoners cannot choose whether they are visible and are unable to hide from the gaze of guards.

When prisoners in segregation are under observation or suicide/self-injury watch, they are under constant monitoring via CCTV (CSC, Commissioner's Directive 709). Prisoners are observed performing bodily functions, thus negating the possibility for dignity in captivity: "humans have adopted norms of keeping excretory functions private and thus experience the vulnerability of being on display as they defecate or urinate as an affront to their dignity" (Gruen 243). For women who have experienced prior sexual and physical assaults, conditions of segregation that include violent cell removals and lack of privacy in toilets and showers can be triggering and retraumatizing (Shaylor). The staff protocol for women prisoners held in segregation states that only women guards are allowed to monitor the CCTV cameras, and that the screens will be positioned in such a way to protect the dignity and privacy of the prisoner (CSC, Commissioner's Directive 577), but this does not negate the fact that prisoners are subject to constant surveillance and are unable to hide from view. In this sense, dignity would entail an ethics of sight where the captive is able to suspend the panoptic gaze, which is always already impossible in a segregation cell (see Gruen). Might dignity be actualized if we recognize the vulnerability of prisoners?

The notion that vulnerability is a dualism of harm/perpetration precludes us from attending to the logic of carcerality. Specifically, this logic entails that intersecting identity categories and social structures of inequality (i.e., race, gender, and sexuality) render certain persons more likely to be considered perpetrators of harm, while their vulnerability to state surveillance and criminalization is negated. It is often the case that "vulnerability is, for the most part, deemed incompatible with criminality" (Gilson 46). Within this cultural imaginary, the vulnerability of those considered threatening to society's victim archetypes (legitimate (white) vulnerable subjects) goes unrecognized. Vulnerability is thus a corporeal and social condition that is politically mediated and differentially distributed.

Within a dualistic understanding of vulnerability, prisoners are reduced to perpetrators who are incapable of being harmed or at least undeserving of protection from vulnerability. In turn, the effect that the violence of solitary confinement is "not recognized as the exploitation of vulnerability that [it is] or the exploitation of prisoners' vulnerability is perceived as warranted" (Gilson 47). This position is echoed in international research findings that show that prison guards overlook or fail to recognize the stress experienced by prisoners in solitary confinement (Fellner and Mariner; Grassian; Jackson, *Prisoners*; Koch; Toch). Other scholars have suggested that prison guards may interpret explicit expressions of distress, including self-harm, as attempts to manipulate or disrupt the prison operations for special treatment (Conover; Grassian; Kupers, *Prison*; for a detailed review, see Scharff Smith). In this sense, the vulnerability of prisoners is recoded as perpetration via their violation of institutional norms of conduct.

Solitary confinement is a process wherein prisoners are rendered corporeally, socially, and psychologically vulnerable, and so we require a relational understanding of vulnerability to account for the harms of this form of confinement.

Gilson suggested that vulnerability is "an experience rather than a social position" (44) and "is a fundamental, shared condition of openness to being affected and affecting" (45). Official state discourse mobilizes the language of vulnerability regarding institutional security, or the vulnerability of the prisoner who is segregated for their own protection, but these rationales rely on a flattened and dualistic understanding of vulnerability that does not account for the specific vulnerabilities that segregation practices produce and that require our ethical attention.

A relational account of vulnerability provides the space to consider how practices of solitary confinement render subjects vulnerable in multiple forms (physically, politically, and emotionally) and their lives precarious (Gilson). In this sense, we are better able to understand the ethical violations that practices of solitary confinement entail, regardless of attempts for reform or oversight.

Conclusion

From its inception, solitary confinement and practices of forced isolation have been subject to scrutiny, investigation, and reform in Canada. Yet, despite legal rulings that sensory deprivation of this kind can constitute cruel and unusual punishment, and research demonstrating the multiple ways that forced isolation precipitates self-harm, suicide, uncontrollable rage, trembling, and the erasure of the self, this practice remains staunchly protected by the CSC as an indispensable tool of security and management that can be reformed and appropriately used and administered. We propose that the indelibility of solitary confinement is tied to its historical roots and investment in dominant ontologies of the human. Because we accept a Cartesian ontology of the human—who by nature is a rational autonomous actor who can flourish without meaningful corporeal relations—we will continue to perpetuate notions that solitary confinement can be reformed and appropriately administered.

Legal challenges to solitary confinement mobilized on the terrain of dehumanization and subsequent calls for the "humane" treatment of prisoners remain constricted within a humanist legal discourse that are unable to account for the ethical violations implicit in solitary confinement (Guenther). Instead, we ought to view practices of solitary confinement as effecting a deontologization of our intersubjectivity, of precluding a relational account of dignity, and of failing to account for the corporeal, political, and psychological vulnerabilities it produces. In so doing, possibilities of reforming this practice are precluded, as these ethical violations are implicit in its logic of sensory deprivation, isolation, and surveillance.

Note

1 The recommendations are too numerous to outline in detail here. For more information, see Arbour.

References

Arrigo, B. and J. Bullock. "The Psychological Effects of Solitary Confinement on Prisoners in Supermax Units: Reviewing What We Know and Recommending What Should Change." *International Journal of Offender Therapy and Comparative Criminology*, vol. 52, no. 6, 2008, pp. 622–640.

Arbour, Louise. *Commission of Inquiry into Certain Events at the Prison for Women in Kingston*. Public Works and Government Services Canada, 1996.

Bonner, R L. "Stressful Segregation Housing and Psychosocial Vulnerability in Prison Suicide Indicators." *Suicide & Life-Threatening Behaviour*, vol. 36, no. 2, 2006, pp. 250–254.

Bottos, S. 2007. *Profile of Offenders in Administrative Segregation: A Review of the Literature. Research Brief 39*. Research Branch, Correctional Service of Canada, Ottawa. Available at: www.csc-scc.gc.ca/research/b39-eng.shtml#Toc195779129.

Brown Commission. *Second Report of the Commissioners Appointed to Investigate into the Conduct, Discipline, and Management of the Provincial Penitentiary*. Rollo Campbell, 1849.

Canadian Human Rights Commission. *Protecting their Rights: A Systemic Review of Human Rights in Correctional Services for Federally Sentenced Women*. Canadian Human Rights Commission, 2003.

Conover, T. *Holding the Key*. Scribner, 2001.

Correctional Service of Canada. Commissioner's Directive 577—Administrative Segregation. Government of Canada, 2013. Available at: www.csc-scc.gc.ca/lois-et-reglements/577-cd-eng.shtml.

——. Commissioner's Directive 577—Administrative Segregation. Ottawa, ON: Government of Canada, 2013. Available at: www.csc-scc.gc.ca/lois-et-reglements/577-cd-eng.shtml.

——. Commissioner's Directive 709—Administrative Segregation. Government of Canada, 2015. Available at: www.csc-scc.gc.ca/politiques-et-lois/709-cd-eng.shtml.

. *Management of Higher-Risk Women: Results of Consultation on an Alternative to Management Protocol*. Women Offender Sector, Correctional Service Canada, 2010.

——. *Response to the Coroner's Inquest Touching the Death of Ashley Smith*. CSC, 2014. Available at: www.csc-scc.gc.ca/publications/005007-9011-eng.shtml.

——. *Ten-Year Status Report on Women's Corrections 1996–2006*. Women Offender Programs and Issues, Correctional Service of Canada, 2006.

Derrida, Jacques and Marie-Louise Mallet. *The Animal that Therefore I am*. Fordham University Press, 2008.

Fellner, J. and J. Mariner. *Cold Storage: Super-maximum Security Confinement in Indiana*. Human Rights Watch, 1997.

Foucault, Michel. *Discipline and Punish: The Birth of the Prison*. Vintage, 1977.

Garland, D. *The Culture of Control*. Oxford University, 2001.

Gilson, E. "The Perils and Privileges of Vulnerability: Intersectionality, Relationality, and the Injustices of the US Prison Nation." *philoSOPHIA*, vol. 6, no. 1, 2016, pp. 43–59.

Grassian, S. "Psychopathological Effects of Solitary Confinement." *American Journal of Psychiatry*, vol. 140, 1983, pp. 1450–1454.

Grassian, S. and N. Friedman. "Effects of Sensory Deprivation in Psychiatric Seclusion and Solitary Confinement." *International Journal of Law and Psychiatry*, vol. 8, 1986, pp. 49–65.

Gruen, L. "Dignity, Captivity, and an Ethics of Sight." In *The Ethics of Captivity*. Edited by Lori Gruen, Oxford University Press, 2014, pp. 231–247.

Guenther, L. *Solitary Confinement: Social Death and its Afterlives*. University of Minnesota Press, 2013.

Hall, Kim Q. "Toward a Queer Crip Feminist Politics of Food." *philoSOPHIA*, vol. 4,no. 2, 2014, pp. 177–196.

Haney, C. "Mental Health Issues in Long-Term Solitary and 'Supermax' Confinement." *Crime & Delinquency*, vol. 49, 2003, pp. 124–156.

Hannah-Moffat, Kelly and Amy Klassen. "Normalizing Exceptions: Solitary Confinement and the Micro-politics of Risk/Need in Canada." In *Extreme Punishment*. Edited by Keramet Reiter and Alexa Koenig. Palgrave Macmillan, 2015, pp. 135–155.

Hayman, Stephanie. *Imprisoning Our Sisters: The New Federal Women's Prisons in Canada*. McGill-Queen's Press, 2006.

Jackson, M. *Justice behind the Walls: Human Rights in Canadian Prisons*. Greystone Books, 2002.

——. *Prisoners of Isolation: Solitary Confinement in Canada*. University of Toronto Press, 1983.

Koch, I.E. "Isolationens psykiske og sociale følgevirkninger." *Månedsskrift for Praktisk Lægegerning*, vol. 60 (June), 1983, pp. 369–372.

Kerr, Lisa. "The Origins of Unlawful Prison Policies." *Canadian Journal of Human Rights*, vol. 4, no. 1, 2015, pp. 91–119.

Kruttschnitt, C. and M. Vuolo. "The Cultural Context of Women Prisoners' Mental Health: A Comparison of Two Prison Systems." *Punishment & Society*, vol. 9, 2007, pp. 115–150.

Kupers, T.A. "How to Create Madness in Prison." In *Humane Prisons*. Edited by David Jones. Radcliffe Publishing, 2006, pp. 47–59.

——. *Prison Madness: The Mental Health Crisis behind Bars and What We Must Do about it*. Jossey-Bass, 1999.

Madrid v. Gomez. 1995. 889 F.Supp. 1146 (N.D.Cal.).

McCann v. Canada. Federal Court of Canada. 1976.

McCoy, Ted. *Hard Time: Reforming the Penitentiary in Nineteenth-Century Canada*. Athabasca University Press, 2012.

Méndez, Juan. "Interim Report of the Special Rapporteur of the Human Rights Council on Torture and Other Cruel, Inhuman or Degrading Treatment or Punishment." United Nations, 2011.

Metzer, J. and J. Fellner. "Solitary Confinement and Mental Illness in U.S. Prisons: A Challenge for Medical Ethics." *Journal of the American Academy of Psychiatry and the Law*, vol. 38, no.1, 2010, pp. 27–31.

Miller, H.A. and G.R. Young. "Prison Segregation: Administrative Detention or Mental Health Problem?" *Criminal Behaviour and Mental Health*, vol. 7, 1997, pp. 85–94.

Motiuk, L.L. and K. Blanchette. "Characteristics of Administratively Segregated Offenders in Federal Corrections." *Canadian Journal of Criminology*, vol. 43, 2001, pp. 131–143.

Office of the Correctional Investigator. *Annual Report 2008–2009*. Her Majesty the Queen in Right of Canada, 2009.

——. *Annual Report of the Office of the Correctional Investigator 2015–2016*. Her Majesty the Queen in Right of Canada, 2016.

——. *Annual Report of the Office of the Correctional Investigator 2014–2015*. Her Majesty the Queen in Right of Canada, 2015.

Reiter, K. "The Most Restrictive Alternative: A Litigation History of Solitary Confinement in US Prisons, 1960–2006." *Studies in Law, Politics, and Society*, vol. 57, 2012, pp. 71–124.

Reiter, K. and T. Blair. "Punishing Mental Illness: Trans-institutionalization and Solitary Confinement in the United States." In *Extreme Punishment*. Edited by Keramet Reiter and Alexa Koenig. Palgrave Macmillan, 2015, pp. 177–196.

Roberts, J.V. and R.J. Gebotys. "Prisoners of Isolation: Research on the Effects of Administrative Segregation." *Canadian Journal of Criminology*, vol. 43, no.1, 2001, pp. 85–97.

Scharff Smith, P. "The Effects of Solitary Confinement on Prison Inmates: A Brief History and Review of the Literature." *Crime and Justice*, vol. 34, no. 1, 2006, pp. 441–528.

Shaylor, Cassandra. "It's Like Living in a Black Hole: Women of Color and Solitary Confinement in the Prison Industrial Complex." *New England Journal on Criminal & Civil Confinement*, vol. 24, 1998, p. 385.

Toch, H. *Mosaic of Despair: Human Breakdowns in Prison*. Princeton University Press, 1992.

"The Ultimate Response." *Fifth Estate*, directed by Michael Smith, CBC Radio-Canada.

Union of Canadian Correctional Officers. 2008. *A Rush to Judgment: A Report on the Death in Custody of Ashley Smith, a Prisoner at Grand Valley Institution for Women*, www.cclanaudierc.csn.qc.ca/Documents/UCCO-SACC/National/documents/Issues/GVI/Full%20Report%20-%20A%20Rush%20to%20Judgment.pdf.

Chapter 10

Non-violent communion versus medieval ships of fools

Engaged citizenry alternatives to Europe's war on refugees[1]

Pablo Ouziel

> Once they had left their homeland they remained homeless, once they had left their state they became stateless; once they had been deprived of their human rights they were rightless, the scum of the earth.
>
> (Arendt, *The Origins* 267)

Introduction

What I would like to do for the purpose of this chapter is to address the state of European Union (EU) and Member State laws, and our conceptions of democracy and the nation-state. In order to do this, I will present the way in which refugees are being treated as they try to arrive (and, in some cases, arrive) to Europe in these early stages of the twenty-first century. As a case in hand, I focus on refugees from war-torn Syria.[2] I make this choice because due to an open debate on the issue of Syrian refugees at the heart of the European project, much of the less obvious behavior of Member States has surfaced in mainstream dialogues across European countries.[3]

The journey of these refugees is part of the greatest exodus of the twentieth and twenty-first centuries. It is well documented that it is mainly caused by Western powers and 100 years of imperialism and destruction in the Middle East.[4] As Tony Blair has admitted, there "are elements of truth" in the claim that the "principal cause" of the rise of Islamic State (ISIS) was the invasion of Iraq (Watt para. 8). In addition, when the US government decided that Syrian President Bashar al-Assad had to go, it began to arm rebels opposing the regime (McKelvey).[5] According to the BBC, there are now over 1,000 armed opposition groups in Syria ("Guide to the Syrian Rebels"). Prior to Western intervention in the country, these factions had been living in relative peace with each other for 100 years.[6]

At first sight, it would seem that refugees entering or attempting to enter Europe in their flight from Syria are facing cruel and unusual punishment as part of a permanent state of exception imposed on them by Western powers. However, when one reflects on the history of the region, things look different. Through this reflection, one understands that, for 100 years, Western imperial interests have been systematically destabilizing and destroying the region. Due to this reality, it becomes unhelpful to think of the response to refugees as cruel and unusual punishment or a permanent state of exception. Instead, I think it is more accurate to speak of an all-out war on refugees.[7]

Western powers include in their war budgets millions of dollars, which are used to hire international lawyers. These lawyers argue that the actions these states are taking toward innocent people are in accord with international law, conventions on refugees, and their pertinent duties to protect innocent civilians. Nevertheless, the process is an historical norm. Western powers bomb, Western powers justify, and Western powers punish those fleeing—a dysfunctional system that is beneficial primarily to the West.

Of course, the cause of their flight elicits an active objection to the Western imperial project, particularly by those claiming to be fighting injustice and claiming concern for law, democracy, and the legitimacy of the nation-state. However, this is a struggle I must leave to one side for now. I want to focus instead on observing the legal, alter-legal, and illegal violences carried out on refugees entering Europe. Doing this reveals how the EU and its Member States are systematically hollowing out whatever remains of their ideal of democracy.[8]

Following this, throughout this chapter I will be thinking of the multiplicity of policies being faced by Syrian refugees entering (or attempting to enter) the EU as an all-out war on refugees. I will try and argue that the distinction between legal and illegal violence in relation to the treatment of refugees does not guarantee any limits. The type of violence one observes as an EU citizen or experiences as a refugee happens within a shifting space. Within this space, policy is constantly moving toward the legalization of ever-increasing violence on refugees.

Discussing these issues is important because it raises the question of whether other alternatives are achievable. We are living times in which we are told that legality sustains the democratic nation-states. Yet, those claiming to be defending democracy are using this legality to legitimate expansionary and imperial violence, including the waging of war on refugees. At the same time, alternatives from "below" stemming from organized EU citizens helping refugees in more or less spontaneous solidarity with them are showing us other possibilities, as are the refugees organizing themselves in a multiplicity of ways that need to be heard. Perhaps it is in these "other" responses to and with refugees, and in the self-organizing of the refugees themselves, that an approach can be found that strengthens democracy, "humanizes" law, and redraws the parameters and aspirations of the nation-state.

It is useful to extract ourselves from solutions coming from "above" in "power-over" form. Orienting ourselves from the spaces of social, political and legal transformation that are opened up by engaged-citizens ("refugee" citizens and "EU" citizens alike) working on solutions from below in a "power-with" manner.[9] The alternative infrastructures developed by these engaged citizens can help change the way we understand our "response-abilities" as democratic citizens. Their modes of being in the world with others are exemplary of the participatory democracies of the planet that we call "the other world that is actual."

Although EU engaged citizen networks have been an important support to refugees, the fact is that the refugees constitute within themselves a whole world of power-with that they themselves have created in their exodus. Although refugees are often portrayed as people with humanitarian needs, they are above all human beings "fighting for freedom of movement, resisting the border regimes, and practicing disobedience of the laws that exclude and criminalize them" ("Make Europe" para. 2). While states try to individualize and isolate them, they "build and defend social ties and networks, that give power to cross borders and power to get inserted into societies of destination" ("Make Europe" para. 2).

On a daily basis, refugees are resisting racist systems that separate between those with papers and those without papers. Their resistance occurs "in the camps, at the borders … in police stations and prisons" ("Make Europe"). Through their journey, they have had to endure enormous hardships and suffering; they have been cheated, betrayed, and many have died along the way. These are people who have left their homes, their histories, and their ancient civilizations. Yet, by working together they have managed to cross country after country and have made their way to Europe. Once in Europe, whilst the whole power-over forces of states and the EU have tried to make them into "bare life," they have "come to life."[10]

The courage, strength, imagination, and love revealed by the everyday practices of refugees are exemplary. Yet, once they arrive to Europe, they are mostly treated as victims and subjects—people who do not need to be heard in order to describe what they have endured. Commentators do not need their voice in order to define them and place them into normative understandings of their realities. Nevertheless, the refugees are agents, and every day they exercise more agency than most looking from outside will ever acknowledge.

It is because of this that we need to switch off our normative frameworks. We need to enter into dialogues with these people and learn from them. We need to listen very carefully to the refugees themselves and pay attention to the multiple ways in which they understand their own situation from their multiple perspectives. This kind of listening and learning elucidation will shed light on our own perceptions of the refugees and of ourselves. It will also reveal how refugees have not been reduced to "bare life," but have indeed "come to life" through their power-with struggle. Understanding this can be helpful for Western commentators. It can reveal to us power-with approaches for confronting and transforming our tyrannical power-over structures of domination.[11]

Attempting to present a sketch of these issues, I will approach the chapter in the following manner. First, I will present a survey of the EU and Member State policies toward Syrian refugees. Second, I will highlight another way to relate to and with refugees that is actual and that stems from different traditions of democratic citizenship found in Europe.[12] Third, I will attempt to present multiple ways in which refugees reveal themselves as agents and not as subjects.[13] By paying attention to what self-politicized refugees crystalize through their work, we are led toward acknowledging the huge blindspots we often find in the manner in which refugees are approached in our academic analyses.[14] And, fourth, in the final section I will reflect on how the absolute destruction of "otherness" is an accepted norm found in EU and Member State policies toward refugees. Furthermore, I will suggest that in response to this reality and in the spirit of democracy and human rights, engaged civic and civil citizens ("refugee" citizens and "EU" citizens alike) challenge our interpretations of law, state, and democracy. Through their actions, they maintain their "human dignity," whilst the conscience of a reasonable and free democratic society continues to be shocked.

A survey of EU and Member State policies toward Syrian refugees

The 1951 UN Convention and the 1967 Protocol are the only international legal norms applying specifically to refugees. These entitle refugees to international protection and to not be returned to their home countries. In the case of mass refugee movements, refugees are "often declared prima facie refugees," but international refugee law and international human rights treaties do not explicitly entitle refugees to asylum or impose obligations on states to grant asylum (Zamfir 1). The Geneva Convention does require that states "refrain from actions that would endanger asylum-seekers," but nobody is "entitled to interpret the Geneva Convention authoritatively"; the task falls on "domestic law-makers and courts" (Zamfir 1).

Hannah Arendt reminds us of the fact that "the nation-state cannot exist once its principle of equality before the law has broken down" (290). She also points to the fact that the reality of the refugee is that of a person "thrown out of the family of nations altogether" (294). As Costas Douzinas suggests, when this person (the refugee) arrives at the door of national law, he or she represents absolute otherness (253). He or she represents the foundational inequality of the law which, although inherent to the law, has to *disappear* so that the law can *appear* to be equal. Douzinas describes very eloquently how the refugee in being the absolute other, and representing "the trauma that marks the genesis of state and self," must be excluded from the state, given no rights, and treated as a lesser human being because of his or her lack of citizenship (253). For Douzinas, the refugee is treated like the medieval mad people "travelling the rivers of Europe in the ships of the fools"; always in movement, "in perpetual flotation or in orbit" (253).

It is along these lines that the EU and its Member States wage war on the refugee. Through their policies, they exclude him or her from the domain of ethical responsibility whilst exposing him or her to violence without any legal consequences (Diken).[15] At the frontline of this war, the two areas in which there has been a strong collective response from the EU toward refugees have been: first, the militarization of the Mediterranean Sea with the collaboration of the North Atlantic Treaty Organization (NATO); and, second, the externalization of EU borders by reaching agreements with states like Morocco and Turkey.

Regarding the first major area of collaboration, under German command, NATO has agreed to send ships to the Aegean Sea for surveillance and intelligence gathering aimed at stopping the influx of refugees.[16] In addition, on December 15, 2015, the European Commission approved the creation of a *European Border and Coast Guard* staffed with Frontex personnel.[17] This move increases Frontex's powers and gives it legal autonomy. It broadens its mandate "to organize 'joint return operations' and authoriz[es] Frontex teams to use force, including service weapons, ammunition, and equipment, with the consent of the home Member State and the host Member State" (Tsangarides para. 5). In cases where the migratory pressure is too high for countries to protect their own borders, the European Border and Coast Guard is in a position to operate without the country's consent (Tsangarides).

In relation to the externalization of EU borders (the second major area of EU collaboration), whilst 45,000 were fleeing Damascus in early February 2016, German Chancellor Angela Merkel traveled to Turkey. The purpose of the trip was to guarantee that the €3 billion offered by the EU to the country in November was effectively being used in order to contain the influx of Syrian refugees to the EU (Albiol).[18]

In addition to EU-wide policies aimed at fortifying the union against refugees, specific countries have dealt with the influx of refugees entering, or attempting to enter, their national territory differently. Following a clear logic of criminalization of the refugee, every country has provided its own interpretation of the Geneva Convention and of EU law. For example, in Denmark, the authorities in August 2015 reduced social benefits granted to refugees by 50%. In September of the same year, the government put out an advertisement in a Lebanese newspaper, making it clear to potential refugees that going to Denmark was not a good idea (Taylor).[19] In addition, recently the Danish Parliament approved legislation that allows the government to expropriate personal belongings and money from refugees, a policy implemented so that refugees will finance their own stay in the country (Taylor).[20]

In Switzerland, refugees who receive a permit to stay and work in the country will need to give 10% of their salary to the authorities for 10 years. The refugees are expected to pay back the estimated €13,600 it costs the state to keep them in the country (Taylor).[21]

In Germany, the federal government has announced that it will apply the Dublin Regulation in relation to Syrian refugees. By this move, refugees will be deported to the EU country in which they registered when they entered Europe ("Alemania").

In the UK, the city of Middlesbrough has marked refugee homes with red doors to facilitate identification. This has led to refugees having dog excrement, eggs, rocks, and logos of the National Front (an extreme right-wing party) being thrown at their homes ("Alemania"). In a similarly discriminatory policy, in the city of Cardiff, asylum-seekers are required to wear at all times a red shiny bracelet in order to be able to receive three meals a day.[22]

In Austria, on the border with Slovenia, the country has begun to build 3.7 kilometers of fence to stop the influx of refugees ("Austria Begins Work"). Parliament has also tightened legislation regarding asylum-seekers and family reunification.[23] In order to reunite with family members, refugees will have to be in the country for three years and to show that they have sufficient income. In addition, after three years, their claim to asylum will be revisited and if the government considers there to no longer be a threat in their home country, they will be deported.[24]

In Greece, Amnesty International (AI) has denounced how the government is arbitrarily and in a discriminatory manner limiting the access of refugees to a transitory camp near the border of Macedonia. The organization reports that although only a third of the 1,200 beds are occupied, entry is only being granted to those refugees heading to Austria or Germany. The rest are apparently forced to sleep outside the camp in below-zero temperatures (Huggler).[25]

In France, a recent study by researchers at the University of Birmingham and backed by Doctors of the World (Dhesi et al.) reveals how the migrant camp in Calais known as "the Jungle" hosts 4,300 people who are potential asylum-seekers. Apart from the fact that the camp is overcrowded, these people do not receive the appropriate information regarding the asylum request process. In addition, the study points to the fact that drinking water is contaminated and that inhabitants only have one toilet per every 75 people (Olías).[26]

In Hungary, fences blocking entry into the country include a 175 km fence with Serbia, and fences separating the country from Croatia and Romania (Luna). Parliament has just approved legislation that includes three-year prison sentences for illegal border crossings and sentences for damaging the border fence (Cernušáková). Claiming that Hungary is for the Hungarians, Viktor Orbán the country's Prime Minister has encouraged police to treat refugees with whatever violence is required (Luna). He has also stated that Muslim refugees put European Christendom at risk (Rodríguez-Pina).[27]

Spain is spearheading the way in which Europe deals with migration. According to AI, between 2007 and 2010, Spain spent €120 million on protecting its exterior borders from "illegal" migration.[28] In addition, since 2006, the country has been cooperating with countries such as Mauritania, Senegal, and Morocco to help block departures of migrants attempting to reach Spain ('How Spain Deals").[29] The "knowhow" developed through this kind of cooperation has served to block the path of Syrian refugees attempting to reach the EU via Spain.[30]

These EU and Member State policies are only examples of the kinds of policies enacted in relation to refugees. Nevertheless, they do indicate the disturbing space in which the EU and Member States policies toward refugees find themselves. They also reveal the crisis in which law's relationship to violence finds itself within Europe, and the way in which the war against refugees is being fought.

Another way to relate to and with refugees

In the previous section, I presented responses to refugees coming from "above" in a "power-over" manner, an approach we are submitted to by EU and Member State policies.[31] In this section, I aim to broaden the horizon of possibility by presenting alternatives to the power-over, institutional, and legal approach to refugees. In this sense, I want to present some of the alternatives that are currently approaching solidarity with refugees from "below" in a "power-with" manner. Through networked civil and civic infrastructures,[32] these engaged citizens are able to develop constructive community-building programs for welcoming and embracing refugees. By this move, citizens are acting as non-violent resistance fighters. By presenting us with alternatives to this war on refugees, they are challenging the current juridical-institutional framework.

Notora, a self-organized civic collective in Greece, presents a good example of this type of activity. The collective has occupied an abandoned Ministry of Labour building in Athens in order to provide accommodation for refugees (Strickland). At Notora, temporary accommodation and medical attention are available for refugees. In the collective, all the decisions are reached by the assembly-based consensus of refugees and volunteers (Strickland).[33]

Also in Greece, the initiative "Solidarity with Areos Park" in Athens cooperates with refugees. It does so on "the basis of practical solidarity and self-organization, away from the logic of philanthropy and volunteerism, and the treatment of refugees as a problem to be managed" ("Greece, Communication" para. 4). Supporting refugees camped at the park, volunteers always prioritize "the desires and needs of refugees, as expressed freely by themselves" ("Greece, Communication" para. 11).

Pikpa is a different refugee camp on the Greek island of Lesbos. The camp was set up on occupied land in 2012. Here the camp receives "highly vulnerable" refugees, women that arrive with their children, terminally ill people, and families without financial resources. It is a self-organized camp with volunteers from different nationalities, including people who have been (or are) refugees themselves (Barranco and Calvo).

In the German city of Hamburg, the initiative "Lampedusa in Hamburg" has received the support of the neighborhood of St Pauli. There refugees have been allowed to sleep at local churches and police have refused requests from authorities to carry out ID checks (Meret and Della Corte). As part of a locally grown community network, in the neighborhood, schools, universities, theaters, social movements, and trade unions have organized to exchange knowledge and experiences with refugees (Meret and Della Corte). Also in Germany, but this time in the city of Berlin, performance-art group *Künstlerkollektiv Peng!* has carried out a performance during which it granted the European Cross of Merit to numerous people for helping refugees entering the EU (Streng).[34]

The Austrian city of Vienna is home to the "Train of Hope," an initiative, which in three weeks counted 1,500 registered volunteers at the Hauptbahnhof,

Vienna's new central train station ("Europe's Refugee Crisis"). Translators in Arabic, Farsi, Urdu, and English are amongst the volunteers who help refugees access food (including Halal), medicines, warm clothing, legal assistance, counseling, and funding for travel ("Europe's Refugee Crisis"). By the end of September 2015, 20,000 people had received assistance from the "Train of Hope" ("Europe's Refugee Crisis").[35]

In the Slovenian city of Ljubljana, we have the "Open Borders Caravan." In its first general assembly at the Rog social center, the group referred to refugees as "neither victims nor villains, but rebels and fighters" ("Make Europe" para. 3). The assembly agreed to do whatever was necessary to open borders and "to construct paths, corridors and passages" ("Make Europe" para. 3). Making a call for a "transnational caravan for open borders," it demanded "open authorized paths for everybody's safe arrival to desired destinations, full citizenship for all and the end of the Dublin Regulation" ("Make Europe" para. 5).[36]

In Spain, *Refugiados Bienvenidos* (Refugees Welcome) has organized the location of empty houses, which can be provided to refugees (Bojovic).[37] Refugees Welcome is an initiative initially developed in Germany that has expanded throughout Europe. It is referred to as the Airbnb for refugees (Hernando). Also in Spain, in the city of Pamplona, open microphone meetings by self-organized, assembly-based groups have dialogically approached responses to refugees. Here people on the street are encouraged to raise issues and present alternative viewpoints on how to best receive refugees ("Formato asambleario").

In the Czech Republic, the "Halavák initiative" is supporting refugees arriving in Prague (Bojovic). Also in the Czech Republic, other volunteers are helping with on-land on-border crossings when refugees enter the country (Bojovic).[38]

In Sweden, at the Stockholm central station, *Vard pa Centralen* (Healthcare at the Central Station) has organized medical care for refugees arriving in the city (Bojovic). A different initiative in the country consists of weekly meetings of refugees and locals at Eskjo, where they meet to "chat over a cup of coffee and cookies" (Bojovic).

In Italy, the *Presidio Permanente No Border* in the city of Ventimiglia has made open calls to networks, individuals, and collectives that have mobilized in solidarity with migrants. Their goal is to "re-launch a transnational convergence against borders, racism and the exploitation and militarization of territories" ("From Lampedusa" para. 5). The aim of this initiative is to continue "relationship building" and the promotion of "active solidarity practices," whilst explicitly supporting the crossing of borders to draw new geographies ("From Lampedusa").

On a pan-European scale, in the summer of 2015, we saw the "Convoy of Hope," via which hundreds of EU citizens in their private cars drove refugees across the Hungarian-Austrian and Austrian-German borders. They did this escorted by the Viennese police (Joorman). This followed a decision by the German and Austrian governments to temporarily halt the Dublin Regulation (Joorman).[39]

All over Europe, people are self-organizing to relate to and with refugees, both individually and collectively. Dionisis Avranitakis is a Greek baker on the island of Kos. As a child, he experienced life as a refugee; now everyday he prepares an extra 100 kg of buns to hand out himself to refugees landing on the island (Rojas).[40] On Lesbos, the volunteers have often become grave diggers, "laying to rest the bodily remains of unknown migrants" (Joorman 15). At the Greece-Macedonia border, the activists have been handing out wire cutters to support attempts by refugees to cross the fence (César and Pérez). The hotline for boat-people in distress is "AlarmPhone," which migrants can call if, having called the coast guards, they are not being rescued.[41]

Across Europe, doctors are self-organizing to provide assistance to refugees (Negrete). Students are organizing strikes in support of refugees (Flakin). Crowds at sport events are holding up banners in support of refugees. People are meeting refugees at borders and stations with food and drink. Legal advice is being given. Psychological and emotional support groups are being formed. Demonstrations in support of refugees are frequent. Petitions are constantly being circulated. Occupations of buildings to house refugees have become a Europe-wide phenomenon. Temples, churches, sanctuaries, and monasteries are opening their doors to receive refugees. And at the same time, local politicians encouraged by civic and civil alliances are seeking to legislate in agonism with nation-state and EU directives in relation to refugees.[42]

Some of these engaged citizenry networks are working-with*in* official institutionality more than others, which, in contrast, are working-without official institutionality as much as possible. Making the distinction concretely is not easy. However, it is clear that the speed of response to the emergencies that some refugees are facing is much faster when official institutions are not involved. In addition, it seems as if those working without official institutionality (as much as possible) are working with*in* alternative infrastructures spread out across Europe. These often stem from the networks that became very visible in 2011–2012 with collective presences such as 15M and Occupy.[43] It seems that despite attempts at subordination and violence toward these collective presences, the networks and infrastructures have remained strong. Due to their resilience, these civic-civil alliances of engaged citizens have been able to offer much-needed solidarity to refugees with their struggles.

One distinction that can be made between people working-with*in* and people working-without official institutionality has to do with the way they approach their support. Those working with*in* usually frame their support within a discourse of the refugee as a subject that is a victim needing charity. On the other hand, those working without for the most part relate to the refugee as an agent. In this sense, those working outside official institutionality seem to see themselves as active social cells, entering into communion with refugees who are exercising agency every day of their lives. They relate to and with refugees, understanding that the refugees themselves are exercising "power-with" in working together, traveling together, suffering together, and hanging together in the most difficult of circumstances.

Refugees as agents not subjects

As Rebecca Solnit clearly demonstrates in *A Paradise Built in Hell*, "the image of the selfish, panicky, or regressive savage human being in times of disaster has little truth to it" (2). She suggests, instead, that the war of all against all for scarce resources that Thomas Hobbes and Immanuel Kant took for granted is in fact promoted by the structures governing our economies and our societies. She argues that once this structures collapse, "we are free to live and act another way" (7). As Solnit suggests, in this alternative form of living, we are not "bare life" with no dignity, but quite the opposite.

In the current exodus, time and time again refugees reveal to us how in their alternative form of living, they are not "bare life." If one cares to listen to the refugees and acknowledges their agency, this becomes quite clear. Listening and learning elucidation with refugees can shed light on our own perceptions of the refugees and of ourselves. It can reveal how in actual fact refugees have not been reduced to "bare life," but have in fact "come to life." For this reason, in this section I want to discuss some of the activities by the refugees themselves. By doing this, I aim to encourage further analysis through dialogues of reciprocal elucidation into their practices and modes of organization. The previous section revealed how refugees have counted on the power-with support of many EU citizens. Yet, the fact is that refugees themselves have been initiators of most of the activities relating to the struggle. Sometimes it has been refugees in the current exodus spearheading initiatives and at other times refugees from previous flights who are now settled in the EU.

It is important to put the phenomenon of self-organization by refugees into an historical context. As Martin Joormann points out, the post-Second World War self-organized refugee activism in Europe can be traced back to at least the 1990s. Then the *sans papiers* (without papers) in France began a series of mobilizations and occupations, which spread across Europe. It marked "the beginning of a process of transnational struggle against borders, racism, exploitation and militarization of the territories" ("From Lampedusa").

Then in the summer of 2012, the refugee struggle captured media attention with the Refugee Protest March from Würzburg (Bavaria) to Berlin. It was then that hundreds of self-organized asylum-seekers marched 600 kilometers. Following this protest march, in October 2012, a "Refugee Protest Camp" was set up by the refugees themselves in *Oranienplatz* in Berlin (Ünsal). In December of that same year, the refugees at the protest camp occupied a school in the same district of Kreuzberg Friedrichshain. They did this in order to protect themselves from the cold (Garaev).

Also in 2012, Austria saw self-organized refugee actions struggling for freedom of movement and residence. Following a protest march from the city of Traiskirchen to Vienna, a protest camp was set up, hunger strikes took place, and a movement developed under the name "Refugee Movement Vienna" ("Resistance is Everywhere").

In March 2013, the Congress of Protesting Refugees in Europe (CPRE) was held in Munich.[44] In the summer of 2014, the "Freedom March" (march4freedom) set out from the German city of Kehl and arrived in the Belgian city of Brussels. They traveled via Strasbourg in France and Schengen in Luxembourg. Here refugees wanted to emphasize "the transnational scope of the social movement as well as the political responsibility of the European border and asylum regimes" ("Resistance is Everywhere").

Almost two years later, in June 2014, the occupied school stemming from the 2012 "Refugee Protest Camp" in Berlin's *Oranienplatz* received an eviction order. A total of 1,700 police officers blocked off the area surrounding the school, demanding that the refugees evacuate the building. At that moment, 40 refugees went up to the roof and threatened to burn the building down unless the city government backed down ("Resistance is Everywhere"). Napuli Paul Lange, a Sudanese woman who became a symbol after occupying a tree for five days stated the following:

> We will do what we have to, for us this is war ... We urge people not to use violence, but the police use weapons, beat people and send dogs to attack us. So I will use the little power I have, and if I'll die or will be taken prisoner, that would be a victory because then I would be treated as somebody.
>
> (Garaev para. 8)

In November 2014, we saw Syrian refugees on a hunger strike in front of the Greek Parliament. They were demanding "the right of being recognized as refuges of war and to have shelter and food" ("Open Event"). At the beginning of 2015, self-organizing refugees from "Rights to the City—Never Mind the Papers" in Dortmund, Germany organized a demonstration of 8,000 people. This local alliance fights for "freedom of movement, self-determination, living space and against racism" ("Two Days Left" para. 1). At around the same time, refugees at the Brügmannhallen camp (in the same city) delivered an open letter to the local government calling attention to the bad living conditions in their camp ("Two days left").

In June 2015 in Ventimiglia at the French-Italian border, migrants and refugees were the first to respond to police repression. They acted by "occupying the rocks near the border and setting up a camp that during these months has become a space of resistance, complicity and struggle" ("From Lampedusa").

In September 2015, Miguel Urban, member of the European Parliament for Spain's political party Podemos, described the situation in the refugee camp set up at the heart of the Brussels financial district. Urban reported on how the coordinating body of undocumented migrants and refugees, together with migrants who have lived in Brussels for some time, kept the camp functioning. He also described the makeshift school which had organized an Erasmus-like exchange program with local schools. This was an attempt to "spur change and solidarity from the ground up" (Urban para. 5).

In early January 2016, self-organized refugees together with the activist refugee support group "Without Frontiers" organized a demonstration in the French city of Calais. Following the demonstration, a direct action initiative was carried out at the city's port. A total of 24 refugees and 11 EU citizens were arrested after boarding the ship *Spirit of Britain* in defiance of EU migration policies ("Detenidos"). Also in January, refugees in the cities of Berlin, Cologne, and Munich self-organized and gave flowers and smiles to German women. This action was in response to allegations in the German media that Syrian refugees had committed mass sexual attacks in the city of Cologne during the New Year's Eve celebrations ("Grupos de refugiados").

The above-mentioned examples of self-organizing refugees are only a fraction of the multiple ways in which refugees are organizing themselves as they arrive to, attempt to enter, and settle in Europe. Refugees have independent radio stations like the "Refugee Radio Awareness Network," an independent social initiative by self-organized refugees committed to human rights and human development (Refugee Radio Network). Their motto is "Empowering people and connecting cultures" (Refugee Radio Network). Self-organized refugees even have universities, such as the Silent University set up by refugees, for refugees in numerous European and Middle Eastern cities.[45]

Refugees are agents, as Nonoi Hacbang, a Filipino who became a refugee in Europe during the Ferdinand Marcos dictatorship, put it: "Through our self-organisation efforts, we continue to build not only communities of survival but vibrant communities of initiative and resistance" (Hacbang). This is a message that we hear again and again when we actually stop and listen to refugees themselves.

The statement by refugees calling on a self-organized refugee conference in Berlin in 2011 stressed the need to build refugee communities. Arguing for the importance of "acknowledging that we are the best persons to tell our own stories," the conference stated that the situation of every refugee in Germany "boils down to the German Apartheid concept of isolation, exclusion and total control of those seen as unwanted in this society" ("Statement on Refugee Self Organization" para. 3). The statement began by the refugees saying that "we are here because you destroyed our countries" ("Statement on Refugee Self Organization").

During a protest song contest at the Rabenhof Theatre in Vienna in February 2013, refugee Salaheddine Najah announced a demonstration demanding rights for refugees:

> We ourselves, the refugees, make the demonstration, and we are the ones who want it. It is our fight. We thank everybody for their help, but we don't allow anybody to use us. This is a self-organized struggle of and by refugees, one that needs your support, your presence on the street on Saturday.
>
> (Gržinić)

In a recent appeal by refugees for the creation of a solidarity network by refugee communities in Germany and Europe, the following could be read:

> The self-organization and networking by the affected victims of the collective oppression is the community and it is also the weapon to self determination of refugees ... We are calling on refugees/Asylum seekers and Migrants to build trustworthy Communities to strengthen our solidarity against the continuous inhumane treatments in Germany and Europe. Self-organization goes beyond telling our stories and our problems to the others. Its objective should be empowering through an independent political platform and self-determination in the refugee community with refugee activists and for the refugees. Your liberation is bound up with mine! Our Liberty is bound together!
>
> ("The Political MOVEMENT").

In the previous section of this chapter, we were able to observe how engaged EU citizens challenge the notions of law, democracy and the nation-state promoted by EU and Member State institutionality. In this section, what has been revealed is that "refugee" citizens are themselves active agents in this struggle. In fact, once we listen to them, it becomes clear that by reaffirming their agency, they represent the vanguard of the struggle.[46]

Closing remarks

Critically analyzing EU and Member State practices and the multiplicity of measures, attitudes, and policies being faced by Syrian refugees, it seems clear that the EU and its Member States are at war with the refugee. At this present moment, law is not a mechanism via which the refugee is being protected; in fact, law is constantly being modified in order to further punish the refugee, as if law in a truly Kafkaian manner is becoming "even more self-enclosed, even more vigilant, even more severe, even more malevolent" (Kafka 86). It is clear that law's open textured conception of punishment is expanding the limits of legitimate violence. It does this by making it seem "reasonable" what is clearly a "shock" to the conscience of democratic society.

Considering this scenario, it would seem that if there is a future to look forward to, it is because of the other world of power-with relationality operating in our societies that was introduced in this chapter. Together, the actions of these engaged citizens ("refugee" citizens and "EU" citizens alike) constitute a transformative climate within which people are acting in concert and taking control of their own fate.

By embracing refugees in defiance of EU and Member State policy, EU engaged citizens cooperating with refugees from below are changing the way they govern themselves. They are in agonistic struggle with the law, the nation-state, and the EU. They are challenging the limits of governmentality and the rights of refugees and EU citizens. Together, these civic/civil citizen networks are sketching a kind of global citizenry, which constitutes itself through cross-cultural mutual aid in a horizontal and from-below manner. In this sense, they are posing a serious challenge to EU and nation-state institutionality and law by presenting an ethically different democratic alternative.

It is for this reason that responses from the EU and Member States to this kind of engaged citizenry have often been vicious. We have witnessed "low-intensity" strategies against these resistances via administrative measures and everyday intimidation by police ("From Lampedusa"). We have witnessed police forces working with traffickers, official charitable organizations, embedded journalists, and politicians to track those working-without official institutionality ("From Lampedusa").

We have seen arrests and deportations of activists; in Ponte San Luigi on the Italian border, there have been 18 charges for occupation, numerous arrests, and seven expulsion orders ("From Lampedusa"). On the Greek island of Lesbos, we have witnessed people being prevented from distributing food to migrants ("Region of Macedonia"). In Thessaloniki the occupied migrants "orphanage" has received threats from the church that owns the property from the first day of the occupation ("Region of Macedonia").[47] On the island of Chios, Greek police together with Frontex personnel have constantly asked volunteer activists for identification. The pretext has been "to prevent robbing of the refugees, plundering the boats or the stealing of the outboard engines" ("End the Criminalization"). In the Southern Aegean islands, doctors have to provide proof that they are doctors and need to acquire the relevant certificates ("End the Criminalization").

In the French city of Calais, activists giving support to the struggle of refugees have been falsely accused of "inciting migrants to riot" ("Against the Criminalization"). According to No Borders, there have been police controls restricting the entry of volunteers to the "Jungle" migrant camp. Police have also questioned volunteers making their way back to England under Schedule 7 to the Terrorism Act of 2000 ("Against the Criminalization").

In Hungary the criminalization of those assisting refugees is already in place. There, a foreign reporter revealed how she had been hit by police and arrested for attempting to help a family of migrants. She was interrogated, locked up, and accused of helping migrants illegally cross the border ("Policías húngaros"). Other reporters have also been arrested under similar circumstances ("Policías húngaros").

In addition, since the beginning of 2016, 12 international volunteers have been arrested on Lesbos while trying to help refugees arriving on shore. Seven have been arrested "on suspicion of stealing used lifejackets from a municipality rubbish dump." Another five have been "arrested and accused of attempted people smuggling and possession of arms (knives)" (Tsangarides para. 8). Efi Latsoudi, a member of Pikpa,[48] recently described how the detainees had been "treated like animals." As Pikpa has reported, they have spent 60 hours in a police station without being able to eat, sleep, or go to the toilet (Tsangarides).[49] Now, according to Statewatch, a new regulation that the EU is secretly drafting will allow the criminalization of humanitarian help given to refugees ("La UE prepara").[50]

In this war, refugees themselves are the enemy. Yet, those who support them are increasingly been persecuted. Nevertheless, together these engaged "refugee" citizen and "EU" citizen networks are working in communion with and from within the tradition of non-violent mutual aid and power-with democratic citizenship to struggle in this war. A tradition, which aligns with the human rights tradition of which Costas Douzinas reminds us, always retains a critical distance from law and stretches its boundaries and limits (355).

These "EU" citizen and "refugee" citizen engaged networks are sustaining their struggle with*in* a shifting space. Within this space, policy is constantly moving toward the legalization of imperial war and absolute punishment of "otherness." A permanent state of war facilitating a legitimized and alter-legal destruction of human dignity is what these engaged citizens are in agonistic struggle against.[51]

These people are, as Jerome Roos eloquently describes them, "ordinary people on the ground—refugees and locals alike—who are self-organizing solidarity beyond borders and creating a different kind of Europe from below" (para. 2).[52] Through their example, they are proposing an alternative approach to understanding our environment and those living beings with who said environment is co-created and co-inhabited. In this sense, they are proposing an alternative way of being in the world with fellow living beings. They present an alternative to EU and nation-state institutionality.

Whilst the EU and Member States "institute" ever-floating ships of fools in their ever-expanding war on "otherness," these multiple *demoi* "constitute" community via interdependent and nonviolent communion. Through their practices, they challenge EU and Member State democratic claims, law's relationship to violence, and the very legitimacy of the institutions claiming to uphold such systems and ideals. As this imperial war continues, perhaps it is the responsibility of Western academics, whose privilege stems from such a reality, to join the struggle and resist the root cause of the hardship, and to oppose the bombings by their own governments of the countries of origin of the refugees. By this act of solidarity, we would be supporting the "refugee" citizen and "EU" citizen engaged networks trying to confront this violent reality on the ground.

Notes

1 The *Merriam-Webster Dictionary* in one of its multiple entries defines "war" in the following manner: "An organized effort by a government or other large organization to stop or defeat something that is viewed as dangerous or bad." It is in this sense that I speak of a war on refugees.
2 According to the United Nations refugee agency, 87% of sea arrivals to Europe in 2015 and 2016 are refugees from Syria, Afghanistan, and Iraq. See Frelick.

3 The extensive media coverage received by the so-called "crisis of refugees" facilitates access to information on how the EU and its Member States are treating refugees. By following the public statements of EU and Member State representatives, analyzing laws being passed, listening to what refugees themselves are describing, and noting opinions expressed by non-governmental organizations (NGOs), citizen/refugee collectives, public intellectuals, and legal scholars, we are able to survey EU and Member State policies toward refugees. We are also able to highlight some of the violence being inflicted on human beings whilst labeling them as refugees. Through this kind of analysis, we cannot determine where the distinction lies between legal and illegal violence. We can, however, gain a better understanding of how different states and the EU itself are interpreting law and creating law, while dealing with refugees in a violent manner.

4 Although in the text I say that the wars and refugees in the Middle East are "mainly caused by" Western imperialism, I do, of course, understand that it is immensely complex. Russia and China are involved. Religious differences are mobilized, power politics between Middle Eastern postcolonial states is being played, and a whole host of other factors are in play. Bassel Salloukh raises our awareness of the internal complexity of the divisive politics of the postcolonial states in the Middle East in his "The Banana Republic of Lebanon."I thank Bassel Salloukh for pointing out in his critique of an earlier draft of this chapter that the problem is not just EU laws and international (Western) conventions, but also the criminality of authoritarian regimes that force people to become refugees. As he puts it, "both Brussels and Bashar are culprits in this demonization." Nevertheless, in this chapter I do claim that ongoing Western imperialism remains the major cause, both historically and today. There are many texts written on the subject; see Khalidi for a good example.

5 It is important to emphasize that the US is not alone in providing weapons; Saudi Arabia, Qatar, and Turkey are also amongst the countries providing arms.

6 Although I speak of relative peace, I acknowledge that the history of authoritarian regimes is a violent one.

7 These are people whose home and civilization Western powers are destroying. I consider this an all-out war on these people because once they flee, they are labeled as refugees and continue to be punished by these same powers.

8 I am drawn to this topic as a European citizen with Spanish nationality, and I write this chapter from the discipline of political science. As I write, I place my contribution in the tradition of non-violent mutual aid and power-with democratic and civic citizenship. I think this tradition is best exemplified today by collective presences such as 15M in Spain and by the work of intellectuals such as Peter Kropotkin, Henry David Thoreau, Mahatma Gandhi, Richard Gregg, Hannah Arendt, Barbara Deming, Gene Sharp, Thomas Merton, Howard Zinn, and James Tully. When we orient ourselves from within this tradition, a whole power-with approach to community building and democracy is revealed. In this sense, alternatives to the war on refugees become apparent, which can contribute to safeguarding our democracies and can help us rethink the nation-state.

9 I differentiate between power-over and power-with to reveal the difference between a relationship of subordination (power-over) and a democratic relationship of equality (power-with). The distinction derives from my engagement with James Tully's work, although it is important to mention that Hannah Arendt also tried hard to get theorists to see outside the ruler-ruled assumption or worldview in *On Violence*. Arendt makes the distinction most fundamentally in "Socrates," in *The Promise of Politics*. For further analysis on these two concepts and their connection with Hannah Arendt's thought, see Tully "Violent Power-over". Tully has also traced this distinction between "power-with" and "power-over" in Follet.

10 Giorgio Agamben suggests that the existence of the refugee represents the point at which the state of exception, "the temporary suspension of the juridical-political order" legally crafted by Carl Schmitt, becomes "a stable spatial arrangement inhabited by … bare life" (175).
11 The *Merriam-Webster Dictionary* in one of its multiple entries defines "tyranny" in the following manner: "Cruel and unfair treatment by people with power over others." It is in this sense that I speak of EU and Member State institutionality as being tyrannical.
12 I present this in the form of a preliminary survey, which I hope reveals the need to enter into dialogues of reciprocal elucidation with these engaged citizens. Through these dialogues, alternatives wisdoms can surface, which present alternative readings of law, democracy, nation, and union.
13 As with the previous section, I present this section with the aim of encouraging dialogues of reciprocal elucidation with the agents.
14 I am grateful to Jen Bagelman for her emphasis (in comments on a previous version of this chapter) on the importance of finding a humble way via which we can follow and learn from those who are taking political action every day. I identify completely with her call for a kind of academy that aims to make more real space for these voices and experiences.
15 According to the Office of the United Nations High Commissioner for Refugees (UNHCR), on May 1, 2017, there were 5,031,622 registered Syrian refugees. For latest updates on this figure, see *Syria Regional Refugee Response— Inter-agency Information Sharing Portal*, http://data.unhcr.org/syrianrefugees/regional.php.
16 Jens Stoltenberg, Secretary General of NATO, describes this mission as "aimed at stopping illegal trafficking and immigration in the Aegean Sea" ("La OTAN").
17 See http://frontex.europa.eu.
18 This externalization of borders is no secret; in the 2015 *Valletta Summit on Migration*, the EU granted €1.8 billion to countries of the African Union in order to guarantee that they would police their own people and those traveling through their countries making their way to Europe. These initiatives are in alignment with previous bilateral agreements between countries like Spain, with Mauritania, Nigeria, Senegal and Morocco, or France with Mali.
19 When denouncing the EU, I am not ignoring the responsibility of Turkey. This is a clear example of how geopolitics trumps refugee rights, and both Turkey and the EU are responsible in this case.
20 The police will confiscate valuables (except those with sentimental value) and any money over €1,340. Amnesty International has labeled these steps as "really serious and cruel," and the UNCHR has referred to them as an "affront against the dignity of these people." Nils Muiznieks, Council of Europe Commissioner for Human Rights, has made clear that "the new Danish law for refugees will have a devastating impact on already vulnerable people" (Luna). Similar measures have also been implemented in Switzerland and the German states of Bavaria and Baden-Württemberg. In the case of Switzerland, this measure relates to quantities above €913. When the money is handed in, refugees receive a receipt form the state ("Suiza sigue"). In Bavaria, any money above €750 has to be handed in to the authorities. In the state of Baden-Württemberg, those asking for asylum can only keep up to € 350 of valuables and money (Rodríguez-Pina).
21 The UNHCR has stated that these policies could be in violation of articles in the European Convention on Human Rights and the Convention on the Rights of Children (Luna).

22 This has led to numerous incidents of harassment toward refugees ("La ciudad de Cardiff").

23 Tightening of legislation regarding family reunification is happening in numerous countries and the UNHCR has expressed deep concern regarding this practice (Rodríguez-Pina).

24 Austrian chancellor Werner Faymann has made clear that the new law is to "signal that asylum is something which is temporary" (Huggler).

25 Amnesty International is also denouncing the fact that thousands of refugees and asylum-seekers are facing inhumane conditions after arriving on the Greek Aegean islands. According to Amnesty International, they are "at risk of violence by police and members of far-right groups."

26 This is clearly insufficient when we consider the UN demands that in emergency situations there should be one toilet for every 20 people (Olías).

27 The country's Ambassador in Spain, Eniko Gyori, recently stated that fences were the only option "when a border is being attacked" (Rodríguez-Pina). In the meantime, refugees entering the country refer to facilities at the border area as feeling like "prisons" or "Guantanamo," and have denounced long detentions, refusals to access sanitation, and lack of food and water. As one refugee described it: "They are treating us like animals; worse than animals" ("Hungría equipara").

28 Between 2005 and 2013, the country spent €22,000 per day on maintaining border fences ("Más vallas para los refugiados").

29 This cooperation includes local police in these countries receiving Spanish money, training and equipment, and generous development-aid programs ("How Spain Deals").

30 José Palazón, member of Prodein, suggests that "in Melilla the right to request asylum has to be bought." Palazón makes this statement because due to an unofficial quota system, in order to enter the city, refugees have to pay traffickers set up on the Moroccan side of the fence (Bengoa).

31 In speaking of "we," I am referring to citizens and non-citizens of the EU currently suffering the consequences of these EU policies.

32 In distinguishing between civic and civil types of citizenship, I am inspired by James Tully's differentiation. According to Tully, civil citizens "participate by exercising their communicative powers in elections, political parties, deliberation in official public spheres and civil disobedience with the hopes of exercising influence power on elected representatives who exercise governmental power through legislative deliberation and law-making." On the other hand, civic citizens "discuss and exercise powers of self-organization and self-government themselves (citizen-citizen relationships) prior to any separation of ruler and ruled or governor and citizen in representative practices of government." For a more detailed account of the differences between civic and civil citizenship, see Tully ("Responses").

33 A similar initiative is Orfanotrofeio, a self-organized squat in the Greek city of Thessaloniki also working with refugees ("(A-Radio)").

34 Also in Berlin, a workshop has been organized by a numerous collectives and groups, which "brings together refugees, volunteers, activists, digital developers, theorists and artists to develop strategies and critically reflect on the current situation." The workshop is called "Civil Society 4.0.—Refugees and Digital Self-Organization." See *Civil Society 4.0—Refugees and Digital Self Organization*, www.hkw.de/en/programm/projekte/2016/civil_society_4_0/civil_society_4_0_start.php.

35 A very active social media desk posts messages on Facebook and Twitter regarding specific needs, and usually the turnaround time from the moment a refugee asks for something to the moment he or she receives it is around 40 minutes.

36 Their public statement closed with the following words: "Their fight is our fight and their future is our future!"
37 By January 2016, 969 houses had been registered (Bojovic).
38 Informally they are referred to as the "Czech Team."
39 At the time, people active in the convoy used the term "Fluchthilfe" ("escape aid") to describe their politically encouraged direct action. "Escape aid" is a term often associated with the help people received to escape Nazi Germany and the German Democratic Republic.
40 His family abandoned the city of Izmir following the Turkish invasion of 1922 (Rojas).
41 At that point, the volunteers at the hotline call the coast guard, but also the public media and politicians to pressure the rescue services ("About").
42 Good examples of these local-institutional responses are numerous. Taking Spain as an example, there are three very promising initiatives promoted by mayors of cities in the country. The first is a proposal for the creation of a humanitarian sea corridor for Syrian refugees reaching the city of Valencia. The second is a commitment by the Mayor of Madrid, Manuela Carmena, to promote and finance a program by which citizens loan their empty apartments to refugees. Finally, the third is a proposal by the Mayor of Barcelona, Ada Colau, to promote a web of European refugee-friendly cities (Fernández-Savater).
43 For a more in-depth look into the infrastructures I am referring to, see Ouziel.
44 See https://refugeecongress.wordpress.com.
45 See www.thesilentuniversity.org.
46 I see this as aligning with Hannah Arendt's notion of refugees representing the vanguard of their people ("We Refugees" 119). When a group of refugees starts a university for and by refugees because their academic titles are not recognized in countries through which they travel, I see them having agency and changing the way they govern themselves. When a group of refugees organizes an occupation or a march for freedom and invites people who are not refugees to attend, I think they are showing agency and are also changing the way they are governed. They displace the position of the refugee as a victim or person in need of charity to an active agent in the struggle; an agent who defines the way the struggle is fought. They govern themselves rather than let others do it for them. Ultimately, I do not see my presentation of refugee agency as being a theorization of it; rather, I think it is simply an engaged observation of everyday examples of this agency. Of course, I wish I had some funding to go and conduct interviews with refugees in order to elaborate on this section. Nevertheless, this section offers a glimpse into the vast world of relational practices of self-governance in which refugees are engaged.
47 The clergy has been active in attempting to cut power to the building. By an "occupied migrants 'orphanage,'" what I am referring to is an orphanage that exists within a building that was occupied illegally by activists for the purpose of creating the orphanage.
48 See www.lesvos.w2eu.net/tag/pikpa.
49 Similar arrests have taken place in the island of Chios, where one volunteer was arrested "on suspicion of spying after photographing a Frontex boat." In addition, the city of Athens police have begun to crackdown on solidarity actions.
50 As part of a strategy for sealing the border between Greece and Turkey, charities, volunteers, holidaymakers, and local people could be criminalized for helping migrants arriving in the EU (Waterfield).
51 The climate in Europe is so disturbing that recently Eva Schloss, the stepsister of Anne Frank, whose family suffered Nazi persecution and passed through

numerous concentration camps, has compared the hardship of Syrian refugees to that of Jews fleeing the Third Reich. As she puts it: "We haven't really learnt anything—I'm depressed by the current situation. The experience of the Syrian refugees is similar to what we went through" (Court-Dobson).

52 Perhaps in this sense, they are the free people striving to make law free that Henry David Thoreau wrote about; those true "lovers of law and order." The kind of citizen suggested by Mahatma Gandhi understood the unconstitutionality of cooperating with the injustice of tyrannical government. See Gandhi 349.

References

"(A-Radio) Mediterranean 3: The Self-Organized Refugee Squat Orfanotrofeio in Thessaloniki." *Anarchistnews.org*, January 16, 2016, www.anarchistnews.org/content/radio-mediterranean-3-self-organized-refugee-squat-orfanotrofeio-thessaloniki.

"About." *AlarmPhone: Watch the Med*, www.alarmphone.org/en/about.

"Against the Criminalization of Support for Migrants." *Calais Migrant Solidarity*, November 14, 2015, www. calaismigrantsolidarity.wordpress.com/2015/11/14/against-the-criminalization-of-support-for-migrants.

Agamben, G. *Homo Sacer: Sovereign Power and Bare Life.* Stanford University Press, 1998.

Albiol, Marina. "La normalización del fascismo en Europa ante la llegada de refugiados." *Publico.es*, February 3, 2016, http://blogs.publico.es/dominiopublico/15746/la-normalizacion-del-fascismo-en-europa-ante-la-llegada-de-refugiados.

"Alemania devolverá a los sirios al país por el que entren en la UE." *20minutos.es*, November 10, 2015, http://m.20minutos.es/noticia/2601522/0/alemania-devolvera-sirios/pais-entrada/union-europea.

Amnesty International. "Urgent Action: Refugees Face Hellish Conditions on Islands," November 5, 2016, www. ua.amnesty.ch/urgent-actions/2015/11/250-15/ua-250-15-english.

Arendt, Hannah. *The Origins of Totalitarianism.* Meridian Books, 1961.

——. "Socrates." *The Promise of Politics.* By Arendt. Edited and Introduction by Jerome Kohn, Schocken Books, 2005.

——. *On Violence.* Houghton Mifflin Harcourt, 1970.

——. "We Refugees." In *Altogether Elsewhere: Writers on Exile.* Edited by Marc Robinson. Faber & Faber, 1994, pp. 110–119.

"Austria Begins Work on Slovenia Border Fence." *The Local*, December 7, 2015, www.thelocal.at/20151207/austria-begins-erecting-fence-on-slovenia-border.

Barranco Riaza, F. and O. Calvo. "Pikpa Camp, el campo de refugiados asambleario y horizontal en Lesbos." *Eldiaro.es*, December 27, 2015, www.eldiario.es/desalambre/Pikpa-Camp-asamblearia-horizontal-Lesbos_0_466853455.html.

Bengoa, A. "No digas que eres sirio." *El Pais*, September 19, 2015, www.politica.elpais.com/politica/2015/09/18/actualidad/1442604574_288079.html.

Bojovic, J. "Special: Civil Society Responses to Refugee Crisis." *Politheor: European Policy Network*, January 2016, http://politheor.net/wp-content/uploads/2016/01/Politheor-Special-Report-on-Civil-Society-Responses-to-Refugee-Crisis.pdf.

Cernušáková, Barbora. "Trains to Nowhere—Hungary's Harsh Welcome for Refugees." *Amnesty International News*, September 4, 2015. www.amnesty.org/en/latest/news/2015/09/trains-to-nowhere-hungary-harsh-welcome-for-refugees.

César, P. and Rodrigo Pérez. "Activistas pro refugiados reparten tenazas en la valla entre Grecia y Macedonia." *La Cuarta Columna*, March 3, 2016, www.lacuartacolumna.com/activistas-refugiados-cizallas.
"Civil Society 4.0—Refugees and Digital Self Organization." Online Workshop, March 3–5, 2016, www.hkw.de/en/programm/projekte/2016/civil_society_4_0/civil_society_4_0_start.php.
Court-Dobson, C. "Anne Frank's Stepsister Warns Us the Situation is 'Worse Than it was under Hitler." *The Canary*, January 28, 2016, www.thecanary.co/2016/01/28/anne-franks-stepsister-warns-us-situation-worse-hitler.
"Detenidos 24 migrantes y 11 manifestantes en el puerto francés de Calais." *Sputnik News*, January 24, 2016, www.mundo.sputniknews.com/europa/20160124/1056022428/Detenidos-migrantes-manifestantes-Calais.html#ixzz421miQ900.
Dhesi, S. et al. *An Environmental Health Assessment of the New Migrant Camp in Calais*, University of Birmingham, 2015, www.birmingham.ac.uk/Documents/college-les/gees/research/calais-report-oct-2015.pdf.
Diken, B. "From Refugee Camps to Gated Communities: Biopolitics and the End of the City." *Citizenship Studies*, vol. 8, no. 1, 2004, pp. 83–106.
Douzinas, Costas. *The End of Human Rights: Critical Legal Thought*. Hart Publishing, 2000.
"End the Criminalization of Solidarity to Refugees NOW!"*Aiktyo*, January 17, 2016, www.diktio.org/node/1203.
"Europe's Refugee Crisis and IES Abroad Vienna." *IES Abroad News*, September 25, 2015, www.iesabroad.org/study-abroad/news/europes-refugee-crisis-and-ies-abroad-vienna#sthash.d0Lrkrny.AOP01nzr.dpbs.
Fernández-Savater, A. "Interferencias: Javier de Lucas: "La Unión Europea está, de facto, en una situación de guerra contra los inmigrantes." *Eldiario.es*, January 29, 2016, www.eldiario.es/interferencias/Javier-Lucas-Union-Europea-inmigrantes_6_478812126.html.
Flakin, W. "Huelga y autoorganización estudiantil en apoyo a los refugiados en Alemania." *Izquierdadiario.es*, November 10, 2015, www.izquierdadiario.es/Huelga-y-autoorganizacion-estudiantil-en-apoyo-a-los-refugiados-en-Alemania.
Follet, M.P. *Creative Experience*. Longmans, Green & Co., 1930.
"Formato asambleario para aportar soluciones." *Noticias de Navarra*, September 15, 2015, www.noticiasdenavarra.com/2015/09/15/sociedad/estado/formato-asambleario-para-aportar-soluciones.
Frelick, B. "Dispatches: Fearmongering about Refugees." *Human Rights Watch*, March 4, 2015, www.hrw.org/news/2016/03/04/dispatches-fearmongering-about-refugees.
"From Lampedusa to Calais, We Will Not Go Back!" *Presidio Permanente No Borders Ventimiglia*, September 3, 2015, www. noborders20miglia.noblogs.org/post/2015/09/03/solidarity-without-borders-11-12-13-september-transnational-meeting-against-borders-racism-exploitation-and-militarization.
Gandhi, M.K. *The Essential Writings*. Oxford University Press, 2008.
Garaev, P. "Berlin's Refugees to the Authorities: Ich bin ein Berliner." *i24news.tv*, April 25, 2015, http://webview.i24news.tv/en/news/international/europe/68946-150425-berlin-s-refugees-say-ich-bin-ein-berliner.
"Greece, Communication from the Self-Organized Initiative for Refugees in the Mars Field." *A-Infos*, August 23, 2015, www.ainfos.ca/en/ainfos31760.html.

"Grupos de refugiados regalan flores a los ciudadanos tras las agresiones a mujeres en Alemania." *Huffington Post*, January 17, 2016, www.huffingtonpost.es/2016/01/17/refugiados-flores-alemania-agresiones_n_9003912.html.

Gržinić, M. "A Refugee Protest Camp in Vienna and the European Union's Processes of Racialization, Seclusion, and Discrimination." *Journal Number 43, e-flux.com*, March 2013, www.e-flux.com/journal/43/60214/a-refugee-protest-camp-in-vienna-and-the-european-union-s-processes-of-racialization-seclusion-and-discrimination.

"Guide to the Syrian Rebels." *BBC News*, December 13, 2013, www.bbc.com/news/world-middle-east-24403003.

Hacbang, N. "Migrants and Refugees: Lessons Being Learned." *Communities of Initiative & Resistance*, Issue 24, 1998, www.aislingmagazine.com/aislingmagazine/articles/TAM24/Migrants.html.

Hernando, P. "La sociedad civil europea se vuelca con los refugiados." *Sabemosdigital.com*, September 3, 2015, www.sabemosdigital.com/hoy/3164-la-sociedad-civil-europea-se-vuelca-con-los-refugiados.

"How Spain Deals with Migrants: Forward Defence." *The Economist*, October 17, 2015, www.economist.com/news/europe/21674726-what-other-europeans-can-learn-spanish-efforts-limit-illegal-migration-forward-defence?fsrc=scn/tw/te/pe/ed/forwarddefence.

Huggler, J. "Austria Tightens Asylum Rules to Counter Record Numbers of Migrants." *The Telegraph*, November 4, 2015, www.telegraph.co.uk/news/worldnews/europe/austria/11975115/Austria-tightens-asylum-rules-to-counter-record-numbers-of-migrants.html.

"Hungría equipara su valla contra los refugiados con las de Ceuta y Melilla en España." *Eldiario.es*, September 15, 2015, www.eldiario.es/desalambre/embajadora-hungara-explicar-Espana-sentido_0_431157259.html.

Joormann, M. "From Malmö to Lesbos: Tracing a Trans European Network of Voluntary Work and Activism for Refugees." *Refugees Welcome*, No. 10, European Group for the Study of Deviance and Social Control, 2015, www.europeangroup.org/sites/default/files/Newsletter%20No%2010%20November%202015.pdf.

Kafka, F. *The Trial*. Translated by Mike Mitchell, Oxford University Press, 2009.

Khalidi, R. *Resurrecting Empire: Western Footprints and America's Perilous Path in the Middle East*. Beacon Press, 2005.

"La ciudad de Cardiff obliga a los refugiados a lucir pulseras brillantes identificativas." *El Economista*, January 24, 2016, http://ecodiario.eleconomista.es/europa/noticias/7300590/01/16/La-ciudad-de-Cardiff-obliga-a-los-refugiados-a-lucir-pulseras-brillantes-identificativas.html.

"La OTAN enviará buques al Egeo para frenar la llegada de refugiados." *Reporte24.net*, February 11, 2016, http://reporte24.net/2016/02/la-otan-enviara-buques-al-egeo-para-frenar-la-llegada-de-refugiados.

"La UE prepara una normativa que obligaría a registrarse para poder ayudar a los refugiados." *Elperiodico.com*, January 1, 2016, www.elperiodico.com/es/noticias/internacional/prepara-una-normativa-para-registrarse-para-ayudar-refugiados-4860253.

Luna, V. "Brazaletes, confiscaciones, casas marcadas … las medidas contra los refugiados en Europa." *20minutos.es*, February 9, 2016, www.20minutos.es/noticia/2664852/0/medidas/europa/refugiados/#xtor=AD-15&xts=467263.

"Make Europe, Open Borders! Call for a European Open Borders Caravan." *Solidarity against Repression*, September 24, 2015, www.change4all.eu/change-in-action/detail/make-europe-open-borders-call-for-a-european-open-borders-caravan.html.

"Más vallas para los refugiados: Amnistía Internacional advierte de que ceder al miedo no protegerá a nadie." *ElPlural.com*, November 17, 2015, www.elplural.com/2015/11/17/mas-vallas-para-los-refugiados-amnistia-internacional-advierte-de-que-ceder-al-miedo-no-protegera-a-nadie/?utm_source=twitterfeed&utm_medium=twitter.

McKelvey, T. "Arming Syrian Rebels: Where the US Went Wrong." *BBC News*, October 10, 2015, www.bbc.com/news/magazine-33997408.

Meret, S. and E. Della Corte. "Between Exit and Voice: Refugees' Stories from Lampedusa to Hamburg." *Opendemocracy.net*, January 22, 2014, www.opendemocracy.net/can-europe-make-it/susi-meret-elisabetta-della-corte/between-exit-and-voice-refugees-stories-from-la.

Negrete, C. "Impresionante demostración de solidaridad de los alemanes en apoyo a los refugiados." *Eldiario.es*, August 31, 2015, www.eldiario.es/desalambre/Asilo-Alemania-voluntarios-ONGs-Siria-refugiados-catastrofe_humanitaria_0_425557671.html.

Olías, L. "Abandono de Francia a los migrantes y refugiados en Calais: sin techo, aseos y ni agua potable." *Eldiario.es*, October 10, 2015, www.eldiario.es/desalambre/abandono-Francia-migrantes-refugiados-Calais_0_439557039.html.

"Open Event: Claiming Voice: Refugee and Migrant Rights and Self-Organization in Host Societies." *Analyze Greece*, June 11, 2015, www.analyzegreece.com/topics/immigrants-rights-and-racism/item/233-pen-event-claiming-voice-refugee-and-migrant-rights-and-self-organization-in-host-societies.

Ouziel, Pablo. "'Vamos Lentos Porque Vamos Lejos': Towards a Dialogical Understanding of Spain's 15Ms." Dissertation, University of Victoria, 2015, https://dspace.library.uvic.ca/bitstream/handle/1828/6734/Ouziel_Pablo_PhD_2015.pdf?sequence=5&isAllowed=y.

"Policías húngaros apalean a periodistas durante un incidente con refugiados." *Sputnik News*, September 17, 2015, https://mundo.sputniknews.com/europa/201509171051529134.

"The Political MOVEMENT: Appeal to Refugee Communities for Solidarity Network in Germany and Europe." *thevoicejena*, February 2, 2016, www.thecaravan.org/node/4425.

Refugee Radio Network. RRAN Radio, www.refugeeradionetwork.wix.com/rran.

"Region of Macedonia: Migrants are CLASS Brothers—Progress of Solidarity with Immigrants." *A-Infos*, January 25, 2016, www.ainfos.ca/en/ainfos32573.html.

"Resistance is Everywhere: Call for Solidarity with the Imprisoned Refugee-Activists." *Solidarity against Repression*, January 2014, www.solidarityagainstrepression.noblogs.org/resistance-is-everywhere.

Rodríguez-Pina, G. "AVISO: Este repaso al maltrato europeo a los refugiados puede herir tu sensibilidad." *Huffingtonpost.es*, January 31, 2016, www.huffingtonpost.es/2016/01/31/europa-verguenza-refugiados_n_9067890.html?utm_hp_ref=spain.

Rojas, A. "Dionisis, el panadero de Europa." *El Mundo*, October 13, 2015, www.elmundo.es/internacional/2015/10/13/561be808268e3e7d688b457b.html.

Roos, J. "Welcoming Refugees: Our Future is Common." *Telesur.tv*, October 12, 2015, www.telesurtv.net/english/opinion/Welcoming-Refugees-Our-Future-Is-Common-20151012-0033.html.

Salloukh, Bassel. "The Banana Republic of Lebanon."' *The New Arab*, March 7, 2016, www.alaraby.co.uk/english/comment/2016/3/7/the-banana-republic-of-lebanon.

Solnit, Rebecca. *A Paradise Built in Hell.* Penguin, 2009.

"Statement on Refugee Self Organization in Lagers by Rex Osa 'Refugees Have a Voice.'" *Refugee Community Germany*, January 20, 2011, www.linksunten.indymedia.org/en/node/33068.

Streng, R. "*Peng!* Helps Undocumented People Cross." *Cities in Transition. EU*, November 11, 2015, https://citiesintransition.eu/cityreport/peng-helps-undocumented-people-cross.

Strickland, P. "Greek Anarchists Organise for Refugees as 'State Fails.'" *Al Jazeera*, January 19, 2016, www.aljazeera.com/indepth/features/2016/01/greek-anarchists-organise-refugees-state-fails-160117032251199.html?utm_content=buffer13c35&utm_medium=social&utm_source=facebook.com&utm_campaign=buffer.

"Suiza sigue a Dinamarca y también confiscará activos a los refugiados." *La Vanguardia*, January 15, 2016, www.lavanguardia.com/internacional/20160115/301423405648/suiza-sigue-dinamarca-confiscara-activos-refugiados.html.

Taylor, A. "Denmark Puts Ad in Lebanese newspapers: Dear Refugees, Don't Come Here." *Washington Post*, September 7, 2015, www.washingtonpost.com/news/worldviews/wp/2015/09/07/denmark-places-an-advertisement-in-lebanese-newspapers-dear-refugees-dont-come-here.

Tsangarides, N. "Why are Volunteers Being Treated Like Criminals in Greece?" *New Internationalist Blog*, January 28, 2016, www.newint.org/blog/2016/01/28/refugees-volunteers-crackdown/#sthash.myzsBPUm.Xgb9VyOw.dpuf.

Tully, James. *Public Philosophy in a New Key: Volumes I and II.* Cambridge University Press, 2008

——. "Responses." In *Freedom and Democracy in an Imperial Context. Dialogues with James Tully.* Edited by Robert Nichols and Jakeet Singh, Routledge, 2014, pp. 223–224.

——."Two Days Left: Refugee Struggle in Hamburg & Dortmun." *Refugees Welcome Dortmund*, April 23, 2015, www.refugeeswelcomedo.noblogs.org/never-stop-resisting-refugee-struggle-in-hamburg-and-dortmund.

——."Tyranny." *Merriam-Webster Dictionary.* Online. www.merriam-webster.com/dictionary/tyranny.

——. "Violent Power-over and Nonviolent Power-with: Hannah Arendt on Violence and Nonviolence." Unpublished article, Oklahoma, 2011.

Ünsal, N. "Challenging 'Refugees' and 'Supporters': Intersectional Power Structures in the Refugee Movement in Berlin." *Journal für kritische Migrations- und Grenzregimeforschung*, vol. 1, no. 2, 2015, http://movements-journal.org/issues/02.kaempfe/09.%C3%BCnsal--refugees-supporters-oplatz-intersectionality.pdf.

Urban, M. "A Refugee Camp in the Brussels Financial District: A Portrait of European Dystopia." *Huffington Post*, September 28, 2015, www.huffingtonpost.com/miguel-urban/a-refugee-camp-in-the-bru_b_8207822.html.

"War." *Merriam-Webster Dictionary*, www.merriam-webster.com/dictionary/war.

Waterfield, B. "Tourists Who Help Drowning Migrants Face Prosecution." *The Times*, January 30, 2016, www.thetimes.co.uk/tto/news/world/europe/article4678348.ece.

Watt, N. "Tony Blair Makes Qualified Apology for Iraq War Ahead of Chilcot Report." *The Guardian*, October 25, 2015, www.theguardian.com/uk-news/2015/oct/25/tony-blair-sorry-iraq-war-mistakes-admits-conflict-role-in-rise-of-isis.

Zamfir, I. "At a Glance: Refugee Status under International Law." *European Parliamentary Research Service (EPRS)*, 2015, www.europarl.europa.eu/RegData/etudes/ATAG/2015/569051/EPRS_ATA%282015%29569051_EN.pdf.

Index

For Product Safety Concerns and Information please contact our EU representative GPSR@taylorandfrancis.com Taylor & Francis Verlag GmbH, Kaufingerstraße 24, 80331 München, Germany

Batch number: 10725973

Printed by Printforce, the Netherlands